Poverty and Inequality in Latin America

TITLES FROM THE HELEN KELLOGG INSTITUTE
FOR INTERNATIONAL STUDIES

Kwan S. Kim and David F. Ruccio, eds.
Debt and Development in Latin America (1985)

Scott Mainwaring and Alexander Wilde, eds.
The Progressive Church in Latin America (1989)

Bruce Nichols and Gil Loescher, eds.
The Moral Nation: Humanitarianism and U.S. Foreign Policy Today (1989)

Edward L. Cleary, O.P., ed.
Born of the Poor: The Latin American Church since Medellín (1990)

Roberto DaMatta
Carnivals, Rogues, and Heroes: An Interpretation of the Brazilian Dilemma (1991)

Antonio Kandir
The Dynamics of Inflation (1991)

Luis E. González
Political Structures and Democracy in Uruguay (1991)

Scott Mainwaring, Guillermo O'Donnell, and J. Samuel Valenzuela, eds.
Issues in Democratic Consolidation: The New South American Democracies in Comparative Perspective (1992)

Roberto Bouzas and Jaime Ros, eds.
Economic Integration in the Western Hemisphere (1994)

Mark P. Jones
Electoral Laws and the Survival of Presidential Democracies (1995)

Dimitri Sotiropolous
Populism and Bureaucracy: The Case of Greece under PASOK, 1981–1989 (1996)

Peter Lester Reich
Mexico's Hidden Revoution: The Catholic Church in Law and Politics since 1925 (1996)

Michael Fleet and Brian Smith, eds.
The Catholic Church and Democracy in Chile and Peru (1997)

A. James McAdams
Transitional Justice and the Rule of Law in New Democracies (1997)

Carol Ann Drogus
Women, Religion, and Social Change in Brazil's Popular Church (1997)

Víctor E. Tokman and Guillermo O'Donnell, eds.
Poverty and Inequality in Latin America: Issues and New Challenges (1998)

Poverty and Inequality in Latin America

Issues and New Challenges

Edited by

VÍCTOR E. TOKMAN

and

GUILLERMO O'DONNELL

UNIVERSITY OF NOTRE DAME PRESS
Notre Dame, Indiana

Copyright © 1998 by
University of Notre Dame
Notre Dame, Indiana 46556
http://www.undpress.nd.edu
All Rights Reserved

Set in 10/12 Electra by The Book Page, Inc.

Thomas McGrath, "Flint and Steel" and "Revisionist Poem: Machado" from *Selected Poems 1938–1988*. Copyright © 1988 by Thomas McGrath. Reprinted with permission of Copper Canyon Press. P.O. Box 271, Port Townsend, WA 98368-0271

Paperback printed in 2001

Library of Congress Cataloging-in-Publication Data
Poverty and inequality in Latin America : issues and new challenges / edited by Víctor E. Tokman and Guillermo O'Donnell.
    p. cm. — (Title from the Helen Kellogg Institute for International Studies)
  Includes bibliographical references.
  ISBN 0-268-03868-6 (pbk. : alk. paper)
  1. Poverty—Latin America—Congresses.   2. Latin America—Social policy—Congresses.   I. Tokman, Víctor E.   II. O'Donnell, Guillermo A.   III. Series.
HC130.P6P69   1998
339.4'6'098—dc21   97-46841
                                                                                                    CIP

∞ *This book is printed on acid-free paper.*

Contents

Preface
    Ernest Bartell, C.S.C., and Guillermo O'Donnell   vii

Introduction
    Víctor E. Tokman   xi

PART I   ISSUES AND CHALLENGES IN THE NEW ECONOMIC ENVIRONMENT

1   Inequality, Employment, and Poverty in Latin America: An Overview   3
    Oscar Altimir

2   The Demographics of Poverty and Welfare in Latin America: Challenges and Opportunities   36
    José Alberto Magno de Carvalho

3   Poverty and Inequality in Latin America: Some Political Reflections   49
    Guillermo O'Donnell

PART II GLOBALIZATION AND THE EMPLOYMENT ISSUE

4 Globalization and Job Creation: 75
A Latin American Perspective
René Cortázar

5 Restructuring, Education, and Training   91
María Antonia Gallart

PART III EMERGING RESPONSES FOR FACING POVERTY AND VULNERABILITY

6 Welfare and Citizenship: Old and New Vulnerabilities   119
Carlos H. Filgueira

7 The Crisis of Old Models of Social Protection in   140
Latin America: New Alternatives for
Dealing with Poverty
Dagmar Raczynski

8 Balancing State, Market, and Civil Society: 169
NGOs for a New Development Consensus
Charles A. Reilly

PART IV A NEW POLITICAL ECONOMY OF POVERTY AND EQUITY?

9 Jobs and Welfare: Searching for New Answers   209
Víctor E. Tokman

Appendix   227

Contributors   231

Index   233

Preface

Since 1993 the Helen Kellogg Institute for International Studies at the University of Notre Dame, through its Project Latin America 2000 (generously supported by The Coca-Cola Company), has sought to enlarge its contributions to the knowledge of significant political, economic, and social issues facing Latin America at the threshold of a new century. It has done so by focusing its own academic research priorities on these issues and by engaging distinguished scholars, senior statesmen and -women, government officials, entrepreneurs, and executives from national and international business, labor leaders, representatives of nongovernmental donor agencies and civil associations, along with the media, in constructive dialogue on the results of its academic research. Our hope is that the research and the dialogue will contribute to the policy agendas of public and private actors by clarifying issues and questions, analyzing options, and pointing the way to more effective and equitable policy alternatives in both public and private sectors.

The format we have followed for these dialogues has consisted of first holding an academic workshop, in which distinguished academics write and comment on topics directly related to the main theme, and immediately after the workshop holding a policy forum, in which leaders from various venues of public and private life discuss the same topic, bringing to a roundtable discussion their own experience and taking into account the findings and questions emerging from the workshop.

The first such event, in 1993, focused on "Economic Integration in the Western Hemisphere." Its main results are presented in a volume of the same title, coedited by Roberto Bouzas and Jaime Ros and published by the University of Notre Dame Press in 1994. For the second event we decided to take stock of the present situation and future prospects of democracy in the Americas. The contributions to the workshop on this topic have been published as Working Papers of the Kellogg Institute and are available upon request.[1] The present volume results from the third Project Latin America 2000 event. The next, in November 1996, focused on the rule of law in Latin America, with special emphasis on ways to improve its effectiveness in relation to various underprivileged sectors. A volume resulting from this event, coedited by Juan Méndez, Guillermo O'Donnell, and Paulo Sérgio Pinheiro, will be published by the University of Notre Dame Press in 1998. "The Changing Status of Children in Latin America: Issues in Child Health and Children's Rights" was chosen as the topic for the last (26–29 September 1997) of the five events originally planned, all hosted by the Kellogg Institute at Notre Dame with the support of The Coca-Cola Company; the vehicle for disseminating the results of this final dialogue in the series has not yet been determined.

The present volume addresses issues and challenges generated by the current situation and probable future directions of poverty and inequality in Latin American democracies as they cope with increasingly competitive markets and open economies in the wake of economic liberalization. The chapters in this book were written by the authors of principal presentations in the academic workshop on "Poverty in Latin America: Issues and New Responses" in fall 1995. The chapters also reflect the contributions made by participants at the workshop and at the policy forum that followed it.

We are grateful to Vilmar Faria, State University of Campinas and presently Special Advisor on social policy to the President of Brazil, who codirected the academic workshop, and to all the authors for their efforts on behalf of the workshop and this volume. We are especially indebted to Víctor E. Tokman, Assistant Director General and Regional Director for the Americas of

---

1. Project Latin America 2000 Working Paper #1, 1994, Catherine Conaghan, "Democracy that Matters: The Search for Authenticity, Legitimacy, and Civic Competence in the Andes"; #2, Scott Mainwaring, "Democracy in Brazil and the Southern Cone: Achievements and Problems"; #3, Jorge G. Castañeda, with comments by Robert Dahl, "Three Challenges to U.S. Democracy: Accountability, Representativeness, and Intellectual Diversity"; #4, Laurence Whitehead, "The Peculiarities of 'Transition' *a la mexicana*"; #5, Terry Lynn Karl, "Central America in the Twenty-First Century: The Prospects for a Democratic Region"; and #6, the summary of the workshop, Volker Frank and Charles Kenney, "Democracy in the Americas: Approaching the Year 2000 (A Rapporteurs' Report)."

the International Labor Organization, who codirected the public policy forum and coedited this volume. He contributed a concluding chapter that goes beyond a synthesis of the other chapters; he addresses basic issues such as job creation and training and further analyzes the evolution of poverty and social policy in Latin America.

We wish to acknowledge with special thanks Joetta Schlabach, formerly Academic Coordinator of the Kellogg Institute, for her exceptionally thorough and consistent performance in the execution of every stage of the project. We are also grateful to the members of the Kellogg Institute staff; Bettye Bielejewski, Caroline Domingo, and Gabriela Mossi assisted in the final preparation of the manuscript and Martha Sue Abbott, Dolores Fairley, Nancy Hahn, and Albert H. LeMay contributed in many helpful ways. Our aspirations for this project were high and the generosity of so many contributors and participants has justified those aspirations. Any failures to reach our goals are thus ours.

      Ernest Bartell, c.s.c.
      Executive Director
      Guillermo O'Donnell
      Academic Director
      The Helen Kellogg Institute for International Studies
      Notre Dame, September 1997

Introduction

VÍCTOR E. TOKMAN

This book contains the papers submitted to the academic workshop "Poverty in Latin America: Issues and New Responses," organized by the Kellogg Institute and sponsored by The Coca-Cola Company. The workshop was followed by a public policy forum which debated the main conclusions from different perspectives. Both events were attended by high-level academics, politicians, governmental officials, congressional representatives, entrepreneurs, union leaders, journalists, and civil society representatives (see Appendix 1). In spite of the richness of comments and interventions in both events, we had to make the hard choice of including in this book only the written contributions to the academic workshop.

Vilmar Faria and I were kindly invited by the Kellogg Institute to design and conduct the academic workshop, as well as to collaborate in the public policy forum. The outcome is thus the result of a collaborative endeavor with Vilmar Faria, Ernest Bartell, C.S.C., Guillermo O'Donnell and Joetta Schlabach from the Kellogg Institute. I undertook the responsibility of coediting this volume with O'Donnell and of writing the final chapter. Not intended as a conclusion, the final chapter is the result of my own reading of the papers which, of course, was very much influenced by the workshop and forum debates in which I had the privilege to participate.

Itinerary

The book is organized in four parts. The first presents the general trends in poverty and equity in Latin America, setting the scenario for policy analysis. The second and third concentrate on the policy discussion from a double perspective: the employment question, including human development aspects, and emerging responses in social policies. The final part contains my own contribution, based on the content of the preceding chapters, to the search for new answers for eradicating poverty and increasing equity.

Chapter 1, written by Oscar Altimir, presents a comprehensive analysis of the evolution of poverty and equity in the region, looking into the relation between them and their links with growth and employment. From his analysis, the reader will have access to the most complete set of data available on these issues. Altimir paints a clear picture of deterioration in the situation of poverty and equity during the economic adjustment period, as well as of the crucial importance of growth (or, during the 1980s, the lack thereof) and of the employment evolution characterized by increased unemployment, predominance of low quality jobs, and diminishing wages.

In chapter 2, José Alberto Magno de Carvalho anticipates the impact of the fertility transition on poverty, identifying a positive outcome in the short run owing to the decrease in the child dependency rate which will liberate resources, particularly in education. However, in the longer run, an increase in the elderly dependency rate will impose additional demands on already fragile social security systems. O'Donnell approaches the poverty and social question from a political perspective and examines the insufficient political support mobilized in the recent past to make an antipoverty strategy feasible. He goes further, looking for new political alliances that could provide the necessary base for a sustainable effort on this front.

The contributions of René Cortázar and María Antonia Gallart contained in part II examine the employment question in a globalized world. Both see a need to redesign labor and human resource development policies in response to changing economic conditions. Cortázar argues, in chapter 4, that the new economic rules require a substantive change of the previous consensus that was based on a strong state, a centralized regulatory system, and a closed economic environment. To progress in a more open, international economy, increased productivity and greater flexibility are needed. Cortázar calls for changes in labor policies, particularly in relation to wage-setting. He suggests that, given the necessarily closer link between wages and productivity changes, collective bargaining will become more efficient as it takes place at the enterprise level. In addition, the search for growth and equity will imply changes in the roles of and relations among the state, the market, and civil society. In Cortázar's view the emerging consensus should be based on an autonomous civil society without weakening the state or forgetting the importance of markets. This strategic change will have important effects on regulations and policies in the labor field, which Cortázar explores in his chapter.

Gallart examines the type of training needed for responding to the transformation of the world economy. She identifies an important change in the demand for able human resources based on flexible competence rather than on specific skills. This calls for new links between education and training. The increased importance of demand aspects leads to an interesting discussion of the more active participation of entrepreneurs and their enterprises in training and reforming national training institutes.

Emerging responses in the social policy field are analyzed from a systemic perspective in part III. Carlos Filgueira looks into new and old social vulnerabilities and identifies changes related to demographic and employment factors. While the majority of vulnerabilities are inherited from the past, new forms of vulnerabilities linked to economic changes are emerging. In chapter 7 Dagmar Raczynski examines the factors determining the crisis of the old model of social protection and identifies new features incorporated in recent generations of social policies, in particular, privatization, decentralization, targeting, and financial sustainability. Charles Reilly adds, in chapter 8, a different vision from the perspective of civil society. He brings into the scenery the active participation of nongovernmental organizations as channels for representation and instruments for implementing social policies.

"The Notre Dame Consensus"

Finally, in chapter 9, I offer some thoughts, based on previous chapters, of an integrated vision, trying to identify whether a new paradigm is emerging. Clearly, a number of values and perspectives are shared by all contributors. The first is that poverty alleviation should be a matter of priority and that increasing equity is both an end in itself and an instrument to reach that objective. There is also recognition of substantial changes in the world economy and in the role of social actors, including government, which necessitate the introduction of reforms. The reforms suggested in this book are wide-ranging, for poverty and equity cannot be tackled by marginal changes in policy orientation; rather, a comprehensive redesigning of policies and sociopolitical relations is required. Interactions between economic and social policies are today more important than ever. Economic success cannot be reached if social and labor conditions are inadequate, and social progress cannot be attained without proper economic conditions.

Job creation is considered a crucial instrument, but labor policies must be adapted to respond to the challenge of international competitiveness and flexibility. This requires a closer relation between wages and productivity, as well as a more decentralized and autonomous process of collective bargaining. Labor regulations should take into account the new needs and adapt by moving progressively to self-regulation by civil society. These changes require a strong, although less interventionist, government. Protection should be adapted to a more mobile labor market to promote mobility and to ensure that those affected by the changes are not left vulnerable. Investing in human resources was considered a necessary condition; thus policies and institutions for education and training are a critical component of the reform package. In the new economy, abilities are replaced by competence, which is more closely related to primary level education; secondary levels are important for technological management. This opens new grounds for interaction between education and training, and with it, the need to respond more closely to market demands by linking entrepreneurs to the training process and by decentralizing, through which the enterprise and training organizations are given the task of providing the necessary skills. A role remains, however, for government: to guide and monitor policy and to respond to the needs of vulnerable groups.

Social responses to new and old vulnerabilities should also be a subject of systemic treatment. Reform in social policies should focus on the poor as a priority, but should go beyond this focus in the search for equity. There are new openings for privatization, decentralization, targeting, and a more careful consideration of financial aspects in social policies. The approach suggested is, however, necessarily cautious; some public spaces must be preserved, and care must be taken so that extreme forms of cost effectiveness and targeting do not diminish poverty, however efficiently, at the cost of widening or perpetuating social inequalities.

The state, the market, and civil society should move to a new balance, where society acquires a primary role without weakening the state and where markets are given due responsibility for economic efficiency. The process will necessarily have to be gradual, since the transfer of power in an unequal society must simultaneously empower the weak to avoid perpetuating present disparities. This is particularly true in cases where the move toward decentralization could affect the bargaining strength of national actors. The redefinition of roles and regulations implies a redesigning of the prevailing social order. To make it sustainable, creative political alliances are needed to support the reform.

The above thus constitutes the basis of the "Notre Dame Consensus," an ambitious and far-reaching proposal for reform. I hope that readers will find the intellectual stimulus in this book that we found in actively participating in the collective search for new responses to poverty and inequity.

Part I

Issues and Challenges in the New Economic Environment

1 | Inequality, Employment, and Poverty in Latin America

An Overview

OSCAR ALTIMIR

The present paper reviews the trends and recent changes in income distribution in Latin America, setting them in the context of the style of development that prevailed in the region during the postwar period and of the "change of regime" involved in ongoing economic and institutional reforms. It also attempts to look into the future, at what will influence the distributive outcomes under the emerging style of development.

Long-Term Trends in Employment, Inequality, and Poverty in Latin American Postwar Development

The Dynamics of the Postwar Style of Development

The style of development that prevailed in Latin America after World War II was characterized by a growth dynamic based on: (i) the export of natural resources in which these countries had traditionally enjoyed absolute advantages; (ii) industrialization protected from external competition and oriented to the domestic market; (iii) expansion and diversification of private consumption; and (iv) the sustained growth of public expenditure.

The expansion of public expenditure provided, first, for the progressive setting up of a *sui generis* welfare state which protected and served emerging social strata. Second, it financed public investments considered strategic. Third, it funded various means of subsidizing private investment. Finally, it led to the establishment of an extensive bureaucracy, required by the considerable state activism involved in the dynamics of postwar development but also needed to absorb middle-class segments that were quickly emerging as a result of the expansion of education but were not yet fully employed by the growing modern sectors.

The postwar style of development entailed both a scheme of accumulation that had to accommodate the drain of resources represented by deteriorating terms of trade and, until the 1970s, a mostly negative net transfer of financial resources. Domestically, accumulation was based on: (i) the appropriation by the state and the expanding urban sectors of a significant part of the rents from the exploitation of natural resources; (ii) the appropriation by the state and urban firms and workers of quasi-rents originating in protection; (iii) transfers of resources to private investors by credit rationing and subsidies or tax exemptions; and (iv) import permits and tax subsidies for promoted investments.

Growth, Accumulation, and Technical Progress

On the basis of this model, Latin American output grew 2.7% per capita a year between 1950 and 1980. At least for the major countries, average growth in this period was not very different from the rates they had experienced under the liberal order prior to World War I or after the Great Depression. While the rate of growth—"golden age" of the world economy—was similar to that of the United States, it was not enough either to prevent a widening of the income gap relative to most of the advanced capitalist economies or to keep pace with the relatively less developed but rapidly expanding economies of East Asia.

Capital accumulation was significant (over 6% a year) and in some countries (Brazil and Mexico) it was comparable to that of Japan, Korea, Germany, or Spain during the same period, although investment ratios remained below the levels attained in these thrifty countries. Labor input also increased relatively rapidly, and the expansion of education raised the educational level of the labor force more quickly than in the developed countries, although not as fast as in Korea or Taiwan. What made most of the difference between Latin America's growth performance and that of Western European or Asian countries was lagging productivity. The average[1] increase of joint factor productivity[2] in Latin America (1.2% a year) was comparable to that of the laggards (the United States and the United Kingdom) among developed countries and was far behind the 3–4% annual gain of the other developed countries and even the Korean 2% increase.

Employment and Underemployment

Postwar development in Latin America involved the dynamic creation of new jobs and an enormous transformation of the labor force. While the labor force grew at an annual rate of 2.5%, rapid urbanization diminished the share of the agricultural labor force from 55% in 1950 to 32% in 1980. Employment in the urban formal sector grew at about 4% a year, involving profound transformations of the occupational structure and generalized social mobility. This was barely enough to absorb the increases in the urban labor force however; about 30% remained underutilized (unemployed or in informal activities) (PREALC 1991).

The Expansion of Education and Social Mobility

Educational enrollment expanded significantly in the 1960s and 1970s. The net enrollment rate of children 6 to 11 years reached 71% in 1970 and 82% in 1980. Secondary school enrollment reached 63% of the 12- to 17-year-old population in 1980 (vs. 15% in 1960), while 24% of the 18 to 23 age group (vs. 6% in 1960) were enrolled in higher education. The quality of education was increasingly deficient, however, characterized by poor quality of basic skills training, the use of obsolete curricula in secondary education, and questionable quality and irrelevance of much of higher education. In addition, the expansion of education took place in an increasingly inequitable style, owing to differential access to public education and to segmentation according to quality (ECLAC-UNESCO 1992).

Changes in production patterns—both in terms of activities and occupations—brought about a sizable structural mobility, with a drastic reduction of the agricultural stratum and a rapid expansion of middle and upper urban strata. The expansion of education was, in the first stages, consistent with these structural changes; education became a basic vehicle of social mobility, enabling people to move from the popular sectors into the middle class. Lack of education was one of the main factors keeping the popular sectors in informal, low-productivity activities. On the other hand, the rapid expansion of secondary and higher education and their emphasis on traditional curricula exceeded the requirements of production, resulting in underutilization of the labor force and diminishing returns to higher education (Filgueira and Geneletti 1981).

Income Inequality

Latin America has traditionally been a region of great income inequalities; most countries of the region have been among the most unequal societies of the developing world. Moreover, in 1980, balancing periods of deterioration and improvement of income distribution, most of the bigger and medium-sized countries reached the end of the long period of postwar inward growth with a greater concentration of income, almost irrespective of their average rate of growth. The only exceptions appear to be Colombia and perhaps Costa Rica and Venezuela (Altimir 1994a).

Multiple factors, many of them structurally interrelated, lie behind traditional Latin American inequality. Among the statistically more significant are those related to agricultural underdevelopment (itself associated with great inequalities in land tenure and access to land), the proportion of the labor force in agriculture, and the educational level of the labor force.[3] On the other hand, although difficult to measure, it is evident to any Latin American that the appropriation of quasi-rents which originated in the style of development through oligopolistic or corporatist structures has added significantly to inequality both of earnings and of incomes from property.

At the beginning of the 1970s, according to a decomposition exercise covering nine countries (Altimir and Piñera 1982), education by itself accounted for between 10% and 15% of total inequality, age accounted for between 12% and 20%, and occupation for between 3% and 17%, while the urban or rural location of earners and jobs with similar characteristics accounted only for between 2% and 7% of total inequality.[4] By themselves personal characteristics (education, age, and sex) and employment characteristics (status, occupation, and kind of economic activity) accounted for roughly similar proportions of total inequality. However, in statistical association with the other variables, education accounted for between 22% and 36% of total inequality.

But how were the *changes* of inequality related to the dynamics of the postwar style of development? An analysis of inequality and growth during the 1960s and 1970s (Altimir 1994a) shows that in a few instances inequality decreased during periods of moderate growth (Mexico 1968–77 and 1977–84) or rapid growth (Colombia 1971–78 and Venezuela 1971–81); in other spells of rapid growth (Brazil 1970–80 and Mexico 1963–68) it was unchanged. In most spells of moderate growth, low growth, or no growth, inequality increased.

The degree to which the human capital hypothesis can explain the recorded evolution of inequality in all those cases and in shorter periods of time is still open to question and research. The equalizing effects of the rapid expansion of education may be visible in the Colombian and Mexican cases of rapid growth. In the Brazilian case of rapid growth, it can be argued that the increased demand for higher skills offset the equalizing effect of the increasing supply of educated workers, given its small initial base (Birdsall, Ross, and Sabot 1994).

But why has moderate growth, in the context of expanding education, almost always been accompanied by increases in inequality? A plausible hypothesis may be that at low and unstable growth rates, labor market segmentation resulting from institutional factors takes precedence over human capital dynamics, maintaining or increasing returns to education in the formal sector while keeping even educated workers in informal activities underpaid.

Poverty

Absolute poverty, which affected about 40% of Latin American households in 1970 (Altimir 1982), tended to decrease during the 1970s, owing to aggregate economic growth and the modernization of some segments of the agricultural sector. During the 1970s the incidence of poverty in the rural areas showed a downward trend in almost all of the major countries irrespective of the rate or stability of their growth, with Chile being the one noticeable exception. Urban poverty decreased in countries that attained high rates of per capita growth (Brazil, Colombia, Mexico, and Venezuela) but tended to increase in countries that experienced increasing inequality with moderate growth (Costa Rica and Uruguay) or low and unstable growth (Argentina, Chile, and Peru) during that last decade of the postwar period of inward development (Altimir 1994a).

Crisis, Adjustment, Reform, and the Transformation of the Style of Latin American Development

In the 1980s Latin American countries suffered a profound crisis, comparable to that at the beginning of the 1930s. How long they could have continued to grow under the postwar style of development had it not been for the triple external shock that unleashed the crisis,[5] is an interesting but unanswerable question. The shocks dramatically exposed the external vulnerability, the lack of structural flexibility, and the fiscal fragility of the Latin American economies.

Latin American countries reacted to the abrupt reversal of foreign finance at the beginning of the 1980s with varied attempts at external adjustment. In most cases such adjustments were unusually large, in accordance with the magnitude of the external shock. But, as a rule and like previous adjustments, they did not alter the main economic institutions. Market-oriented reforms had previously occurred only in Argentina, Chile, and Uruguay, and in Argentina they were reversed or suspended at the beginning of the crisis. It was only later, as a second reaction to pervasive macroeconomic imbalances and an attempt to set the foundations for future sustained growth, that various reform packages were adopted in various countries.

Although national reform processes vary considerably, they all pursue goals of macroeconomic stability and international competitiveness through fiscal discipline, freer trade, market mechanisms, and private investment. Opening the economies to trade (both to the competition of imports and to competing in export markets), privatizing state enterprises, deregulating markets, and resorting to taxes for securing public revenues are the main pivots of the reform strategy. This involves a radical turnaround of the accumulation and growth model.

Capital accumulation becomes primarily the responsibility of private enterprises (whether domestic or foreign appears to be less relevant), responding to market signals and—at least in tradables—exposed to international prices. Even investment in utilities and other infrastructure comes under the aegis of the private sector, in some cases in association with the state, which retains regulatory power over monopolies. The scope for industrial policy is limited to the use of trade instruments recognized under GATT (General Agreement on Tariffs and Trade) and to subsidies and tax expenditures from public revenues to reinforce private investment and technological development.

Growth dynamics have changed in favor of exports and private investment and against public expenditure. Private consumption, however, has retained its key expansionary role, enhanced by the availability of imports and finance.

Income Distribution, Employment, and Poverty through Crisis and Adjustment

Income concentration increased further during the crisis and adjustments of the 1980s. Almost all Latin American countries experienced acute redistribution of income during the decade of crisis, adjustment, and reforms, in most cases with regressive net outcomes at the end of the decade. Only Uruguay has clearly emerged in the 1990s with a lesser income concentration than the one existing before the outbreak of the crisis (see Table 1.1, end of chapter).

However, synchronic distributive changes in the different countries of the region are not uniformly comparable. The countries did not all suffer adverse external shocks at the same time. Furthermore, national circumstances and policy responses entailed different sequences of adjustment, which in some cases included spells of instability and further adjustment. Therefore, the vicissitudes of income distribution, poverty, and employment in different countries through the 1980s must be compared for similar phases of macroeconomic adjustment. In particular, the balance of the whole adjustment process cannot be drawn until each economy has regained its production frontier.

Distributive Changes in Different Phases of the Adjustment Process

In a previous paper (Altimir 1994b) I analyzed in detail the evolution of income concentration and poverty through the different macroeconomic phases each of nine countries experienced during the 1980s and early 1990s. The results of that analysis are summarized in Table 1.2. The main highlights follow:

i) In most cases recessive adjustment to external shocks at the beginning of the decade had adverse effects on inequality. Colombia stands out as an exception owing to the mild nature of its adjustment and to increasing real wages. In Brazil inequality apparently remained invariant through the rapid adjustment of 1981–84; this fact may also be associated with the rise in real wages. The small improvement of inequality in Costa Rica during the 1980–83 period is less explicable, except for the possible influence of the drastic abatement of inflation.

ii) Only in two countries (Colombia and Uruguay) did the recovery after external adjustment improve the distribution of income. It is no wonder that inequality increased in Argentina (in 1983–86) and Venezuela (in 1986–89), where recovery was hesitant. But it is noteworthy that inequality also increased in Brazil, Chile, and Costa Rica, amid vigorous growth in economic activity.

iii) Countries that, after initially recovering from external adjustment, again plunged into recession owing to pervasive internal imbalances, additional external shocks, and accelerating inflation *cum* stabilization efforts, experienced even further increases of inequality. In Argentina and Peru such imbalances drove the economies to hyperinflation; real incomes and wages went down and labor underutilization increased. In Mexico the combination of external shocks, accelerated inflation, and the stabilization efforts in 1985–87 determined a new recessionary spell with an increase of informal labor and a drop of real wages. This suggests that part of the observed increase of inequality up to 1989 may have taken place during this period. The post–1986 acceleration of inflation in Brazil coincided with an almost stagnant level of economic activity and the eventual fall (in 1990) of real wages; this more gradual path was, up to that point, compatible with a slight decrease of concentration.

iv) The cases of stabilization and recovery from high inflation and recession in Argentina (1990–92) and Mexico (1987–89) had different distributive outcomes. In the Argentine case income concentration and the high level of urban poverty both declined. This was probably associated with getting out of hyperinflation, for employment and wages did not improve significantly. In Mexico, on the contrary, evidence indicates that inequality may have increased.

As the above summary reveals, the notion that income concentration has been countercyclical, as stated by Morley (1994), is only a broad contour, subject to important qualifications. In the first place, the depth or type of adjustment to external shocks may make a difference as to whether or not it brings about more inequality, as the cases of Brazil, Colombia, and Costa Rica highlight. Second, recovery from external adjustment did not, in most cases, bring about distributive improvements; on the contrary, it was usually accompanied by further deterioration. Of course, in countries where internal imbalances and attempts at stabilization eventually brought about another recessionary spell, the corresponding rise of income concentration added to the previous deterioration in a process of increasing inequality attributable to instability and recession. Third, the distributive effects of recovery and disinflation were not symmetrical to those of recession and inflation, as evidence summarized in Table 1.1 and the following discussion reveals. Finally, for cases where recovery turned into growth at approximately full capacity, the countercyclical explanation should give way to more structural factors.

A Distributive Balance of the "Lost Decade"

As the 1990s began most Latin American countries were in the process of stabilizing their economies and some were already growing at full capacity. Since 1991 the region as a whole has grown at moderate rates and has tended to consolidate price stabilization and fiscal adjustment, aided by the resumption of large-scale capital flows and by their own new modalities of macroeconomic management.

The "lost decade" thus came to an end, leaving behind it the social and distributive costs of instability, adjustment, and the (mostly forced and forcible) introduction of reforms. The losses of social welfare are unrecoverable, and analyses of the losses may give way to deceptive counterfactuals. But now that the crisis and its immediate aftermath have passed, we can look at the scars in the social tissue and the feebleness of its different segments.

In 1990 aggregate social welfare for the region as a whole, as measured by real per capita national income, was 15% less than in 1980. Among the countries we are considering here, only Colombia and Chile had recovered and surpassed their precrisis levels (see Table 1.1).

During the 1980s, the fragile structural balance of employment under the postwar style of development, in which the growth of formal employment was barely enough to absorb the increase of the urban labor force (PREALC 1991), broke down. Urban labor underutilization (unemployment and employment in the informal sector) grew apace at an annual rate of 5%, while employment in formal activities expanded at half that rate, with most of the increase located in small firms of lower productivity (data from ECLAC and PREALC). By 1990 only Chile had surpassed, and Colombia and Costa Rica almost attained, the precrisis degree of utilization of the urban labor force.[6] But Mexico and Brazil, as well as the still recovering economies of Argentina and Venezuela, showed degrees of underutilization of the labor force much higher than before the crisis.

Real wages were maintained during the 1980s in Colombia and Panama and, by 1990, had more than recovered in Chile. Preadjustment Brazil also maintained a high real wage, but recovered economies like Costa Rica, Mexico, and Uruguay and unrecovered ones like Argentina, Peru, and Venezuela entered the 1990s with significantly lower real wages (see Table 1.1).

Only Colombia, Costa Rica, and Uruguay emerged from the crisis with a lower degree of income concentration than before its outbreak.[7] Chile's inequality in 1987 was still somewhat higher than before the crisis (and significantly higher than before the structural reforms of the 1970s), despite the improved labor situation.[8] In Mexico, in a slow-growth path by 1987, both the distributive situation and the labor indicators were worse than in the late 1970s. On the other hand, those countries that still had not completed their recovery into sustained growth (Argentina, Brazil, Panama, Peru, and Venezuela) also showed a concentration of income significantly greater than before the crisis (see Table 1.1).

Real income improvement spread across all classes in Colombia (1980–92), but distributive changes brought about significant increases in the incomes of the poorest half and the middle stratum of the population, favoring much less the highest quintile. In Uruguay, with a more modest increase of real per capita income, the decrease of inequality resulted in rising incomes for the middle half, a lesser rise for the poorest quintile, and a decrease in real income for the richest. In Chile between 1987 and 1992 the modest improvement of income concentration along with a significant average increase of real income per capita entailed greater real income gains for the poorest half than for the middle classes and the richest.

In Mexico, the rise in per capita real income between 1984 and 1992 favored only the richest quintile, owing to the increase of inequality over that period. In Venezuela a lower real income per capita and distributive deterioration affected the real incomes of the poor and of the middle classes much more than those of the richest quintile. In Argentina and Brazil they translated into significant declines of real incomes for the poorest half of the population, less severe losses for the middle classes, and increases of real incomes for the richest.

The different behaviors of real wages help explain the diverse outcomes in terms of inequality, which in turn correspond to contrasting changes in the relative position of occupational groups. The decrease of inequality in Uruguay and its upsurge since 1990 in Colombia and Costa Rica reflect gains by different groups of wage earners (including those in the public sector) with respect to employers and both professional and nonprofessional self-employed workers. Symmetrically, greater inequality in Argentina and Venezuela corresponds to relative losses by wage earners and relative gains by employers and (in Argentina, to a lesser extent) self-employed workers[9] (see Table 1.4).

These changes in relative incomes are generally consistent with the changes in the composition of employment during the adjustment of the 1980s and early 1990s (see Table 1.5). The main changes included: i) an increase in the proportion of the urban labor force occupied in low productivity sectors; ii) a decrease in the share of the public sector in total urban employment; iii) a significant rise in the proportion of the urban labor force occupied as professional and technical employees in the formal sector; and iv) a trend toward the reduction of nontechnical jobs in the formal sector as a proportion of total employment.

The combined effects of recession, adjustment, and restructuring during the 1980s apparently affected relatively more the earnings of medium- and higher-skilled workers, probably because the indicated relative shift of demand for labor in the formal private sector towards technical and professional staff was outpaced by a rapidly growing supply.[10] Average incomes of the urban labor force with secondary and university education generally fell relative to the incomes of those with basic education (see Table 1.6).[11]

Changes in relative incomes and the fall of real per capita income during the first half of the 1980s, when most economies suffered recessionary adjustments or had just begun to recover, involved significant increases in urban poverty. Only in a few cases were these increases partially reversed with the stabilization and growth processes of later years. By 1992 Chile and Uruguay were the only countries where the incidence of poverty in urban areas had fallen below the precrisis marks (see Table 1.7).

Figures for Latin America as a whole (ECLAC 1991, 1992) estimated that 35% of households lived in poverty in 1980, 37% in 1986, and 39% in 1990. This deteriorating trend is almost entirely attributable to the aggravation of urban poverty, which affected 25% of urban households in 1980, 30% in 1986, and 34% in 1990, thus almost doubling the absolute numbers living in poverty in urban areas, 22.7 million households and 115.5 million people in 1990.

In contrast, the incidence of rural poverty in the region as a whole remained relatively stable during the decade, close to 54% of rural households and 60% of the rural population, with absolute numbers increasing slightly more than 1% a year, to 80 million people. Consequently, around 60% of the Latin American poor now concentrate in urban areas, compared with less than half in 1980.

Distributive Trends at Full-Capacity Growth

The distributive changes recorded by available income distribution and employment measurements, upon which the above very broad picture has been drawn, incorporate the effects of external shocks, macroeconomic adjustment, institutional changes involving policy reform and underlying restructuring processes, as well as those of failed adjustments and the acceleration of inflation. It may be impossible to disentangle the distributive changes involved in production restructuring (both the processes already underway before the crisis and those induced later by economic reforms) from those associated with the vicissitudes of shocks, instability, adjustment, and economic recovery. Economic policy reforms may have contributed to the short-term effects that the stabilization packages and adjustment policies, implemented at the same time, have had on income distribution and employment. Moreover, some of these effects may have been imposed by the political economy of reforms.

We can look with more certainty at the trends of income distribution once the economies were growing at full capacity or close to their production frontiers,[12] under more or less stable macroeconomic conditions. From 1986 to 1990 Colombia approximately maintained its previously diminished degree of inequality, but in 1991–92 the Gini value of its distribution jumped to a mark higher than the precrisis level, remaining stable thereafter. Inequality in Chile has virtually remained stable since 1987; a slight improvement between 1987 and 1992 had faded by 1994. Costa Rica's inequality tended to increase after 1990. Mexico experienced a modest rise between 1989 and 1992. Only Uruguay, as mentioned, significantly decreased its income concentration between 1990 and 1992.

For the other countries considered, the last available observation of income distribution corresponds precisely to the point when the economies regained their production frontiers: Brazil in 1989, Panama in 1991, Argentina, Mexico, and Venezuela around 1992. Therefore, similar indications cannot yet be drawn from their more recent experience. Furthermore, in these cases (except Panama) growth was not sustained and spells of capacity underutilization reappeared.[13]

Urban poverty decreased in Chile, Mexico, Uruguay, and Argentina. In the first case, the decrease is attributed solely to the significant growth of real income. In Mexico and Uruguay most of the observed attenuation of poverty occurred during periods when these economies were operating at close to full capacity and thus is largely due to growth. Nevertheless, one-fourth of the decrease in Mexico and one-third in Uruguay is attributable to the reduction of inequality (ECLAC 1994). In Argentina the decrease from historically high levels of incidence coincided with the recovery from hyperinflation. By contrast, in Colombia and Costa Rica, urban poverty tended to increase. In both cases the increase was owing to a retrogression of the relative income of the lower strata; in Costa Rica this offset the effect of real income growth.

Regarding the employment situation in the cases of sustained growth, the degree of labor force utilization was maintained in Colombia, Costa Rica, Mexico, and Uruguay, and improved significantly in Chile. The real wage was maintained in Colombia and Costa Rica and improved steadily in Chile, Mexico, and Uruguay (see Tables 1.1 and 1.3).

Changes in the composition of employment during these spells of full-capacity growth prolonged the decrease in public sector employment and the rise in the proportion of professional and technical occupations but not the trend toward reduced nontechnical jobs in the formal sector observed during adjustment (see Table 1.5). On the other hand, in Colombia, Costa Rica, and Uruguay, the trend toward the fall of relative incomes of the medium and higher skills was reversed in this phase, more than offsetting the previous fall. In these three countries, as well as in Mexico, this reversal coincided with a relative expansion of the demand for those skills. This may represent a future characteristic of the new style of development.

Other more detailed analyses of the relative wage structure find that in Chile the relative wages of more educated, skilled workers increased during the 1975–90 period (between the first economic reforms and the return to a full-capacity growth path) owing to intra-industry upgrading of training and occupational shifts (Robbins 1994). In Argentina, during the present reform and stabilization program relative wages for more educated workers increased between 1990 and 1993 (Pessino 1994).

Income Distribution, Employment, and Poverty under the Emerging Economic Order: The Challenges Ahead

How are these trends related to the emerging economic order, bearing in mind the varying chronology of individual country reform processes and the radical or gradual pace of their reform strategies? In most cases we have considered, the combined processes of adjustment (including the spells of imbalances) and structural transformation, impacted or reoriented by institutional reforms, have resulted in asymmetrical changes of inequality, rendering greater inequality at present than before the crisis.

This is by no means strange, given the fact that structural adjustment and reform involved a change in the growth and accumulation model. When the reform process is quick and drastic (as in Chile and more recently in Argentina and Mexico), the "capitalist shock," represented by the switch of the accumulation process to private hands, abruptly opens new investment opportunities, and the changes in asset prices offer opportunities for speculation. This gives rise to rapid gains for a relatively small number of firms and people in positions to take advantage of those opportunities,[14] in a process similar to that highlighted by Kuznets (1966) for the phases of early modernization.

Whether the distributive deterioration is only a temporary effect—however extended—of economic and institutional restructuring or whether the new development style being deployed tends to involve structurally a more unequal distribution of primary incomes is still a matter for speculation. Nevertheless, some hints can be drawn from the experiences reviewed above.

The case of Chile is instructive for it is the only one where the process of transformation has matured beyond the introduction and consolidation of structural reforms to a remarkable and sustained growth. Seventeen years after the first reforms and seven after the second round of reforms—and after a profound restructuring—income inequalities are still clearly wider than before structural adjustment, and they are not being reduced by sustained growth.

More recently, the change of development style is evident in Argentina and Mexico. In both cases income inequality after adjustment and reform was greater than before the crisis, and it was associated with increasing labor underutilization and lower real wages. The Mexican currency crisis of 1994 and its subsequent effects on Argentina underline the fact that consolidating reforms and maturing structural changes can take time. Furthermore, under the new growth model these processes are very exposed to external shocks.

In Colombia, Costa Rica, and Uruguay, reforms and the change of the accumulation model have been gradual. Institutional reforms were introduced in Uruguay beginning in the 1970s; the gradualism that has characterized both trade liberalization and macroeconomic and labor policy is associated with an improvement of the distribution of income once growth had been reinitiated. Reforms in Costa Rica and Colombia have been more recent and have in general proceeded apace, gaining speed in the early 1990s. In both countries, the gradual reforms of the 1980s coexisted with improvements in the distribution of income, while the eventual acceleration of reform in the 1990s coincided with an increase of inequality, though in neither case to a degree much greater than the precrisis mark (see Table 1.1).

Summarizing the above evidence, the completed change of the accumulation and growth model in Chile resulted in a more unequal distribution of primary income—even after it recovered from the "temporary" worsening during recession—than the one prevalent under the old style of development. Such a change of style, even when radically pursued—as in Argentina and Mexico—takes more time than expected to become consolidated and is vulnerable to external shocks (as the Chilean experience of the 1970s also bears witness), thus extending the period and depth of the "temporary" distributive deterioration. Gradual reformers (e.g., Colombia, Costa Rica, and Uruguay) might eventually suffer from further equity deterioration if they follow the path of the forerunners, deepening reform and accelerating structural change. On the other hand, Brazil may become a special case of gradual reform and structural change if it manages to navigate the reform without worsening its already extremely high concentration of income.

Can further deployment and modifications of the growth dynamics under the new style of development bring about distributive improvement? How can more rapid and sustained growth be attained under these new circumstances and how will the pattern of that growth affect employment and income distribution in the long run?

The Sustainability of Growth

It has been amply illustrated that low growth and recessive adjustments have a regressive impact on income distribution and particularly the incidence of poverty. But the sustainability of growth is not only crucial for aggregate and distributive welfare in the short run; low growth hinders modernization and future growth potential by weakening investment and technical progress, impairing international competitiveness.

The Mexican episode and its repercussions in some other countries of the region did not amount to a regional crisis. But they highlighted the external vulnerability of Latin America's transformation processes, in which adjustment has become endemic. If Argentina, Mexico, and Uruguay eventually become regional examples of a new kind of stop-go pattern under the new style of development, resulting in slow medium-term growth, the prospects for equity and social advancement will be bleak.

Such extremes of vulnerability may result in part from macroeconomic management, but they are rooted in insufficient national saving, which exaggerates the dependency on external finance. Limited national saving also impedes technical progress, slowing the pace of total factor productivity increases and holding back progress in international competitiveness.

The Pace of Growth and Poverty Reduction

The pace of growth is crucial for the alleviation of poverty. Assuming no changes in the present relative distribution of incomes and no more vigorous social policies, reducing the total number of the poor to about half of today's mark (and improving the lot of a good portion of the extremely poor) would take 42 years at the present 1.5% per capita growth[15] and 25 years at the historic average of 2.5%. That target would be reached in 16 years[16] with 4% sustained per capita growth. At less than this pace, poverty reduction in most countries of the region appears so parsimonious as to be disheartening, counterproductive for social integration and, ultimately, for sustained growth.

Employment Creation

Rapid growth is the only hope for creating enough employment—at the very least to restore the postwar balance between the expansion of the labor force and the creation of formal or higher-productivity jobs. The demographic background is not very encouraging for the near future. The working-age population is still growing faster than total population[17] and participation rates are strongly increasing.

The creation of higher-than-average productivity jobs is crucial. Productivity in medium and large industrial enterprises across the region has been increasing rapidly,[18] but employment in that segment has been declining at more than 3% a year. This kind of productive restructuring is probably more intense in industry than in the formal segments of other sectors,[19] but it underlines the fact that productivity for the rest of the labor force is advancing very slowly and that new jobs of higher-than-average productivity are relatively scarce.

Until and unless the dynamics of modernization spread over significant segments of the productive system so that growth is geared to higher production rates and becomes system-wide, the creation of productive employment may be insufficient to absorb the increases of the labor force, not to mention alleviating poverty.

Investment and National Saving

The endeavour to create widespread high-productivity jobs calls for an important investment effort. With the exceptions of Colombia, Costa Rica, Chile, and Panama, Latin American countries in 1994 still had lower investment coefficients than before the crisis (ECLAC 1995). Although growth based on unutilized capacity may partially explain this fact, per capita investment in countries close to their production frontier was in most cases still low, except in Colombia and Chile.

Notwithstanding the tendency during ongoing restructuring in some activities to adopt "soft" technologies (i.e., reorganization of production, management techniques, marketing technology, etc.), there is evidence that most countries coming out of recovery return to the long-term trend of declining productivity of capital. In such circumstances, to attain growth rates of, say, 6% a year would require increasing present investment rates by several points (more than five, in most cases). Only huge and widespread efforts to catch up with the international frontier of best productive practices would enable increases in total factor productivity to substitute for additional fixed investment.

Under the new style of development such an effort relies decisively on private investment. Since a significant part of the reduction of total investment during the 1980s corresponded to the contraction of public investment, both in public enterprises (some of them privatized since then) and infrastructure, private investment must take over these requirements.

Because the propensities to save a portion of additional income are low, sustaining such an investment drive would require a substantially greater proportion of external financing than the one represented by the extraordinary inflow of capital of the early 1990s. Given the vulnerability for growth this would entail, the alternative is a significant shift of the national saving functions.

Demand and Supply of Skills

As long as the adoption of "soft" technologies is strengthened, technical change is biased in favor of demand for skilled labor, reducing the need for unskilled labor and capital. In the structural conditions of Latin American countries, such a trend involves, in the medium-term, the creation of more skilled and better paid jobs per unit of investment relative to the number of jobs and pay levels for unskilled workers. Plausible as this speculation is, it offers few clues about the actual amounts of the different kinds of jobs rapid growth may create or the degree to which relative earnings may differ. It follows, however, the already noted trend recorded between 1990 and 1992 in countries growing at full capacity.

The supply of educated workers will continue to grow apace, as a consequence of the higher enrollment rates during the 1980s. Whether the expanding demand for higher skills will outpace supply, causing relative wages to increase—as occurred during 1990–92 in the economies growing at full capacity—is a matter for speculation. If that happens, the inequality of earnings would temporarily increase, and only further investment in human capital, in response to those differential rates of return, would eventually flatten relative wages.

But "temporarily" may mean a considerable time span. Moreover, the growing demand may be for better-than-average quality education at each level, for which supply is scarcer. This would force a good part of the workforce within secondary and even tertiary education to "downgrade" occupationally at lower relative wages, as happened during the 1980s.

The Scope for Social Policy

For the distribution of income to improve in the long run and at the same time foster systemwide productivity enhancement, the supply of skilled labor must not only continue to grow but must also be more equally distributed and more suited to production and to handling information technology. Educational systems must be reformed toward those ends, improving access to education for the poor, combining education with training for unskilled workers, improving the relevance of curricula and, in particular, significantly raising the quality at all levels of the system with the aim of granting everybody effective equal access to high quality education.

Social security (mainly health care and pensions) should at least provide a safety net to prevent situations of extreme deprivation. The instances of social exclusion implicit in the previous style of development, the impact of the crisis and adjustment processes, and the distributive differentiation stemming from the emerging style of development add up to a daunting and varied universe of deprivation, of which estimates of poverty provide only a glimpse.

Social expenditures, which were already ineffective for meeting the challenge of social exclusion before the crisis, were diminished by fiscal adjustment during the 1980s. By 1992, when fiscal balances were under control as part of the new style of macroeconomic management, only Colombia had surpassed its precrisis level of per capita social expenditure, while in Costa Rica, Chile, and Uruguay that level had barely been regained. In the other countries considered here, per capita social expenditures were significantly lower than during the previous phase of growth (see Table 1.1).

States like Argentina, Costa Rica, Chile, or Uruguay, which already spend around 15% of GDP and more than 60% of their total expenditure for social purposes, may find it difficult to expand social expenditures without affecting their structural fiscal balance. Others, like Colombia, Mexico, and Venezuela, which devote little more than a third of their budgets and less than 9% of GDP to social expenditures, have more room to maneuver (see Table 1.8).

The fiscal restriction highlights the importance of reforming social welfare systems to increase their efficiency, improve the quality of services, make their distribution more equitable, and enhance the effective access of the lower strata to services of equal quality.

Concluding Remarks

Almost all Latin American economies are now working on new foundations, characterized by a firmer orientation toward exports, trade liberalization, principles of fiscal austerity, and a greater reluctance to resort to public regulation of economic activity. What is perhaps more important and permanent is that there has been restructuring at the sectoral and microeconomic levels which tends to enhance productivity and international competitiveness.

Nevertheless, the combination of market-oriented reforms and overoptimistic economic policies, on the one hand, and the retarded and ambiguous impact of reforms on savings, investment, and total factor productivity, on the other, have opened a window of vulnerability—of varying width, depending on the country—on Latin American growth.

From this viewpoint, the Mexican crisis and its sequels have laid bare a twofold problem for the sustainability of reform and transformation processes:

the economic policy problem of guaranteeing the stable functioning of the economies in the short run and the political economy problem of their medium-term outcomes for growth, employment, and inequality.

To secure rapid and sustained growth and at the same time launch processes for improving social equity, a second stage of policy reforms is needed. Lessening external vulnerability is an immediate priority, and in the longer run policymakers should actively promote national savings, together with productivity-enhancing investment and technical change. These variables are crucial for accelerating growth and necessary for eventually improving equity. Macroeconomic management, institutional reforms, the development of factor markets, and microeconomic policies should be coordinated and geared to those ends. Incentives should supplement market signals to focus the dynamism of the private sector in those directions.

Within the rationale of the new economic order, the state should assume a coordinating role through four basic strategies to support accumulation and productive development: (i) helping develop technological and entrepreneurial capabilities; (ii) providing and financing education and training; (iii) fostering infrastructure investment; and (iv) mobilizing and channeling savings to long-term financing of productive investment.

On the basis of rapid growth and systemwide productivity enhancement, it is possible to build more just societies. The distribution of primary incomes can be influenced by policy, primarily through appropriate policies for education and training and for technological development, but also improving the access of the poor to land and credit. Social policy should be able to correct undesired distributive outcomes of the transformation process and also support investment in human capital, enabling the poor to advance on the basis of their capabilities. Taxes can be raised in less regressive ways, shifting some of the burden from the worse-off to the better-off. Such a program requires a profound reform of the public tax and welfare system, active policies, and a solid commitment of fiscal resources to that end.

Table 1.1 Income Distribution and Labor Situations in the Early 1990s (Indices, precrisis levels = 100)

Countries and years[a]		Number of years since trade reform	Real per capita income	Urban poverty	Income concentration[b]	Labor force utilization[c]	Real wage	Real per capita social expenditure
I. Countries and spells of growth at close to full capacity								
Colombia	1986	—	105	100	92	92	120	109
	1990	—	112	97	94	99	116	117
	1992	2	113	106	101	99	117	128
	1994	4	123	...	101	100	124	...
Costa Rica	1990	5	89	138[h]	99	98	87	93
	1992	7	95	156[h]	101	101	86	97[e]
Chile	1987	12	90	118[g]	102	100	87	85
	1990	15	103	103[g]	99	108	96	82
	1992	17	111	87[g]	100	112	106	97
	1994	19	125	75[g]	101	108	114	105[f]
Mexico	1989	2	83	122[d]	110[d]	86	75	59
	1992	5	88	107[d]	112[d]	86	90	74[e]
Uruguay	1990	15	90	133	93	...	85	101
	1992	17	102	89	79	...	91	...
II. Countries and spells with unutilized productive capacity								
Argentina	1990	—	72	320	116	88	79	75
	1992	2	85	200	112	87	82	89
Brazil	1990	—	98	130	104	94	116	125[g]

Table 1.1 continued

Countries and years[a]	Number of years since trade reform	Real per capita income	Urban poverty	Income concentration[b]	Labor force utilization[c]	Real wage	Real per capita social expenditure

II. Countries and spells with unutilized productive capacity (cont.)

Panama 1989	–	93	110	115	...	114	...
1991	–	85	110	112	...	111	...
Peru 1990	–	72	190	...	...	44	40[g]
Venezuela 1990	1	75	183	105	91	44	65
1992	3	78	178	106	95	43	...

Source: Author's estimates, based on ECLAC's data.

[a] Base years: Argentina, Colombia, Costa Rica: 1980; Chile, Mexico, Panama, Uruguay, Venezuela: 1981; Brazil and Peru: 1979.
[b] Measured by the Gini coefficient. Income distribution: Brazil, Mexico, and Venezuela: national; Colombia, Costa Rica, Panama: urban; Argentina, Chile, and Uruguay: metropolitan area.
[c] Percentage of the nonagricultural labor force employed in formal activities.
[d] Base 1984=100.
[e] 1991.
[f] 1993.
[g] Base 1980=100.
[h] Base 1981=100.

Table 1.2 Latin America (9 countries): Changes in Macroeconomic and Labor Variables and Distributive Changes in Different Macroeconomic Phases, 1980–94 (percentage over each period)

Country	Period	Macroeconomic variables[a]			Labor market[b]						Distributive changes[c]	
		RNIpc	RER	INF[d]	RW[f]	RMW	NALU	IE	UU	GCpc	Concentration (Gini)	Urban poverty

I. Periods of recessive adjustment to external shocks

Argentina	1980–83	−16	77	I	−8	53	10	−15	81	−18	I?	I+?
Brazil	1979–83	−11	22	I	10	−10	20	...	8	−7	M	I
Colombia	1980–83	−6	−10	D	10	7	12	−16	21	7	D	M?
Costa Rica	1980–83	−24	41	I/D	−22	−1	12	−4	42	−30	D	I+
Chile	1981–83	−21	34	I	−11	−21	32	−25	111	−8	I	I
Mexico	1981–84[c]	−12	40	I	−28	−32	12	−13	36	−14	I?	I?
Peru	1982–84	−13	12	I	−21	−20	45	−15	35	−22	...	I+
Uruguay	1981–86	−17	53	I	−13	−14	...	...	60	−14	I	I+
Venezuela	1981–86	−29	48	—	...	6	24	3	78	−22	I	I+

II. Periods of recovery after external adjustment

Argentina	1983–86	−2	−3	D	17	−28	10	−5	19	14	I	I?
Brazil	1983–87	19	13	D/I	11	−26	−11	14	−45	42	I	D
Colombia	1983–86	12	64	I	9	6	3	−2	15	−3	D	M
Costa Rica	1983–88	12	14	I	8	16	−4	9	−26	11	I	D?
Chile	1983–87	14	74	—	−2	−26	−25	39	−37	−23	D?	I?
Panama	1982–86	10	—		9	13	...	30	26	−3	...	M?
Peru	1984–87	16	−2	D/I	25	−3	−15	14	−46	28	...	D?
Uruguay	1986–89	12	10	M/I	6	−12	...	—	−20	—	D	D
Venezuela	1986–89	−5	53	I	−43	−15	−5	12	−20	−20	I	I

III. Periods of recession due to internal imbalances

Argentina	1986–89	−13	43	I/H	−30	−62	14	−8	36	...	I	I+
Brazil	1987–90	−7	−36	D/I	−5	−28	1	−3	16	25	D	I
Mexico	1984–87	−7	42	I	−4	−17	21	1	−32	−20	I?	I

Table 1.2 Continued

Country	Period	RNIpc	RER	INF[d]	RW[f]	RMW	NALU	IE	UU	GCpc	Concentration (Gini)	Urban poverty
Panama	1986–89	−25	−	−	−	−1	…	3	61	−21	I?	I
Peru	1987–90	−29	−47	I/H	−64	−64	…	−15	73	−53	I?	I

IV. Periods of disinflation and recovery

Argentina	1990–93	25	−27	D	1	25	12	−	28	…	D	D
Panama	1987–89	2	−24	D	8	−16	9	1	−26	−4	I?	I?
Mexico	1989–91	−8	−	−	−3	−2	…	3	−7	−10	D	−

V. Periods of growth beyond recovery

Colombia	1986–90	6	30	I	−3	−7	−12	9	−22	15	M	D
	1990–92	4	−10	D	1	−3	−	2	−3	10	L	I
	1992–94	9	−16	D	6	1	−1	−1	−13	33	M	…[g]
Costa Rica	1988–93	17	−5	D	12	−3	−6	10	−37	18	D	D
Chile	1987–90	15	5	I	11	27	−15	30	−45	5	D	D
	1990–92	12	−5	D	10	14	−7	9	−25	14	M	D
	1992–94	8	−	D	8	9	8	5	26	2	M	D
Mexico	1989–92	6	−19	D	19	−18	−	−5	−3	25	L	D
Uruguay	1989–92	9	−5	D	−2	−24	…	−19	5	6	D	D
Venezuela	1989–90	10	4	D	−6	−29	6	−1	13	−8	D	…
	1990–92	5	−11	D	−1	10	−8	7	−26	22	M	D

Source: Changes in the macroeconomic and labor variables: ECLAC and PREALC. Distributive changes: Tables 1.3 and 1.4.

[a] RNIpc: real national income per capita; RER: real effective exchange rate; INF: inflation. [b] RW: real urban or industrial wages; RMW: real minimum wage; NALU: nonagricultural labor force underemployed (per active person) equivalent to NALFIA+UU; NALFIA: nonagricultural labor force in informal activities (as defined by PREALC); UU: urban unemployment; IE: industrial employment; GCpc: per capita real government consumption expenditure. [c] I: increased; I+: increased notably; D: decreased; M: maintained; "?" indicates the most probable assumption for the phase (see text) on the range of the changes observed during a longer period. [d] I: increased; D: decreased; M: maintained inflation rate; H: entered into hyperinflation. [e] This period includes a transitory recovery. [f] Argentina: average wage in manufacturing; Brazil: industrial wage (average of São Paulo and Rio de Janeiro); Colombia: wage of workers in manufacturing; Costa Rica: average remuneration declared to the social security; Chile: average wage of nonagricultural workers; Mexico: average wage in manufacturing; Panama: average remuneration in manufacturing in Panama City; Peru: private sector workers' wage in Lima; Uruguay: average wage; Venezuela: average urban wage. [g] 1988–92.

Table 1.3 Evolution of the Labor Market, 1991–95

	1991	1992	1993	1994[a]	1995[a]
a) Real urban average wage	(1990 average = 100)				
Argentina[b]	101.3	102.7	101.0	102.0	100.9
Brazil[c]					
Rio de Janeiro	79.3	79.5	85.7	87.1	87.9
São Paulo	88.3	85.3	94.6	98.0	98.2
Chile[d]	104.9	109.6	113.5	118.8	123.3
Colombia[e]	97.4	98.6	103.2	104.1	104.2
Costa Rica[f]	95.4	99.3	109.6	113.8	111.5
Mexico[g]	106.5	114.3	124.5	129.1	112.0
Panama[h]	103.8	106.2	106.1	...	...
Peru[i]	115.2	111.1	110.2	127.4	122.6
Uruguay[j]	103.8	106.1	111.2	112.2	109.1
Venezuela[k]	89.5	98.7	75.3	...	...
b) Urban unemployment[l]	(average rates)				
Argentina[m]	6.5	7.0	9.6	11.5	18.6
Brazil[n]	4.8	5.8	5.4	5.1	4.7
Chile[o]	7.3	5.0	4.1	6.3	5.6
Colombia[p]	10.2	10.2	8.6	8.9	8.6
Costa Rica[q]	6.0	4.3	4.0	4.3	...
Mexico[r]	2.7	2.8	3.4	3.7	6.4
Panama[s]	16.0	14.7	13.2	13.7	14.3
Peru[t]	5.9	9.6	9.9	8.8	8.2
Uruguay[u]	8.9	9.0	8.4	9.1	10.7
Venezuela[v]	10.1	8.1	6.8	8.7	10.3

Source: ECLAC, *Economic Survey of Latin America and the Caribbean 1994* (1995); ECLAC, on the basis of official figures.

[a] Preliminary figures.
[b] Total average wages in manufacturing.
[c] Wages of workers protected by the social and labor laws.
[d] Until April 1993, average wages of nonagricultural sector workers. Since May 1993, general index of wages per hour.
[e] Wages of workers in the manufacturing industry; 1994: average from January to November.
[f] Declared average wages of workers paying into the social security system.
[g] Average wages in manufacturing; 1994: estimated annual variation is based in the average variation from January to November in relation to the same period for the previous year.
[h] Industrial wages Panama City from 1990, estimates.
[i] Wages of private sector manual workers in the metropolitan area of Lima.
[j] Average wages.
[k] Average income of persons working in the urban zones.
[l] The time periods covered by the rates shown are those originally established by each country.
[m] Nationwide urban, May and October average.
[n] Metropolitan areas of Rio de Janeiro, São Paulo, Belo Horizonte, Porto Alegre, Salvador, and Recife, average for twelve months.
[o] Metropolitan area of Santiago, average for twelve months.
[p] Seven metropolitan areas, average for March, June, September, and December.
[q] Nationwide urban, up to the month of July.
[r] Includes a growing number of urban areas from October 1994: 39 urban areas.
[s] Metropolitan region.
[t] Metropolitan Lima.
[u] Montevideo, average for twelve months.
[v] Average for two semesters; 1994 nationwide total.

Table 1.4 Changes in Mean Relative Incomes of Urban Household by Occupational Categories (percentages)

Occupational category	Argentina[a] 1980–92	Brazil 1979–90	Costa Rica 1981–92	Colombia 1980–92	Uruguay 1981–92	Venezuela 1981–92
Employers	25.9	-9.5	-1.2	-23.6	-27.6	69.3
Microenterprises	20.4	...	-7.7	...	-31.8	49.6
Rest	43.3	...	14.2	...	-25.8	95.2
Wage earners	-6.8	5.1	2.7	10.1	27.4	-22.9
Public sector	...	...	0.3	12.7	17.4	-20.8
Private sector	...	5.1	15.3	13.4	33.7	-24.1
Professional and technical	...	-1.0	27.7	2.7	75.8	-17.6
Establishments employing more than 5 persons	...	-10.0	34.5	...	77.5	-17.0
Establishments employing up to 5 persons	...	29.1	21.8	...	44.9	-48.1
Nonprofessional, nontechnical	...	4.1	6.9	8.2	24.2	-24.2
Establishments employing more than 5 persons	...	3.9	1.5	8.2	24.6	-25.0
Establishments employing up to 5 persons	...	15.0	14.6	...	21.7	-20.8
Household employees	...	4.1	6.6	-16.0	30.4	9.2
Self-employed and unpaid family workers	5.7	-18.8	-23.8	-4.2	-33.9	64.4
Professional and technical	...	-26.5	-31.9	-30.4	-24.1	56.9
Nonprofessional, nontechnical	...	-19.2	-26.9	-1.4	-39.4	61.5
Manufacturing and construction	...	-21.1	-28.4	5.5	-42.8	58.3
Commerce and services	...	-21.9	-21.6	-3.5	-38.9	61.3
Other[b]	—	-4.5	-33.9	...	7.6	63.3

Source: ECLAC (1994).
[a] Greater Buenos Aires.
[b] Includes wage earners in the agricultural, forestry, hunting, and fisheries sectors.

Table 1.5 Participation of Selected Occupational Categories in the Urban Labor Force (percentage)

	Argentina	Brazil	Chile	Colombia	Costa Rica	Mexico	Uruguay	Venezuela
I. Low-productivity employment[a]								
1981	42.9[f]	45.7[e]	...	...	37.7	...	35.2	34.7
1990	43.1	48.8	...	...	37.6	...	39.5	37.1
1992	45.0	...	43.4	...	33.9	44.3	39.6	37.9
II. Public sector employees								
1981	...	...	...	10.6[f]	29.9	...	23.7	24.8
1990	...	...	...	10.4	25.0	...	21.8	22.5
1992	...	...	...	9.3	25.0	...	18.7	19.5
III. Professional and technical employees in the private formal sector[b c d]								
1981	5.9[f]	5.8[e]	...	4.9[f]	4.4	4.8[g]	2.4	4.0
1990	8.7	5.8	12.0	6.9	5.2	7.3[h]	3.4	5.5
1992	...	...	12.3	6.7	5.7	6.6	4.4	4.2
IV. Other employees in the private formal sector[b c d]								
1981	46.0[f]	43.2[e]	...	47.4[f]	26.0	64.5[g]	35.4	34.4
1990	43.0	39.0	54.8	46.8	29.5	66.4[h]	31.5	31.3
1992	...	...	55.4	46.4	32.3	66.9	32.7	34.8

Source: ECLAC (1994).
[a] Includes workers in establishments employing up to 5 persons, self-employed workers and unpaid family workers engaged in nonprofessional nontechnical occupations, and household employment.
[b] Occupied in establishments employing over 5 workers.
[c] In Argentina, Brazil, Chile, and Mexico includes public sector employees.
[d] In Chile, Colombia, and Mexico includes those occupied in all establishments.
[e] 1979.
[f] 1980.
[g] 1984.
[h] 1989.

Table 1.6 Change in Relative Incomes of the Urban Labor Force, by Educational Levels (percentages)

Educational level	Brazil 1979–90	Colombia 1980–90	Colombia 1990–92	Costa Rica 1981–90	Costa Rica 1990–92	Uruguay 1981–90	Uruguay 1990–92	Venezuela 1981–90	Venezuela 1990–92
No education	-4.5	-5.5	3.2	-9.3	-10.9	-6.5	15.8	2.6	5.2
1 to 3 years	-2.2	-8.3	7.0	-12.4	-2.1	-13.1	21.0	0.7	5.4
4 to 6 years	0.0	0.0	0.0	0.0	0.0	0.0	0.0	0.0	0.0
7 to 9 years	-3.7	-11.3	1.5	-1.7	-7.5	13.8	-6.4	0.1	-1.3
10 to 12 years	-1.1	-24.8	3.3	-14.0	2.6	1.7	-1.6	-0.7	-2.6
13 to 15 years	6.2	-22.4	10.0	-18.8	4.4	-16.2	19.6	-10.4	-2.5
16 years and more	-4.0	-35.5	6.5	8.7	1.0	-10.9	-4.2	-16.1	6.3

Source: ECLAC, on the basis of household surveys.

Table 1.7 Latin American Countries: Incidence of Poverty and Destitution in the 1980s and Beginning of the 1990s (percentages of households)

Country and years	Poverty Urban areas	Poverty Rural areas	Poverty National level	Destitution Urban areas	Destitution Rural areas	Destitution National level
Argentina						
1980	7	16[a]	9	2	4[a]	2
1986	12	17[a]	13	3	6[a]	4
1990	16[b]					
1992	10[b]					
Brazil						
1979	30	62	39	10	35	17
1987	34	60	40	13	34	18
1990	39	56	43	17	31	20
Colombia						
1980	36	45[a]	39	13	22[a]	16
1986	36	42	38	15	22	17
1990	35			12		
1992	38			15		
Costa Rica						
1981	16	28	22	5	8	6
1988	21	28	25	6	10	10
1990	22	25	24	7	12	10
1992	25	25	25	8	12	10
Chile						
1980	32[c]	41[c]	33[c]			
1987	38	45	39	13	16	14
1990	33	34	33	11	15	12
1992	28	28	28	7	9	7
1994	24	26	24			
Mexico						
1977			32			10
1984	28	45	34	7	20	11
1989	34	49	39	9	23	14
1992	30	46	36	7	20	12
Panama						
1979	31	45	36	14	27	19
1986	30	43	34	13	22	16
1989	34	48	38	15	25	18
1991	34	43	36	14	21	16
Peru						
1979	35	65[a]	46	10	38[a]	21
1985/86	45	64	52	16	39	25
Uruguay						
1981	9	21[a]	11	2	7[a]	3
1986	14	23[a]	15	3	8[a]	3
1989	10	23[a]	15	2	8[a]	3
1990	12			2		
1992	8			1		
Venezuela						
1981	18	35	22	5	15	7
1986	25	34	27	8	14	9
1990	33	38	34	11	17	12
1992	32	36	33	10	10	11

Source: ECLAC (1991, 1992, 1994).
[a] These estimates should be considered "educated guesses" based on relevant but indirect information.
[b] Metropolitan area.
[c] Author's estimates, based on Pollack and Uthoff (1987). See Altimir (1994a).

Table 1.8 Latin America (12 countries): Social Expenditure (Averages)

	Social expenditure/GDP			Real per capita social expenditure (1985 dollars)[a]			Social expenditure/total public expenditure		
	1980–1981	1982–1989	1990–1993	1980–1981	1982–1989	1990–1993	1980–1981	1982–1989	1990–1993
High									
Uruguay	14.9	14.9	15.1	304.7	276.0	309.1	57.4	43.9	58.2
Argentina	14.9	16.3	17.5[b]	278.1	277.2	329.6[b]	63.6	50.1	64.4[b]
Costa Rica	16.8	15.1	16.7	569.9	470.8	516.5	49.0	39.4	63.3
Chile	15.2	15.2	15.9[b]	251.3	230.8	261.1[b]	66.1	51.0	63.2[b]
Brazil[d]	17.7	18.7	14.6	264.5	243.7	260.9	61.7	49.3	63.1[c]
	9.7	9.4	10.8[b]	159.6	157.5	177.3[b]	46.5	29.7	36.8[b]
Moderate									
Venezuela	9.6	8.3	7.5	243.7	189.0	171.5	34.9	29.4	36.4
Colombia	11.5	9.5	8.5[e]	475.5	346.5		35.9	27.6	32.0[e]
Mexico	7.8	8.1	7.9[c]	91.4	97.9	306.1[c]	33.9	33.7[f]	...
Ecuador	8.6	6.8	7.1[b]	224.8	163.0	107.2[c]	31.1	24.9	40.7[b]
	10.3	8.9	6.4[b]	182.9	148.6	167.4[b]	38.8	31.4	36.6[b]
Low									
Bolivia	5.1[g]	4.2[g]	3.3[g]	55.5[g]	41.2[g]	29.3[g]	25.8[g]	19.5[g]	25.2[g]
Paraguay	5.7	4.7	4.5[c]	73.0	49.2	45.0[a]	1.0	23.8	34.5[c]
Peru[d]	3.9	4.2[h]		52.1	52.1[h]		37.7	57.5[h]	
	4.5	3.6	2.0[b]	38.0	33.1	13.6[b]	20.6	15.2	15.8[b]
Regional average[g]	11.2	10.6	10.2	237.2	201.7	108.2	43.5	34.2	45.0

Source: ECLAC, El gasto social en América Latina: Un análisis cuantitativo y cualitativo. *Cuadernos de la CEPAL*, no. 73. Forthcoming.
[a] The values for Bolivia, Venezuela, and (to a lesser degree) Colombia appear overestimated, while those for Peru and (to a lesser degree) Brazil appear underestimated due to the selection of 1985 as the base year.
[b] 1990–91.
[c] 1990–92.
[d] Underestimated due to limited institutional coverage.
[e] 1990.
[f] 1982–88.
[g] Simple average. Excludes Paraguay due to the change in institutional coverage in 1988.
[h] 1982–87.

NOTES

The views expressed are the author's sole responsibility and do not necessarily reflect those of the Commission. The present version of the paper benefitted greatly from comments by Víctor Tokman on a previous one, although he is by no means responsible for remaining weaknesses.

1. The figures mentioned here correspond to the simple arithmetic average of the six major countries (Argentina, Brazil, Chile, Colombia, Mexico, and Venezuela) covered in ECLAC's growth accounting exercise for 1950–94 (Hofman 1995).

2. Labor-adjusted joint factor productivity; that is, the portion of growth "unexplained" by the accumulation of factors minus the increase of "labor quality" (in the present case, represented by the weighted average of years of education of the labor force). See Hofman 1995.

3. These factors are, at least, significantly associated with the differences of income concentration among Latin American countries. In 1970 the following Spearman rank correlation coefficients were calculated between inequality and: per capita product, 5%; share of the labor force in agriculture, 96%; underemployment in agriculture, 97%; relative productivity of agriculture with respect to manufacturing, 75%; years of education of the labor force, 7% (Altimir 1992).

4. These are the ranges of variation of the marginal contributions (i.e., controlling for other variables) to total inequality (as measured by the Theil index) of each variable considered in 14 surveys of nine Latin American countries. Joint contributions of all variables considered in this exercise "explained" between 68% and 88% of total inequality of individual earnings, which were not adjusted for under-reporting (Altimir and Piñera 1982).

5. The combination of falls of the terms of trade, the rise of the international interest rate, and eventually the reversal of external finance.

6. As indicated by the percentage of the nonagricultural labor force employed in formal activities (thus excluding the unemployed and the nonagricultural labor force in informal activities, according to the definition of ILO-PREALC).

7. During the 1980s Colombia showed a lesser degree of concentration than in 1980, but the increase of inequality in 1992–94 brought the Gini coefficient back to the 1980 mark. Something similar is observed in Costa Rica where, in 1992, inequality reached a somewhat higher degree than the one existing in 1980.

8. In Chile inequality in 1990–94 may have been similar to that existing in 1981 (as indicated in Table 1.1), but contrasting evidence on the distribution of expenditure suggests that inequality may have increased much more during the eighties, making present levels still higher than precrisis ones.

9. In Brazil, the comparison is blurred by the fact that 1990 was a year of recession.

10. Gross enrollment rates in secondary and higher education jumped from 26% and 6% in 1970 to 45% and 14% in 1980 and to 53% and 17% in 1990, respectively (Schiefelbein 1995).

11. This finding is in agreement with the results obtained by Psacharopoulos and Ng (1992).

12. Such points in time have been identified by ECLAC (Hofman 1995) on the basis of the estimates of total and nonresidential reproducible capital. According to that analysis, the Mexican economy may have been operating at close to full capacity during the 1989–92 spell.

13. In the case of Brazil, between 1990 and 1992; in Venezuela, since 1993; and in Argentina and Mexico, after the economic crisis and devaluation *(tequilazo)* of late 1994.

14. The likelihood that a good portion of those incomes may not be captured by the household survey measurements used to assess inequality only underlines the fact that this analysis most probably underestimates the distributive deterioration taking place during these phases of the reform process.

15. The average annual rate of growth of per capita product for the region as a whole was 1.5% during 1991–94. As a consequence of the recessions in Argentina and Mexico, the average rate was negative (−1.1%) in 1995, but the rest of the countries continued growing at the previous moderate rate (ECLAC 1995).

16. These calculations are based on the optimistic assumption that poverty norms (lines) can validly remain constant over such long periods of sustained growth, which neither the evolution of consumption patterns nor the change of societal values may support.

17. For the region as a whole annual population growth for the 1990–2000 period is projected to be 2.3% for the economically active, compared to 1.7% for the entire population. However, in the demographically more mature countries of the region, the dependency ratio (population of inactive ages/population of active ages) is increasing (ECLAC 1993).

18. In some cases this is owing in part to economic recovery. In most cases, however, productivity enhancement due to technical change probably amounted to between 2% and 3% a year in the 1990–93 period.

19. In particular, modernization with significant job creation has been taking place in commercial agriculture linked to agroindustries or exports, large-scale mining projects, and *maquila* activities.

REFERENCES

Altimir, O. 1982. *The Extent of Poverty in Latin America*. World Bank Staff Working Papers no. 522. Washington, D.C.: The World Bank.

———. 1992. Crecimiento, distribución del ingreso y pobreza en América Latina. Paper presented at a seminar organized by the Inter-American Development Bank, March, Washington, D.C.

———. 1994a. Cambios de la desigualdad y la pobreza en la América Latina. *El Trimestre Económico* 61 (January–March), no. 241.

———. 1994b. Income Distribution and Poverty through Crisis and Adjustment. *CEPAL Review* 52 (April).

Altimir, O., and S. Piñera. 1982. Análisis de descomposición de las desigualdades de ingreso en la América Latina. *El Trimestre Económico* 49 (October–December), no. 196.

Birdsall, N., D. Ross, and R. Sabot. 1994. Inequality and Growth Reconsidered. Paper presented at the Annual Meeting of the American Economic Association, January, Boston.

ECLAC (Economic Commission for Latin America and the Caribbean). 1991. La Equidad en el Panorama Social de América Latina durante los Años Ochenta. Divisón de Desarrollo Social, LC/G.1686 (October). Santiago: ECLAC.

———. 1992. El Perfil de la Pobreza en América Latina a Comienzos de los Años 90. División de Desarrollo Social, LC/L.716 (November). Santiago: ECLAC.

———. 1993. Población, Equidad y Transformación Productiva. División de Desarrollo Social, LC/G.1758 (March). Santiago: ECLAC.

———. 1994. Social Panorama of Latin America. División de Desarrollo Social, LC/G.1844 (November). Santiago: ECLAC.

———. 1995. Preliminary Overview of the Economy of Latin America and the Caribbean 1995. ECLAC publication no. 1892-P (December). Santiago: ECLAC.

ECLAC-UNESCO (United Nations Education, Science, and Culture Organization). 1992. *Education and Knowledge: Basic Pillars of Changing Production Patterns with Social Equity*. Santiago: United Nations.

Filgueira, C., and C. Geneletti. 1981. Estratificación y movilidad ocupacional en América Latina. *Cuadernos de la CEPAL* no. 39 (October).

Hofman, A. 1995. Economic Growth and Fluctuations in Latin America: The Long Run. Paper presented at the conference on Development Strategy after Neoliberal Economic Restructuring in Latin America, 24–25 March, North-South Center, University of Miami, Miami.

Kuznets, S. 1966. *Modern Economic Growth*. New Haven: Yale University Press.

Morley, S. 1994. *Poverty and Inequality in Latin America: Past Evidence, Future Prospects*. Overseas Development Council Policy Essay, no. 13. Washington, D.C.: Overseas Development Council.

Pessino, C. 1994. Labour-Market Consequences of the Economic Reform in Argentina. Paper presented by the IDB/OECD at the International Forum on Latin American Perspectives, 2–4 November, Paris.

Pollack, M., and A. Uthoff. 1987. *Pobreza y Mercado de Trabajo en el Gran Santiago, 1969–1985*. Documento de Trabajo no. 299. Santiago: ILO-PREALC.

PREALC (Programa Regional de Empleo en América Latina y el Caribe). 1991. *Empleo y Equidad: El desafío de los 90*. Santiago: PREALC.

Psacharopoulos, G., and Y. C. Ng. 1992. *Earnings and Education in Latin America: Assessing Priorities for Schooling Investments*. The World Bank Policy Research Working Papers no. 1056. Washington, D.C.: The World Bank.

Robbins, D. 1994. *Relative Wage Structure in Chile, 1957–1992: Changes in the Structure of Demand for Schooling*. Estudios de Economía, Departamento de Economía de la Facultad de Ciencias Económicas y Administrativas de la Universidad de Chile, special issue, no. 21 (November). Santiago: Universidad de Chile.

Schiefelbein, E. 1995. La reforma educativa en América Latina y el Caribe: Un programa de acción. Paper presented at the Annual Conference of The World Bank on Development in Latin America and the Caribbean, 12–13 June, Rio de Janeiro.

2 | The Demographics of Poverty and Welfare in Latin America

Challenges and Opportunities

JOSÉ ALBERTO MAGNO
DE CARVALHO

This chapter deals with fertility transition in Latin America and some of the opportunities and challenges it will generate. In its first stage fertility transition creates favorable conditions to solve some serious social problems, mainly affecting the young population. In its second stage it will cause significant population aging, which will require new social arrangements, particularly those related to social security.

During the last decades, the Latin American countries, with a few exceptions, have experienced a rapid fertility decline that encompassed the various social groups and urban and rural populations. This decline began in the more affluent social groups and then spread quickly among workers and the poor. The region is replicating the European demographic transition but at a different pace; Latin America took considerably less time to show a significant decline both in mortality and fertility as compared to Europe. Accordingly, the transition will produce its demographic effects in a shorter period of time. The two most important effects of fertility decline will be a lower population growth rate and a demographic aging process.

Fertility transition in Latin America creates new opportunities and poses new challenges. In the beginning fertility decline leads to a rapid decrease in the child dependency ratio and a slight increase in the elderly dependency ratio. At a later stage the child dependency ratio tends to level out, accompanied by a steep increase in the elderly dependency ratio. The majority of Latin

American countries are still in the first stage of their fertility transition when a sharp decline in the child dependency ratio sharply eases the need for the definition and implementation of policies oriented towards the welfare of children and youth (nutrition, health, education, etc.). These opportunities should not be neglected because improving the general living conditions of the current young generations is, in itself, an important goal and because the members of these young generations will be those who, in the future, will have to provide the resources to support the needs of the fast-growing elderly population.

The second stage will be characterized by an extremely rapid increase in the proportion of elderly in the population. This outcome will put enormous pressure on the national social security systems which are already extremely fragile or on the verge of bankruptcy. This new challenge, the worst consequences of which may become clear within only two or three decades, must be anticipated through policies to prepare and train adequately the current young generations and to reformulate the social security systems.

The first stage of fertility transition corresponds to what may be called a "golden age" in demographic terms, extremely favorable for social investment in the young population. This first stage signals a rare opportunity to diminish and even to eradicate poverty in Latin American societies. The subsequent aging of the population will generate extremely serious social burdens which will contribute to deteriorating living conditions if the right measures are not taken well in advance. This chapter will limit its focus to the opportunities and challenges that fertility transition brings to Latin American societies through its effects on the population growth rate and age structure. From a demographic point of view, it is essential that the changes in the population growth rate and social demand profile be taken into account in the definition of social policies.

In undertaking a comparative analysis of the region and its component countries, data and estimates from CELADE (1994) are used.

Fertility Transition in Latin America

Until the 1960s the Latin American countries, except for Argentina, Chile, Cuba, and Uruguay, showed high and basically stable fertility, with total fertility rates (TFRs) varying from 5.6 live-born children per woman (Panama) to 7.4 (Honduras) in 1965/70. Cuba and Chile were at the intermediate level, with TFRs of 3.7 and 4.3, respectively. At the end of the decade Argentina and Uruguay had already experienced fertility transition, with TFRs of 3.1 and 2.8, respectively (Chackiel and Schkolnik 1990; CELADE 1994).

In 1970, the 16 countries with high fertility[1] contained 84% of the total Latin American population. These countries had experienced a significant decline in mortality in the postwar period and had started to show higher and increasing population growth rates. Their annual average population growth rate was higher than 2.5% in 1965/70, except for Bolivia (2.3%) and Haiti (1.7%). Costa Rica, the Dominican Republic, Ecuador, El Salvador, Mexico, Nicaragua, and Venezuela grew at annual rates of 3.0% or higher.

The mortality decline had the demographic effect of accelerating the growth rate while only slightly affecting the population age structure. The relatively constant high fertility rates maintained a stable age distribution in this group of countries, characterized by extremely young populations. In 1970, 44.4% of the population in the set of high fertility countries was under 15 years of age, compared to 42.1% in 1950. In the countries with low and medium fertility, this proportion was 32.5% in 1950 and 1970.

At the end of the 1960s and in the beginning of the 1970s it was widely believed by population studies experts and others in the region that Latin American countries were bound to grow at very high rates. Even in countries experiencing high economic growth rates, a significant decline in fertility was not expected for the outcomes of economic growth were not shared by the majority of the population. (It was an economic growth process, not a development process.) The mortality decline that had already occurred would not be followed by fertility decline, rendering demographic transition incomplete in contrast to the cases of European and other First World countries.

The assumption that the great social investment required by the rapid pace of demographic growth would impair the necessary investment in the economic infrastructure and in the productive sectors was rapidly and extensively accepted by Latin American elites.[2] An exogenous inducement or even enforcement of fertility decline, by introducing family planning or birth control policies, was considered necessary to break out of the vicious circle of poverty.

For the Latin American countries with high fertility in the 1960s, Table 2.1 shows the average TFRs observed in 1965/70 and 1985/90 and those projected by the United Nations (UN) for 2005/10, as well as their proportional variations in the three periods. In the period between the last quinquenniums of the 1960s and 1980s, a significant decline was observed in all 16 countries, varying from 12% in Guatemala to 54% in Colombia. Generally speaking, those countries with higher decreases initiated a process of persistent fertility decline in the early 1970s.

Of the 16 countries under analysis, 10 have experienced a sharp fertility decline, higher than 30%, in a span of only 20 years. The populations of these 10 countries represented 92% of this group's total population in 1970. Fertility decline was also significant among the remaining six countries.

In the 1970s and 1980s fertility decline undoubtedly occurred among all social groups, including the destitute, for it would be mathematically impossible to achieve such magnitudes if only the elites had benefited—the most privileged strata are only a small proportion of the total population. And it is worth noting that this process occurred in most countries in the absence of any effective family planning or birth control policy.

The main determinants of the process are to be found in the profound structural changes that occurred in Latin America during the last decades, not necessarily accompanied by social and economic improvement in all social groups. The general improvement in educational levels, a growing consciousness among women of their rights, the increasing share of the female labor force participation in a social and economic context of an expanding market economy, and the role of television in the diffusion of new values for less educated women are among the most important factors (Faria and Potter 1990).

The experiences of the countries that experienced a higher fertility decline, documented over the 20 years since the decline began, suggest that this is an irreversible process, tending to spread to all countries and social strata.[3] The United Nations (which is traditionally very conservative in its projections of fertility decline) foresees significant fertility decline in all countries in this group between the quinquenniums 1985/90 and 2005/10, varying from 16% in Haiti to 41% in Honduras. The United Nations also projects that Latin America as a whole (with its TFR declining from 5.0 in 1965/70 to 3.4 in 1985/90) will reach a TFR of 2.5 in the quinquennium of 2005/10, a value not too distant from that which will produce zero population growth in the long run in a closed population.[4]

The magnitude of fertility decline in Latin America in such a short time is surprising when compared with the experience of European countries. Figure 2.1 contrasts the evolution of the TFRs of England and Sweden with those of Brazil, Colombia, Mexico, and Peru.[5] Sweden and England took approximately half a century (from 1870 to 1920) to achieve TFR declines of 53% and 44%, respectively. Although departing from different levels, Brazil, Colombia, Mexico, and Peru experienced declines of 40%, 54%, 47%, and 42%, respectively, in only 20 years (from around 1970 to 1990).

The first and most obvious effect of fertility decline is a decrease in the population growth pace. For Latin America as a whole the average annual growth rate declined from 2.6% in the 1965/70 quinquennium to 1.9% in the 1985/90 quinquennium. This decline has already had a significant effect on the region's total population. If there had been no decreased growth pace, the total population would have been 459 million people in 1990 instead of the observed 427 million people, i.e., there would be around 30 million more children and youngsters.

A second demographic outcome of a fertility decline is a remarkable change in the population age structure which occurs in the medium and long run as the relatively larger generations born before the beginning of the fertility decline progress through the age structure, followed by relatively smaller post decline generations. Increasing population aging is the outcome of this process.

Population aging is mainly a consequence of fertility decline and not mortality decline as might be commonly believed. Because the fertility decline in Latin America is occurring at a much faster pace than it did in the First World, it is expected that aging in the region's demographic structure will occur in a much smaller time span than that observed in the developed countries.

Table 2.2 shows the proportions of Latin America's population in the age groups from 0 to 14, 15 to 64, and 65 and over as observed in 1970 and 1990 and projected for 2010 and 2030. In Latin America as a whole and in those countries with higher rates of fertility decline (Brazil, Colombia, and Mexico), a significant decline in the proportion of youth was observed between 1970 and 1990. This trend is projected to continue in all countries of the region.[6] The proportion of people in Latin America under age 15 is expected to decline from the 1970 level of 42% to 28% in 2010 and 23% in 2030. In consequence, the proportion of people over 65 is increasing. The increase began slowly (from 4.1% to 4.8% between 1970 and 1990) but is projected to accelerate between 2010 and 2080 when the proportion will grow from 6.5% to 11.2%.

Table 2.1 Latin America: Total Fertility Rates (TFRs) of High Fertility Countries in the Region, 1965/70–2005/10

Countries	TFRs 1965/70	TFRs 1985/90	TFRs 2005/10	Proportional Change (%) 1985/90 1965/70	Proportional Change (%) 2005/10 1985/90
Latin America	5.6	3.4	2.5	−39.3	−26.5
Bolivia	6.6	5.3	3.5	−19.7	−34.0
Brazil	5.3	3.2	2.3	−39.6	−28.2
Colombia	6.3	2.9	2.3	−54.0	−20.7
Costa Rica	5.8	3.4	2.6	−41.4	−23.5
Dominican Republic	6.7	3.5	2.4	−47.8	−31.4
Ecuador	6.5	4.0	2.5	−38.5	−37.5
El Salvador	6.6	4.5	2.9	−31.8	−35.6
Guatemala	6.6	5.8	4.0	−12.1	−31.0
Haiti	6.0	5.0	4.2	−16.7	−16.0
Honduras	7.4	5.4	3.2	−27.0	−40.7
Mexico	6.8	3.6	2.3	−47.1	−34.3
Nicaragua	7.2	5.6	3.5	−22.3	−37.5
Panama	5.6	3.2	2.3	−42.9	−28.1
Paraguay	6.4	4.7	3.2	−26.6	−31.9
Peru	6.6	3.8	2.6	−42.4	−31.6
Venezuela	5.9	3.7	2.5	−37.3	−32.4

Source: CELADE (1994).

Figure 2.1 Brazil, Peru, Colombia, Mexico, Sweden, and England: Total Fertility Rate (TFR) for selected years

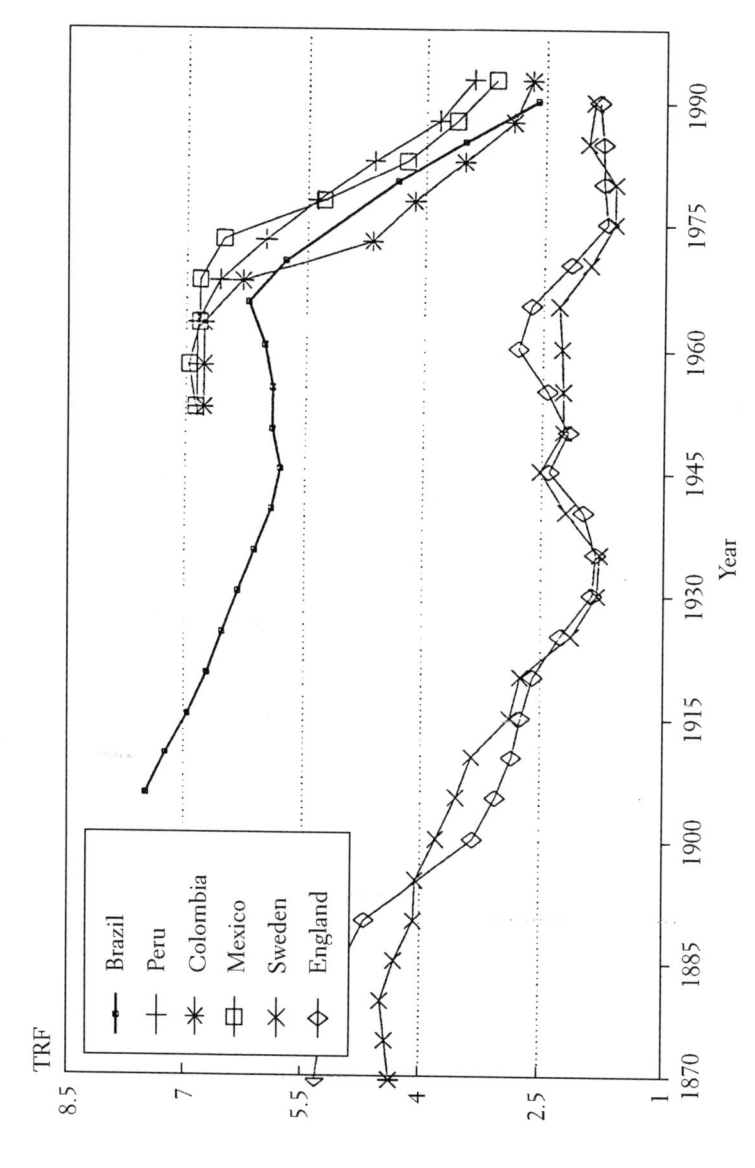

Source: Carvalho and Wong (1995) and CELADE (1994).

Table 2.2 Latin America: Age Distribution of the Region and Countries (%) 1970/2030

Countries	0–14 1970	0–14 1990	0–14 2010	0–14 2030	15–64 1970	15–64 1990	15–64 2010	15–64 2030	65 and over 1970	65 and over 1990	65 and over 2010	65 and over 2030
Latin America	42.4	35.9	28.2	22.7	53.5	59.3	65.3	66.1	4.1	4.8	6.5	11.2
Argentina	29.4	30.6	25.5	21.7	63.6	60.5	64.2	65.0	7.0	8.9	10.3	13.3
Bolivia	43.0	41.2	36.0	27.1	53.6	55.2	59.5	66.1	3.4	3.6	4.5	6.8
Brazil	42.3	34.4	26.6	21.5	54.3	60.9	66.5	66.0	3.4	4.7	6.9	12.5
Chile	39.2	30.1	24.9	21.4	55.7	63.8	66.5	64.0	5.1	6.1	8.6	14.6
Colombia	46.0	35.3	26.7	21.8	50.7	60.5	67.6	66.6	3.3	4.2	5.7	11.6
Costa Rica	46.1	36.5	29.2	24.0	50.7	59.3	64.7	64.6	3.2	4.2	6.1	11.4
Cuba	37.0	22.8	19.3	18.4	56.9	68.8	68.7	62.5	6.1	8.4	12.0	19.1
Dominican Republic	47.3	37.0	28.2	22.2	49.7	59.5	68.8	66.4	3.0	3.5	5.7	11.4
Ecuador	44.4	39.0	29.2	22.5	51.4	56.9	65.2	67.9	4.2	4.1	5.6	9.6
El Salvador	46.5	43.5	34.7	25.9	50.7	52.7	60.3	66.5	2.8	3.8	5.0	7.6
Guatemala	45.9	45.4	39.3	30.1	51.3	51.4	56.8	64.4	2.8	3.2	3.9	5.5
Haiti	41.0	40.2	38.3	34.1	54.3	55.7	57.9	61.0	4.7	4.1	3.8	4.9
Honduras	48.2	45.2	36.1	26.4	49.3	51.8	59.9	66.8	2.5	3.0	4.0	6.8
Mexico	46.5	38.6	28.4	22.1	49.2	57.4	65.7	67.0	4.3	4.0	5.9	10.9
Nicaragua	48.4	47.9	38.4	28.2	49.1	49.1	58.0	66.0	2.5	3.0	3.6	5.8
Panama	43.9	35.3	26.8	21.1	51.8	51.8	66.4	66.7	4.3	5.0	6.8	12.2
Paraguay	46.4	40.7	33.6	26.3	50.2	50.2	55.7	65.1	3.4	3.6	4.4	8.6
Peru	44.0	37.8	29.4	22.5	52.5	58.4	65.0	67.5	3.5	3.8	5.6	10.0
Uruguay	27.9	25.8	23.0	20.8	63.2	62.6	64.5	65.1	8.9	11.6	12.5	14.1
Venezuela	45.6	38.2	29.5	23.0	51.5	58.2	65.0	66.5	2.9	3.6	5.5	10.5

Source: CELADE (1994).

Social Policy Implications of the New Demographic Pattern

The new demographic reality in Latin America has been creating extremely favorable conditions for the solution of some chronic social problems while also posing new challenges. It would be naïve to believe that certain social problems would be solved automatically as the population started to grow at a slower pace, with the reduced relative weight and even the reduced absolute size of some target populations. Opportunities are created, but "they will only be fully utilized if priorities are defined, decisions taken, and programs really implemented" (Carvalho and Wong 1995, 17). Generally speaking, societies are not conscious of the new demographic reality and thus do not take advantage of the opportunities created or prepare themselves to cope with future challenges. This is clearly the Brazilian case!

As a result of a reduced relative number of births in Latin America, the child dependency ratio[7] is decreasing and will decline at an accelerated rate in the next decades. In 1970 the ratio for the entire region was 79%; it dropped to 61% in 1990 and is projected to decline from 43% to 34% between 2010 and 2030 (see Table 2.3 and Figure 2.2). The reduced relative proportion (and, in some countries, declining absolute number) of youths offers a unique opportunity to solve some crucial social problems that afflict Latin American children and youth, since pressures on the demand side are reduced. Unfortunately, this favorable circumstance might be used as an argument for diminishing the already scant resources spent for social policies (such as health, nutrition, and education) oriented to youth.

It should be noted that a change in age structure resulting primarily from fertility decline is accompanied by a broader process of social change which will result in new demands from children and youth. For example, with a greater female participation in the labor force, the demand for preschool services will tend to increase proportionally more than the relative decrease in the number of children in this transition phase. Educational planners must be alert for theses changes and should reevaluate resource allocation with a view to ensuring the best possible social return.

In countries faced with so many social needs and dramatic economic crises, social investment must be selective and concentrated in sectors that ensure the greatest social returns in the medium and long run. Investing in children and youth today will help guarantee the rights they are entitled to and will prepare future generations of young adults to enter the next century equipped to compete in an increasingly specialized labor market and to face the new challenges to come.

Table 2.3 and Figure 2.2 show the evolution of the elderly dependency ratio[8] in Latin America, which will rapidly grow in the next decades as a result of fertility decline. This ratio increased from 7.7% to 8.0% between 1970 and

Table 2.3 Latin America: Children, Elderly, and Total Dependency Ratios 1970/2030

Countries	Children dependency ratio				Elderly dependency ratio				Total dependency ratio			
	1970	1990	2010	2030	1970	1990	2010	2030	1970	1990	2010	2030
Latin America	79.3	60.5	43.2	34.3	7.7	8.1	10.0	16.9	87.0	68.6	53.2	51.2
Argentina	46.2	50.6	39.7	33.4	11.0	14.7	16.0	20.5	57.2	65.3	55.7	53.9
Bolivia	80.2	74.6	60.5	41.0	6.3	6.5	7.6	10.3	86.5	81.1	68.1	51.3
Brazil	77.9	56.5	40.0	32.6	6.3	7.7	10.4	18.9	84.2	64.2	50.4	48.5
Chile	70.4	47.2	37.4	33.4	9.2	9.6	12.9	22.8	79.6	56.8	50.3	56.2
Colombia	90.7	58.3	39.5	32.7	6.5	6.9	8.4	17.4	97.2	65.2	47.9	50.1
Costa Rica	90.9	61.6	45.1	37.2	6.3	7.1	9.4	17.6	97.2	68.7	54.5	54.8
Cuba	65.0	33.1	28.1	29.4	10.7	12.2	17.5	27.8	75.7	45.3	45.6	57.2
Dominican Republic	95.2	62.2	41.0	33.4	6.0	5.9	8.3	17.2	101.2	68.1	49.3	50.6
Ecuador	86.4	68.5	44.8	33.1	8.2	7.2	8.6	14.1	94.6	75.7	53.4	47.2
El Salvador	91.7	82.5	57.5	38.9	5.5	7.2	8.3	11.4	97.2	89.7	65.8	50.3
Guatemala	89.5	88.3	69.2	46.7	5.5	6.2	6.9	8.5	95.0	94.5	76.1	55.2
Haiti	75.5	72.2	66.1	55.9	8.7	7.4	6.6	8.0	84.2	79.6	72.7	63.9
Honduras	97.8	87.3	60.3	39.5	5.1	5.8	6.7	10.2	102.9	93.1	67.0	49.7
Mexico	94.5	67.2	43.2	33.0	8.7	7.0	9.0	16.3	103.2	74.2	52.2	49.3
Nicaragua	98.6	97.6	66.2	42.7	5.1	6.1	6.2	8.8	103.7	103.7	72.4	51.5
Panama	84.7	68.1	40.4	31.6	8.3	9.7	10.2	18.3	93.0	77.8	50.6	49.9
Paraguay	92.4	81.1	60.3	40.4	6.8	7.2	7.9	13.2	99.2	88.3	68.2	53.6
Peru	83.8	64.7	45.2	33.3	6.7	6.5	8.6	14.8	90.5	71.2	53.8	48.1
Uruguay	44.1	41.2	35.7	32.0	14.1	18.5	19.4	21.7	58.2	59.7	55.1	53.7
Venezuela	88.5	65.6	45.4	34.6	5.6	6.2	8.5	15.8	94.1	71.8	53.9	50.4

Source: CELADE (1994).

Figure 2.2 Latin American Dependency Ratios, 1970/2050 (per cent)

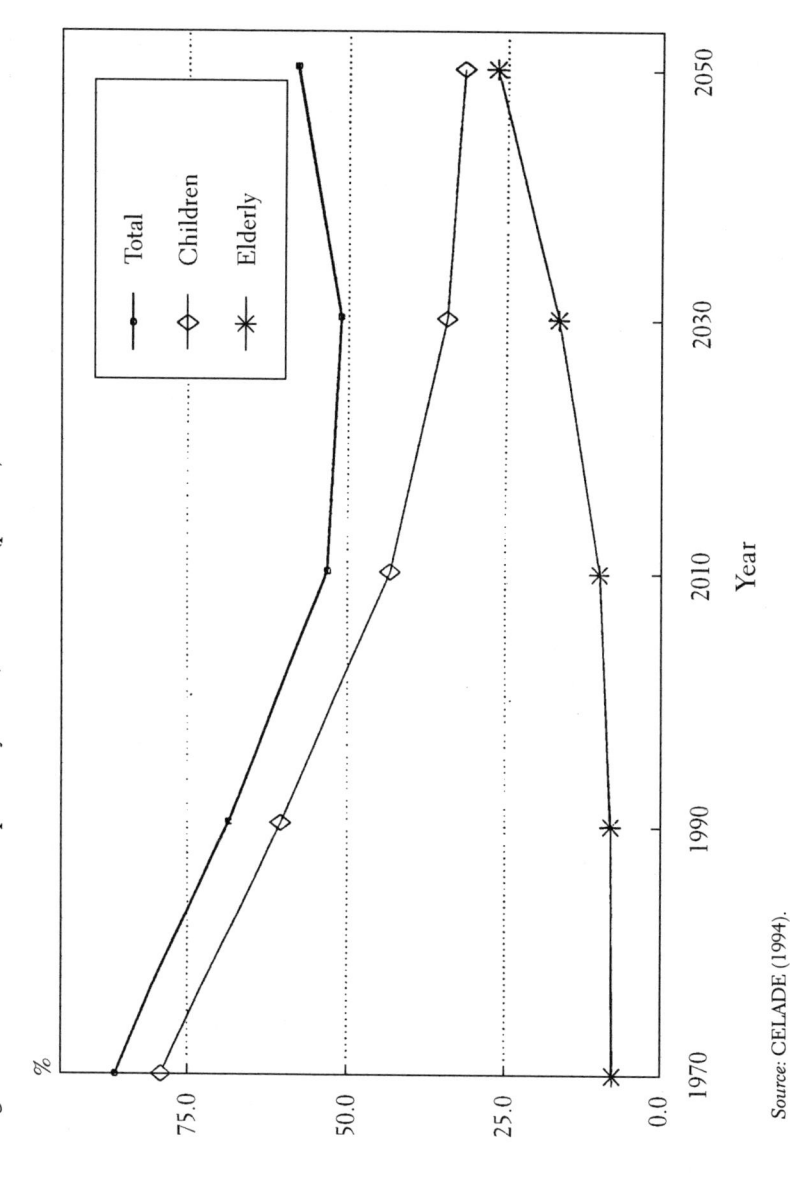

Source: CELADE (1994).

1990 and is projected to grow from 10.0% to 17.0% between 2010 and 2030. The elderly dependency ratio, like the aging of the population, will occur at a faster pace in Latin America than was previously observed in First World countries.

The probable evolution of dependency ratios between 2030 and 2050 is also shown in Figure 2.2. The rapidly increasing elderly dependency ratio will cause the total dependency ratio[9] to rise again after decades of decline. But the total dependency ratio will never reach the extremely high values observed before the beginning of the fertility transition. The children and elderly dependency ratios will eventually tend to converge. It should be emphasized that the evolution of the elderly dependency ratio in the 2030–50 period depends on the assumptions used in the population projections relative to the fertility behavior until 2030.

The rapid aging of the population that will occur during the next decades, combined with the expansion of social security coverage during the last decades, challenge the long term viability of national social security systems.[10] The present crises in the systems have little to do with population aging, since the magnitude of this phenomenon is still limited. The irreversible aging acceleration of the next decades, however, clearly signals the failure of the present systems and the urgent need for reflection and debate in order to create new social security systems that will provide humane conditions for the elderly of the future. The aging of the population will also put increased pressure on health care expenditures because per capita health care expenditures are higher for the elderly than for other age groups.[11] One may conclude that an increasing proportion of national incomes will be required in the next decades for social expenditure for the elderly, mainly in the social security and health areas.

The future social outlook based on the new Latin American demographic dynamics need not be pessimistic if correct measures are taken in the short run. Returning to Figure 2.2, we observe a rapid decline in the child dependency ratio and a slow increase in the elderly dependency ratio. The total dependency ratio is also steadily decreasing. Demographically this represents a "golden age" for Latin America.

Assuming no change in the age-specific participation rates, the labor force will keep growing above the total population [growth] average but at declining rates as the proportion of workers born since the beginning of fertility decline increases.[12] For this reason, Latin America still experiences a sharp drop in child dependency and a slight increase in the elderly dependency ratio. Within a few decades, however, the child dependency ratio will become stable while the elderly dependency ratio will rapidly grow to very high levels. This will generate serious social problems if the present social and economic situation in Latin America persists.

The present demographic situation is extremely favorable for reorienting and redefining social policies to prepare Latin American societies to live in the future context of a remarkably aged population. It is not a question of choosing between investment in children and youth or expenditures for the elderly; rather, present investment in youth is absolutely vital to ensure adequate levels of future support for the high proportions of the elderly. The education and productive sectors must search for better ways to prepare the population about to enter the labor force and to invest in ongoing training for the economically active population, through opportunities within and outside the formal educational system. Social security systems must also be redesigned in response to the changing demographic reality in order to guarantee future old-age benefits for the present young and adult generations.

NOTES

Many thanks are due to Laura Wong for her comments and advice.
  1. Bolivia, Brazil, Colombia, Costa Rica, the Dominican Republic, Ecuador, El Salvador, Guatemala, Haiti, Honduras, Mexico, Nicaragua, Panama, Paraguay, Peru, and Venezuela.
  2. For a classic work in this line of thought, see Coale and Hoover (1958).
  3. Two scientific meetings were held to discuss and analyze fertility transition in Latin America: the April 1990 seminar on Fertility Transition in Latin America in Buenos Aires and the March 1993 IV Conferencia Latinoamericana de Población in Mexico City. For papers presented at the latter conference, see INEGI-IISUNAM (1993), and for the papers presented in Buenos Aires, see IUSSP (forthcoming).
  4. A TFR that ensures perfect population replacement corresponds to a value around 2.1 live-born children per woman at the end of her childbearing period.
  5. In 1970 the total population of these four Latin American countries represented 66% of region's population and 79% of the total population of the region's high fertility countries.
  6. The Brazilian case is illustrative. It is now projected that the population under 30 years in Brazil in 2000 will be at least 40 million fewer than what was officially projected in 1973. This means that the population under 30 in 2000 would be 44% greater if the unforeseen rapid decline in fertility had not occurred. Between 1990 and 2020 the Brazilian population under 5 years of age is expected to increase at an average annual rate of 0.2%, while the 5- to 15-year population will remain practically constant (Carvalho and Wong 1995).
  7. The relation between the population under 15 and that of 15 to 64 years of age.
  8. The relation between the population of 65 and over and that of 15 to 64 years of age.
  9. The relation between the population under 15 and 65 and over and that of 15 to 64 years of age.

10. In social security systems that function on a "pay-as-you-go" basis the population age structure is demographically more important than life expectancy. The latter is fundamental in a fully funded regime which characterizes the private social security systems.

11. Health systems in Latin America presently spend proportionally more for curative than preventive health care. Since the elderly have not yet reached the high proportions existing in developed countries, health planners in Latin America should focus on defining a more preventive health care system to help diminish the need for future curative actions when the elderly will comprise a larger proportion of the population.

12. The growth of the relative labor force participation of the population between 15 to 64 years of age together with the increase, at a declining rate, of the absolute number of people in this age group create favorable conditions for reducing or even eradicating child labor, allowing greater opportunities for children to receive an education and professional training.

REFERENCES

Carvalho, J. A. M. de, and L. R. Wong. 1995. The Rapid Fertility Decline in Brazil: Some Socioeconomic Implications from the New Demographic Age Pattern. Paper presented at the workshop on Rapid Fertility Decline in Brazil and India: Social Determinants and Consequences, April, Harvard Center for Population Studies, Cambridge.

CELADE (Centro Latinoamericano de Demografía). 1994. América Latina: Proyecciones de población 1950–2050. *Boletín Demográfico* yr. 27 (June), no. 54.

Chackiel, J., and S. Schkolnik. 1990. América Latina: Transición de la fecundidad en el período 1950–1990. Paper presented at the seminar on Fertility Transition in Latin America, April, Buenos Aires.

Coale, A. J., and E. M. Hoover. 1958. *Population Growth and Economic Development in Low Income Countries*. Princeton: Princeton University Press.

Faria, Vilmar E., and J. E. Potter. 1990. *Development, Government, Policy, and Fertility Regulation in Brazil*. Texas Population Research Paper no. 12.02. Austin: University of Texas.

INEGI (Instituto Nacional de Estadística, Geografía e Informática)-IISUNAM (Instituto de Investigaciones Sociales de la Universidad Nacional Autónoma de México). 1993. *IV Conferencia Latino-Americana de Población: La transición demográfica en América Latina y el Caribe*. 3 vols. Mexico City: Universidad Nacional Autónoma de México.

IUSSP (General Secretariat of the International Union for the Scientific Study of Population). Forthcoming. *Fertility Transition in Latin America*. Oxford: Clarendon Press.

3 | Poverty and Inequality in Latin America

Some Political Reflections

GUILLERMO O'DONNELL

The social situation of Latin America is a scandal. In 1990 about 46 percent of Latin Americans lived in poverty. Close to half of these are indigents who lack the means to satisfy very basic human needs. Today there are more poor than in the early 1970s: a total, in 1990, of 195 million, 76 million more than in 1970. These appalling numbers include 93 million indigents, 28 million more than in 1970.[1] The problem is not just *poverty*. Equally important is the sharp increase of *inequality* in most of the region during the 1970s and/or the 1980s (Tokman 1991, 1995); rapid economic growth in some countries in the late 1980s and/or early 1990s has not reversed this trend.[2] The rich are richer, the poor and indigent[3] have increased, and the middle sectors have split between those who have successfully navigated economic crises and stabilization plans and those who have fallen into poverty or are lingering close to the poverty line.

Furthermore, since around 1970 countries that were partial exceptions to the general pattern (Chile and Argentina) have greatly increased their poverty and inequality, in spite of recent years of rapid economic growth. Costa Rica and, to a lesser extent, Uruguay have held their own; only Colombia has improved, but marginally and with higher levels of poverty than the previously mentioned countries. Looking at this matter from another angle, indicators of literacy, infant mortality and life expectancy have improved.[4] But even in countries that by the 1960s had developed the rudiments of a welfare state (Argentina, Brazil, Chile),[5] the access to, and quality of, social services for the poor have deteriorated. These include health, housing, and the real value of pensions; education is more ambiguous—overall increases in enrollment have been accompanied by numerous indications of the deterioration of the quality of public education, the only one that the poor may hope to access. Of the 'welfare pioneer' countries, only Uruguay has escaped the general decay.[6] In Latin America as a whole, the informal sector has grown from 25.6 percent in 1980 to 31.9 percent in the 1990s as a proportion of the nonagrarian work force, while the per capita and family incomes of the informal sector have fallen and its internal segmentation has increased.[7] Finally, but certainly not least, women and children have been and continue to be the most victimized by poverty and impoverishment.[8]

Here I do not deal in any detail with the relevant data.[9] I am a generalist, a political scientist interested in processes of democratization in Latin America and elsewhere. I will limit myself to presenting some broad issues and to proposing some criteria that might contribute, from a political perspective, to the emerging debates on poverty and inequality in Latin America.

Extensive poverty and deep social inequality are characteristics of Latin America that go back to the colonial period. We have not overcome these conditions; we have aggravated them.

One may point out that some problems in some countries did not turn out so badly, especially among those that have registered high rates of economic growth in recent years; but even these countries' present poverty and inequality data look bad indeed when compared with data from the 1960s and early 1970s.[10] Or, as the dominant mood in the 1980s dictated, one may argue that the current increases in poverty and inequality are the unavoidable consequence of correcting past errors. Or one may simply ignore these trends, availing oneself of some of the many mechanisms that human beings invent for justifying their callousness toward others. One way or the other, these stances naturalize poverty and inequality: although different from arguments of centuries past, they still cast poverty and inequality as inevitable consequences of the natural ordering of things. From this point of view, while one may regret some of the visible manifestations of such ordering, it would be senseless, if not worse, to try to change it.[11]

We should begin by recognizing some hard facts:

1) Poverty-generated needs are so many and so vital that one is morally and professionally impelled to alleviate them. But these efforts, and the highly specialized knowledge required, should not detract from attempting to grasp the overall picture and forging alliances that are premised on broad agreements about a non-naturalized vision of what poverty and inequality are and what might be done about them. Of course, remedial action should be praised: in terms of actual human beings it does make a lot of difference. Also praiseworthy is moral indignation leading to energetic condemnations of the situation and

proposals for a much better world—but too often we are not told how to get from here to there, and in the meantime these invocations often include a disparaging tone toward 'mere' remedial actions.

2) Somewhere in the middle there are various policy prescriptions, typical of reports of various commissions and international organizations, with which in most cases I agree.[12] These include improving tax collection and making the tax system less regressive; investing more resources in social policies and finding more creative means of cooperation between the state and nongovernmental organizations (NGOs), churches, and business; correctly targeting some social policies; promoting popular participation; and other good ideas that I need not detail here. Although some progress in some policy areas has been registered in some countries, an obvious question is why so little of so much good advice has been actually implemented.

3) The third hard fact is that the poor are politically weak. Their permanent struggle for survival is not conducive, excepting very specific (and usually short-lived) situations and some remarkable individuals, to their organization and mobilization. Furthermore, this weakness opens ample opportunity for manifold tactics of cooptation, selective repression, and political isolation. Democracy makes a difference, in that the poor may use their votes to support parties that are seriously committed to improving their lot. But, if elected, these parties face severe economic constraints. In addition, they must take into account that determined pro-poor policies will mobilize concerns not only among the privileged but also among important segments of the middle class who, after their own sufferings through economic crises and adjustments, feel that it is they who deserve preferential treatment.[13] These concerns, to which I will return, may coagulate in a veto coalition that threatens not only the policy goals of those governments but also whatever economic stability or growth has been achieved.

What Can Be Done?

Good intentions and good advice are necessary but not sufficient to redress the appalling problems of poverty and inequality in our countries. The overall political and economic conditions are not congenial to giving top priority to the eradication of poverty and to a significant diminution of inequality. What, then, can be done? There are three time-honored tactics of would-be reformers:

1) *Appeal to the fears of the privileged.* Instead of exit or voice (Hirschman 1970), the all-too-human situation of the poor, particularly the poorest, is silent suffering. But sometimes they angrily rebel. Chiapas is the most spectacular but not the only recent reminder. Even though nowadays nobody seriously believes in the possibility of a social revolution (which diminishes the effectiveness of this kind of appeal), these episodes give some credence to arguments that the

winners should make some 'sacrifices' if 'everything' is not to explode. This allows at least for the rebellious regions to obtain some new resources from domestic and international agencies. But it is a hard law of policy that these problems disappear from the national agenda soon after the regions in question return to silent suffering. Furthermore, the way these problems are usually dealt with include, in addition to providing some resources, measures such as repression, attempts at coopting (if not murdering) the leaders, splitting the rank and file of the movements, and other niceties.

2) *Appeal to the enlightened self-interest of the privileged.* This consists in arguing that in the medium or long run the privileged themselves will be worse off if they do not begin to address at least some aspects of a given problem right now. A prominent example is the argument (which I believe is correct) that the future growth of the country is severely jeopardized by a work force that lacks the skills to be competitive in the world economy.[14] Except for its effect on altruistic individuals among the privileged, as a general appeal this one tends to get locked into a collective action problem: Why should I sacrifice part of my personal or corporate income for an outcome which I cannot be sure that others will contribute to sufficiently to make it come about?[15] Furthermore, if I am convinced that the grim prognosis of economic stagnation is correct, would not this be a good reason to become wary about keeping my present and future savings or investments in such a country?

Thus, both kinds of appeal may produce some beneficial results, but their overall consequences are deemed to be limited and ambivalent. Notice that both are appeals to the *private* interests of the privileged. Neither is a substitute for the recognition that in redressing poverty and inequality there is a *public* interest that goes well beyond any private interest. The assertion of such a public interest can only be based on the conviction that all human beings share in the same dignity and that they are entitled to freedoms and resources that are denied by the kind of poverty I am discussing here.[16]

The Need for a Strong State

I admit that this kind of language is alien to the mood of the present times, not only in Latin America. Worse still, my argument leads toward sharply devalued currencies: politics, politicians, and the state. It is only through politics, in its dialogues and conflicts, that a persuasive and effective argument about the public interest can be built. And it is through the state that such interest can be mobilized and made effective, by its own policies and by the stimulation of concurrent actions by private agents (beginning by extricating them from collective action problems such as the one I depicted above). This means building the kind of state that, with few and partial exceptions, we do not have after the hurricanes of socioeconomic crises, stabilization programs, and various strands of *enragé* antistatism: a strong state. 'Strong' does not mean big. By 'strong' I mean several interrelated features: a reasonably well-motivated, noncorrupt, and skilled civil service; capacity to formulate and implement policies; openness to, but not colonization by, society; at least some transparency and accountability; and responsiveness to goals and priorities formulated through a democratic political process.[17]

Moisés Naim (1994) correctly argues that after the application of economic stabilization policies—which did not demand extensive bureaucratic capabilities—more and more difficult tasks for the state have emerged. Now the challenges of resuming economic growth, especially of putting growth on a sustainable path, require complex and well-calibrated actions by the state. As a consequence, Naim persuasively stresses the need for greatly enhancing the state institutions directly linked with economic policies.

Everything indicates that this need is even greater in relation to the social policies' area of the state. Those who can afford it have extricated themselves from dependence on the state by means of private transportation, private or privatized health and education services, and in some cases private pension plans. On the other hand, the salaries, working conditions, and career prospects of the 'street bureaucrats' who typically deliver services to the poor (health workers, teachers, *asistentes sociales*) have greatly deteriorated. The same is true of officials in the central bureaucracies, national and especially local, of the social policy apparatus. Admittedly these areas of the state have often been bastions of clientelism and inefficiency. But the *blitzkrieg* conducted against them for deficit-reducing purposes or out of sheer antistatism has done nothing to improve their performance.[18] To the contrary, in several countries this offensive has practically amputated the arm of the state that is most needed for implementing reasonably effective social policies. The problem is compounded by the high motivation and varied skills that are required for effective performance by state agents in the delivery of these services.[19]

It says a lot about actual policy priorities that, while in several countries, efforts have been recently made to enhance the economic policy-making area of the state, to my knowledge no effort, except in Chile, has been made in relation to the social policy area of the state. Despite overwhelming evidence to the contrary, the belief that the market will take good care of everything, including the poor, still seems to hold the upper hand.

I finish this section with a piece of advice similar to the policy prescriptions I mentioned above: Devote serious attention and necessary resources to strengthening the social area of the state; this will have beneficial effects in itself and may generate new and more effective paths of cooperation between the state and private agents.

Anyone driving around a large city in the United States realizes how difficult it is, in spite of more favorable conditions than in Latin America, to eradicate poverty.[20] Also, since the 1980s inequality has increased in most

Organization for Economic Cooperation and Development (OECD) countries, especially in those, such as Great Britain, New Zealand, and the United States, that followed neoliberal economic policies, akin to the ones most of Latin America has adopted since that same period.[21] Even without considering how much deeper and more ingrained poverty and inequality are in Latin America, these are sobering references. What can we really hope for, and in what time span?

As noted above, the sheer dimension and complexity of raising our countries to decent levels of social welfare, encourage—with important help from conservative ideologies, some of them dressed as scientific economic arguments—the naturalization of these problems. In view of this, it is tempting to adopt the posture of an unflagging optimist: because it is too unwieldy, forget the overall picture; concentrate, in policy and academic circles, on topical policies and their eventual successes and dismiss as 'pessimists' those who insist in also looking at the overall picture. This 'optimism' is helpful, because it stimulates and lends broader justification to the remedial actions I praised above. But I would like to insist that we need to keep the overall situation very much in mind. Whatever optimism we feel has to be filtered through the highly structured situation of poverty and inequality that, both for historical and contemporary reasons, we are now facing.

A Dualistic Scenario

I have just begged a huge question: What is this 'overall picture'? Here I will limit myself to sketchily mentioning some characteristics that seem to me particularly relevant. They are the expression of what Altimir (1990) calls a historical pattern of development that is "structurally disequilibrated and socially exclusionary." This may be summarized by an image that has been frequently used by students of Latin America: dualism. Many countries have been dualist since colonial times; others that were not, such as Argentina and Chile, became dualist in the last two decades; only Costa Rica and Uruguay do not fit this category. The idea of dualism points to the coexistence of two worlds within the same national boundaries. One is the world of the rich, as well as of the segments of the middle class and the working class that have been able to attain reasonable levels of income, education, housing, personal security, and related goods. The other is the world of the dispossessed, composed predominantly, but not exclusively, of the poor as classified by the studies to which I have referred. These are not worlds apart. They are closely interlinked. They cannot be understood without taking into account these linkages—among others, the relationships between the formal and the informal sectors studied by the authors already cited and the massive presence of indigents in the cities that the rich also inhabit are two among many other possible examples.

The numbers of the poor have increased. Also, although we do not know the exact numbers, many others hover above the low line that defines the upper limit of poverty. These are segments of the middle class or of the old working class at risk of falling into a category that the social disasters of the last two decades invited sociologists to invent: the 'new poor.' This is well known. Perhaps less notorious is that the privileged are, so to speak, moving away. The contrast between the amount and the quality of the goods and services they enjoy and those of the poor is bigger and more evident than ever. Furthermore, in a world that is rapidly globalizing, the poor cannot do much more than contemplate consumption booms that, following a Latin American tradition, make our rich even more ostentatious than those in the countries of origin of the goods and services that our rich enjoy. Aside from this contemplation, what the poor receive from globalization, and from the way requirements for national competitiveness in a global economy are usually read, are damaging fiscal policies and labor reforms whose likely effect on them is far from clearly beneficial. To what extent this situation will lead to popular rebellions based on unmet expectations or will reinforce patterns of social exclusion and individual anomie is a moot question that I do not have the elements, theoretical and empirical, to answer here.

As Tokman (1991 and 1995) argues, actions that seriously tackle poverty and inequality can only be based on an effective solidarity. This, in turn, can only be based on recognizing the basic duty of, to name it somehow, human decency toward all individuals. The sharp, and deepening, dualism of our countries severely hinders the emergence of broad and effective solidarity. Social distances have increased, and the rich tend to isolate themselves from the strange and disquieting world of the dispossessed. The fortified ghettos of the rich and the secluded schools of their children bear witness to their incorporation into the transnationalized networks of modernity, as well as to the gulf that separates them from large segments of the national population.[22]

Room for Improvement

So, what can be done? Not much, I am afraid, in terms of changing the overall situation, at least in the short and medium term. A lot in terms of concrete remedial actions, not only because of how much difference they make to concrete individuals but also because they are a source of learning that, with proper precautions, can be usefully disseminated. And we should not underestimate what can be achieved by stubbornly hammering away with policy proposals and with data about the overall situation.

There are some things we could arguably do better.

1) Analyze more systematically and comparatively public and private social policies (including some of the many that, one may suspect, have as yet gone unregistered) to increase learning and potential for dissemination.

2) As noted above, one puzzling question is why so much good general policy advice is not being heeded. I believe that this is in part because we have not sufficiently worked out potential trade-offs between those policies and, especially, the extent to which their implementation may require changes in the content and general orientation of current economic policies. This is a very important intellectual task. At this moment I would offer a general suggestion: It is high time that social policy regain some autonomy in relation to economic policy. No reasonable person disputes today that responsible and skilled economic policy-making is needed, even for effectiveness in social areas. But in recent times economic policy has completely ignored the social dimension or has addressed this dimension exclusively in terms of its (narrowly defined) economic implications. At best, economic policy has paid attention to social issues when they seemed to threaten the achievement of economic goals. No decent society was ever built on such a unilateral basis. In particular, after the depths of economic crises have been (one hopes) left behind, there is no reason to keep treating the social dimension as the *pariente pobre* [poor relation] of the economic one. Of course, this plea will be dismissed by some as an excuse for 'economic irresponsibility.' Persuading them that this is not the case, and that in the medium and long run a socially more balanced situation will be helpful even for economic growth, is a very important political task.

3) Since *lo mejor es enemigo de lo bueno* [the best is the enemy of the good] and since economic and political constraints do exist, I do not argue for an immediate and full-fledged enhancement of the state's social policy apparatus. Through a political process that is open to many voices, the poor somehow included, some policy areas should be chosen because of their particular importance or urgency and because they seem amenable both to effective results and to learning-disseminating consequences. Among these it would be a good idea to include programs that promise fruitful interactions with private agents—NGOs, churches, foundations, and business, especially. In all cases, it is necessary to invest in the enhancement of the bureaucratic agencies that will be involved and in finding out what the intended beneficiaries really expect and want. The designers of these policies should make sure to create opportunities for exchanging experiences with participants in similar or convergent programs and for truly independent and skilled evaluations.

Enormous social energy, political skill, and intellectual clarity are needed for progress in these directions. Altruistic individuals find in themselves the main resource and motivation for these actions. As we saw, their efforts may find support from appeals to fear and/or to enlightened self-interest. This is a lot but it most likely falls short of getting us, *antes de las Calendas griegas*,[23] to the eradication of indigence and most[24] poverty and to reasonable[25] levels of social (in)equality.

Linking Poverty and Democracy

There may be still another possibility. By itself it will not take us to the promised land but, combined with the ones I have discussed (and others that escape me), it may get us closer. I am referring to another typical maneuver of the would-be reformer:[26] *causally link your preferred issue to another one that is likely to attract more support than the former*. Actually this is not new in this paper: appealing to fears and to enlightened self-interest are instances of the general rule I have just transcribed. But fear does not appeal to the noblest of human predispositions, and the effectiveness of the appeal is not likely to endure after the specific motive has disappeared. Furthermore, insofar as the appeal to self-interest refers to private interests, the consequences are likely to be limited and ambivalent. What I am going to suggest is linking poverty and inequality to something that is, arguably, a public and general interest: democracy.

This, I hasten to add, is rather tricky. To begin with, even if the causal links are carefully worked out (a tall order, indeed), for the argument to be persuasive one has to really care about democracy. Why should the privileged *really* care? Several answers have been given, none of them guaranteeing that this should be the case:

1) The privileged sectors, particularly but not exclusively business, should care because the demise of democracy will likely lead to a military regime, and the military have proved that they are unreliable allies in supporting, implementing, and maintaining 'market-oriented' policies.[27] In extreme cases, these regimes may go berserk, terrorizing the whole population and even entering into crazy wars.

2) By and large, the present democratic governments are supporting, implementing, and maintaining policies under which the privileged sectors are faring very well. This includes, for these sectors, better access to policy-making than was the rule under military regimes.[28]

3) There are not, nowadays, serious threats that parties determined to produce a radical overhaul of society will win elections.

4) The present international climate of opinion would make it costlier than it was decades ago to undertake and support the adventure of an authoritarian regression.[29]

5) As I found out watching even strong supporters of our past authoritarian regimes, it is rather embarrassing when abroad to be asked questions such as: "Your country is under some kind of dictatorship, isn't it?" Individuals, particularly those who are members of transnationalized networks, prefer not to be put into the category of belonging to some primitive tribe. Furthermore, part of the international climate of opinion is that international business and political leaders have also learned the scant reliability of armed forces' governments and

are at least as satisfied as their domestic counterparts with the current policies of most Latin American governments—more rigorous payments of the external debt, fewer obstacles to profit remittances, financial and commercial liberalization, high domestic interest rates, and privatizations *mediante*.

These are pragmatic reasons, subject to reversal if the contextual conditions that support them change. This is not insignificant, but we should do better, hoping for a more principled commitment to democracy. In this sense one should make the moral and political argument that democracy is grounded on values that dictate a respectful attitude toward the dignity and autonomy of every human being. To the obvious retort that respect for these attributes is not exactly paramount in our new democracies, one can answer that, however deeply imperfect today, since democracy *is* based on those values, it offers better chances than any other regime to make them effective some day.[30] Some contemporary authors, following Schumpeter (1975 [1942]), define democracy in narrow terms as a mechanism that, through competitive elections, decides who will govern for a given period. I do not agree: if democracy were not also a wager on the dignity and autonomy of individuals, it would lack the extraordinary moral force that it has evinced many times in modern history.

In contemporary Latin America the gap between those values and their effectiveness is extraordinarily wide. But one cannot jump to the conclusion that, per se, this gap will eliminate democracy.[31] India shows that democracy can long survive in the midst of enormous poverty and inequality,[32] and some of our new democracies have endured crises (including rapid impoverishment of broad sectors of the population) that not too long ago would have immediately provoked military coups and/or revolutionary upheavals.

The real issue is the *quality* of democracy. Citizens are the individual counterparts of a democratic regime. Citizens are supposed to be protected and empowered by the clusters of rights sanctioned by modern constitutionalism. The basis of citizenship is the assumption of the autonomy and, consequently, of the basic equality, of all individuals. Without this assumption even the narrowest definitions of democracy would be senseless: autonomy and equality are presupposed in the act of choosing among competing candidates and in fairly counting each vote as one, irrespective of the social condition of the voter. Effective citizenship is not only uncoerced voting; it is also a mode of relationship between citizens and the state and among citizens themselves. It is a continuing mode of relationship, during, before, and after elections, among individuals protected and empowered by their citizenship. Citizenship is no less encroached upon when voting is coerced than when a battered woman or a peasant cannot hope to obtain redress in court or when the home of a poor family is illegally invaded by the police. In these and related senses, ours are democracies of truncated, or low-intensity, citizenship. In many regions and cities, and for large parts of the population, it is the same old story: *La ley se acata pero no se cumple* [the law is acknowledged but not obeyed]. A corollary of citizenship and a central component of democracy, the rule of law, extends only intermittently across our countries.[33] Widespread violence, weak and unpredictable courts, and unpunished abuses of all sorts of powers, public and private, compound in many parts of Latin America a sense of unpredictability and ugliness in daily life, especially for the losers but also for the winners.[34]

Admittedly, as noted before, many of the rich opt for an exit: living in fortified ghettos, sending their children to well-guarded schools where they meet only the children of people like themselves, moving their offices out of downtown or other dangerous areas, mistrusting the inefficient and often corrupt police and hiring private guards,[35] and making transnational society the frame of reference of as many of their activities as possible. This process is also observable in the United States, but it is my distinct impression that it has advanced much more in Latin America. On the other hand, as suggested by the data of note 33 and numerous journalistic reports, the realities of an extremely impoverished and unequal society inexorably filter into the lives of the privileged: fear while going back and forth to work and school, manifold horrors highlighted on TV, the pervasive threats of the drug trade, the fear of kidnapping, and the like invade even the most secluded lives.

Literary talent is needed for depicting these situations. Here I want to point out their profound ambivalence. On one hand, they may lead to further exit, as the privileged sometimes seek added protection by supporting repressive measures against the *classes dangereuses*. This support entails indifference toward the gulf that separates winners and losers and further deterioration of values of solidarity and shared human dignity. Also, despite its many inconveniences, the present situation has important advantages, especially cheap and abundant labor, both at work and at home.[36] There are many, albeit unsystematic, indications that this mix of exit with support for repression may be the direction being taken. In this scenario, democracy, narrowly understood as a reasonably competitive and clean electoral process, may survive; but its quality would be dismal.[37]

On the other hand, perception of this bleak scenario may mobilize values and solidarities that could reverse the overall situation. Because nobody can completely extricate him- or herself from the consequences of extended poverty and deep inequality, and because these characteristics deeply offend the values on which democracy is grounded, a general argument for committing oneself to enhancing the quality of these democracies can be derived. As noted above, this argument can be made, through politics, a *public* one only if it is embraced by a broad coalition of social and political forces.

I have noted some of the difficulties that, if created, this coalition is likely to face. For thinking a bit further about this matter, it is useful to note that the image of dualism, like every dichotomy, is a simplification of limited value. It serves to underline the sad fact that there are in our countries two poles and they have been getting farther apart. But this image ignores the layers of the population that do not properly belong at either pole. 'Middle sectors' is too diffuse a category for designating these layers, but for want of a better concept I will use it here. The term itself alludes to those who are somewhere in between the truly rich and the truly poor.

Unfortunately, we know too little about these layers, especially after the changes provoked by the economic crises and adjustment programs of the last couple of decades.[38] Assorted indications,[39] however, plausibly suggest that, just as with the rest of society, a strong differentiation has occurred within the middle sectors themselves. Considerable decreases in pensions and in the salaries of public employees, particularly the lower ranking ones, unemployment resulting from privatizations and various 'rationalization' programs, high rates of bankruptcy of small enterprises during economic crises and at least during the first phases of economic stabilization, and the deterioration (or disappearance) of various social services to which these sectors had good access have combined to bring about a sharp fall of the income and the standard of living of significant numbers of people in the middle sectors.[40] On the other hand, various indications suggest that some layers, especially those composed of individuals who cater to the rich—highly educated professionals and owners of firms dedicated to luxury goods and services—have notably improved their situation throughout these years. It seems, consequently, that 'the middle' has significantly differentiated itself, with some moving toward the poor and some toward the rich poles, while the 'middle of the middle' has become thinner. Thus, despite the simplification it entails, the image of dualism still fits Latin America—now better than ever.

Some time ago the Latin American middle sectors were supposed to be the main carriers of social modernization, economic development, and democracy.[41] For reasons I will not delve into here, these hopes were dispelled. I am not aiming at resurrecting these expectations here, but I believe that some layers of the contemporary middle sectors will have to play a pivotal role in any political alliances that effectively attack poverty and inequality. Because poverty entails that the poor are poor in many resources, not only economic, they are unlikely to organize autonomously and, especially, to sustain collective actions appropriate for overcoming their condition. On the other hand, I surmise that the exit option is likely to be preferred by most of the rich. Toward the other pole of the middle, those whose income and welfare have sharply diminished and/or who linger dangerously close to poverty probably are, at best, as likely to support as to oppose policies aimed at improving the situation of the poor.[42]

This leaves us basically with the middle of the middle sectors. Many of the individuals belonging to this category are socially active, politically aware, highly educated, reasonably well informed about the world in which they live, and have strong aspirations of ascending social mobility. Particularly among the young, lack of employment (or of reasonably good employment) and the extremes of poverty and affluence they confront every day may thoroughly alienate them. But, still, those who have the aforementioned characteristics and, consequently, enjoy many of the advantages of modern life but—in terms of housing, transportation, education, health services, and the like—cannot exit as the rich can, seem the more likely to be mobilized by, and mobilize, the kind of political coalition I postulated above.

The structural position of other segments of the middle sectors generates, as I have argued, serious constraints for collectively playing an active role in efforts to redress poverty and, even more so, inequality. But constraints are not impossibilities. They can be partially overcome[43] with clear-headed actions, imaginative policies, persuasive arguments, good examples and, underlying and reinforcing all this, the emergence of an adequate political coalition. This coalition should have as its dynamic core the valuable if often intermittent collective efforts of the poor, the middle layers referred to above, and the altruists who exist at all levels of the social structure. As soon as it eventually emerges, the coalition will face some hard tests. One will be how to further link itself with the poor with a minimum of clientelism and paternalism. Another test will be to persuade a majority of public opinion, not only the privileged, that the policy orientations of the coalition are not inimical to the stability of basic macroeconomic parameters. A third test relates to the relations of this coalition with the unions. This is a topic in which generalizations across countries, and even across economic sectors and regions, are particularly risky.

With this caveat in mind, it seems clear that, if they were willing to voice the interests of workers in general (i.e., including those who are unemployed and not formally employed), the unions would become a weighty component of the coalition. On the other hand, I fear that, given the social and economic conditions prevailing in Latin America, most of the unions are likely to limit themselves to the defense of the interests of workers employed in the formal sector. In this case the relations between the aforementioned coalition and the unions will be punctuated by serious (albeit, hopefully, not mutually self-destructive) conflicts.

Clearly, the creation and the successful development of the kind of coalition I have sketched is a very tall order.[44] Ultimately the glue of this coalition can only be a moral argument: the decent treatment that is due to every human being. An additional argument is one of public interest: the improvement of the quality of our democracies is tantamount to advancing toward such decency. On the other hand, if the polarizing tendencies I have registered in this text continue unabated, what I have said here may well be a futile exercise in wishful thinking.

NOTES

The author thanks Vilmar Faria, Gabriela Ippolito-O'Donnell, and Víctor Tokman for their useful commentaries on earlier versions of this paper.

1. Data from ECLAC (1994, 157). Concerning the operational definition of these categories, see Feres and León (1990), and Altimir (1994a) and the sources cited thereafter, including the important work that Altimir has been undertaking, and inducing others to undertake, on poverty and inequality in Latin America.

2. As a publication of the International Monetary Fund (IMF) puts it: "Not only is poverty widespread in Latin America and the Caribbean, it has increased during the past decade. The unequal distribution of income is generally seen to be at the heart of poverty in the region—the bottom 20 percent of the population receive less than 4 percent of total income" (Burki and Edwards 1995, 8).

3. From now on, except when the context requires otherwise, I will apply the generic label of 'poor' to both categories. It should be noted that in the ECLAC methodology developed by Altimir and his associates those placed at the upper limit of the operational definition of poverty barely satisfy basic needs. This is even more true of studies by the World Bank, which established an even lower cutting point of U.S. $60 (1985 U.S. $) per person per month, corrected by a purchasing power parity exchange rate index for each country (World Bank 1990, 1994). For a useful discussion of these indicators, see Morley (1994).

4. See, among other sources, Cardoso and Helwege (1992); ECLAC (1994); and World Bank (1994).

5. See Mesa-Lago's classic study (1978).

6. See ECLAC (1994, 1995). Valuable studies of some important social policy areas are found in Mesa-Lago (1989, 1991, 1992).

7. See Tokman (1989a, 1989b, 1991, 1994) and, in general, the important work of PREALC, an institution that this author led for many years. See also C. Filgueira (1993) and Rakowski (1994), especially the chapters by Frank, Márquez, de Oliveira and Roberts, and Portes.

8. See, especially, ECLAC 1994 and the more general assessments in UNICEF (1993) and UNRISD (1994, 1995). An analysis of several important issues on this matter is in Crummett and Buvinic (1994).

9. Within a large and diverse literature, in addition to the sources already cited I have found particularly useful Altimir (1990, 1993, 1994a, 1994b); ECLAC (1995); Emmerij (1994); Lo Vuolo and Barbeito (1994); and Lustig (1992, 1994). For more detailed studies on Argentina, Brazil, Chile, and Uruguay, I refer to the studies resulting from the Kellogg/CEBRAP "Social Policies" project: Brandão Lopes (1994); Draibe et al. (1995); Faría 1994; C. Filgueira (1994); F. Filgueira (1995); Golbert and Tenti Fanfani (1994); León Batista (1994); Lo Vuolo (1995); and Raczynski (1994). For overviews of the economics of the period, among others see Fishlow (1989) and Ros (1993).

10. The authors cited in the preceding footnotes disagree as to how effective economic growth per se would be in diminishing poverty—assuming that economic growth may be achieved and sustained for a reasonably long period. But whatever the answer to

this question, it is hard to imagine that, even if it is a necessary condition for effectively addressing poverty (not to say anything of inequality, a much harder problem), economic growth will in itself be sufficient without criteria and policies that specifically focus on poverty and inequality. Altimir (1990), Borón (1992), Emmerij (1994), and Tokman (1994, 1995) argue persuasively along these lines.

11. For an interesting analysis of the repertoire of arguments supporting the status quo, see Hirschman (1991, 1993).

12. With some exceptions. There seems to be widespread agreement that 'decentralization' is a good thing. In abstract I agree. But transferring resources to highly inefficient, utterly clientelistic, and often corrupt local administrations reinforces circuits of power that worsen the problems that decentralization is supposed to address. On the other hand, 'decentralization' by way of transferring responsibilities to local administrations without the necessary resources has been an effective, if somewhat cynical and in the medium run counterproductive, way of showing 'progress' in the reduction of national fiscal deficits.

13. For a discussion of this scenario, see Nelson (1992).

14. Although the results are open to methodological dispute, there is some evidence that inequality is inimical to economic growth (e.g., Muller 1988). This theme has attracted the attention of mainstream economists in view of the economic successes of the rather egalitarian 'East Asian Tigers,' especially after the report on these countries by the World Bank (1993b). Among the discussions that this report has provoked, see Fishlow et al. (1994) and, from a different angle, Streeten (1994) and Hewitt de Alcántara (1993). But it is very difficult to assess the impact of equality independently from other factors that seem just as likely to have fostered those economic successes.

15. This remark does not ignore the fact that, whether out of altruism, enlightened self-interest, technological need, or a combination of these, some enterprises do take care of adequately training, and retaining, some of their workers. This is excellent for both these enterprises and workers, but it includes only a small proportion of the work force.

16. For recent discussions on this matter by economists who would not usually be classified as 'soft-headed' (as moralists and the present author may be argued to be), see Sen (1992) and Dasgupta (1993). In Sen's terms, poverty does not only matter by itself but also because it curtails capabilities that are essential for the choice of functionings compatible with the human condition. For a convergent philosophical discussion, see Taylor (1985).

17. For recent discussion of these aspects, see Bradford (1994) and Evans (1995). Also O'Donnell (1993).

18. Commenting on the sharp and generalized fall of social expenditures by the state in the 1980s, Cominetti (1994, 35) says: "by the end of the decade, the social expenditure indicators evinced a generalized deterioration, particularly in real per capita terms as well as in relation to GNP, showing that the deterioration did not correspond only to the fall in the level of economic activity but also to the orientation of the policies implemented" [my translation]. For a more general picture on state employment, see Marshall (1990).

19. The classic study of these workers is Lipsky (1980), to whom the term italicized above belongs. The concerns I express in the text do not preclude the possibility that, as Tendler and Freedheim (1994) show in the case of health policies in Ceará, Brazil, some

successful programs may be devised and implemented. But this and other similar cases are, at least for the time being, no more than encouraging exceptions.

20. Or, for that matter, several cities in Great Britain, France, Italy, and Spain, even though poverty there is more recent and less extensive. For thoughtful discussions about the United States, see Sawhill (1988) and Danzinger and Gottschalk (1993). Wilson stirred interesting controversies on this topic (1987), which are recapitulated in Wilson (1991–1992).

21. A recent assessment of the welfare state in OECD countries is in Esping-Andersen (1994).

22. Others, like myself, have migrated to the center, not just partially, as in these ghettos, but entirely. From here we observe a situation of which we arguably are the worst example.

23. Before the Greek Calends: the Greeks did not reckon time by calends, so to plan to settle one's bills at the Greek Calends means that one will pay at a time that will never arrive (Ed.).

24. I write 'most' because, after numerous studies in the highly developed countries, it seems clear that everywhere some pockets of permanent poverty remain, requiring specific interventions for alleviating its more damaging consequences, especially for children. But the Latin American rates of poverty and indigence go much beyond the small numbers and proportions implied by the metaphor of the 'pocket.'

25. The term 'reasonable' is admittedly ambiguous. There is no way of establishing an objective and indisputable criterion of what would be an acceptable, or fair, degree of equality nor of deciding which of the various dimensions of equality should be given priority, see Rae (1981).

26. As will be immediately obvious to the reader, the source here is Hirschman (1963).

27. In this respect Chile is a notorious exception. But nothing guarantees that it would be so again, if unfortunately the occasion should arise.

28. For studies supporting the conditions stated in paragraphs 1) and 2), see, especially, Acuña and Smith (1994); Conaghan and Malloy (1994); and Stepan (1988).

29. Caveat: in Peru Fujimori seems to have found a solution. If you carry out a coup that is openly supported by the military but still keeps an elected president at the top, if the economic policies of the government are blessed by the domestic and international agents who matter, if you defeat one of the ugliest guerrilla movements in history, if the economy begins to grow at a fast pace, and if the same coup-president is re-elected, then you can get away with the coup, even if congress and the judiciary are utterly subordinated to the executive, gross human rights violations continue, and the elections were not exactly immaculate (see the election reports in *LASA Forum* 1995). In a similar, if bloodier, coup in a larger and geopolitically much more important country, Yeltsin got away with less than Fujimori.

30. To which the 'Singapore argument' (or, until sometime ago, the oddly similar 'Cuban argument') will hasten to retort that, with no constitutional democracy whatsoever, some populations enjoy much higher and widespread welfare than our democracies. Since our countries are far more likely to produce predatory authoritarian regimes than Singapore (and since the Pinochet regime is not a very good example in terms of poverty and inequality), this argument does not concern me here.

31. Although, admittedly, such an assertion can be, in certain contexts, a rhetorically persuasive argument.

32. But it should be noted that some comparative quantitative studies have found that income inequality (Muller 1988) or poverty (Przeworski and Limongi 1994) tend to negatively affect the likelihood of survival of democratic regimes.

33. The rule of law in our countries (or, rather its absence for vast sectors of the population) is a complicated and extremely important topic, on which I cannot elaborate here. A preliminary discussion, which I will expand in future publications, is in O'Donnell (1993). This text is also available as Kellogg Institute Working Paper no. 192 (1993). Interesting and eloquent analyses of some of these matters can be found in Pinheiro and Poppovic (1993) and Pinheiro, Poppovic, and Khan (1994). For another, convergent, perspective, see Fox (1994).

34. As one indication of these problems, a recent survey of 320 persons in top private and public positions in Brazil asked the following question: "In your opinion, what is the most important negative consequence of the increase in poverty in the large Brazilian cities?" [my translation]. Of the interviewees 65.3 percent gave answers that reflect how these problems impinge on their own lives: violence, crime, insecurity (51.4 percent); possibilities of social chaos (8.4 percent); and diminution of the quality of life for all (5.5 percent); Reis and Cheibub (1995); see also Soares de Lima and Boschi (1995).

35. In addition to the texts already cited, see Caldeira (1992).

36. An interesting thought experiment is to imagine the incredible disruptions that would be caused in well-to-do families by the disappearance of domestic laborers.

37. It is thought-provoking, if disquieting, that in a comparative quantitative study Muller and Seligson (1994) found that inequality is the strongest negative factor in changes in the level (or quality, as I call it here) of democracy.

38. I concur with C. Filgueira (1993) in his plea for devoting more attention and resources to basic studies of the present social structure of our countries. Various recent projects would have greatly benefitted from the knowledge generated by the type of research C. Filgueira advocates. In particular, studies on the political correlates of adjustment programs that speculate about the classes or social sectors that are likely to support or oppose these programs presuppose a social structure that is dated or about which they have no information (see, e.g., relevant chapters in Williamson 1994).

39. Among others, ECLAC (1994); Davis (1994); Díaz (1994); C. Filgueira (1993); ILO (1995); Tokman (1994); and Torrado (1992).

40. For recent data on and discussion of this matter, see Tokman (1995).

41. Johnson (1958) is the classic statement. It may be worth noting that these conceptions strongly influenced the Alliance for Progress.

42. We saw that the social expenditures that, in general and often against stated policy goals, have benefitted these layers more than the poor (education, housing, urban services, and some health services) have lately deteriorated in many of our countries. In addition to their loss of income, this diminution in their welfare goes a long way in making understandable the demands of these layers to receive preferential treatment from the state—and their, at least implicit, opposition to diverting resources to the poor. For a discussion of these issues, see Nelson (1992). Here lies another major political and intellectual challenge: devising pro-poor policies that would overcome or sidestep these obstacles. One clear but politically difficult way to advance in this direction would be to

decrease the present reliance on regressive indirect taxes (especially value added ones) and emphasize direct taxes on income and wealth; see, especially, Borón (1992).

43. I write 'partially' because it would be a serious mistake to expect some kind of angelic consensus around these issues. Politics means both consensus and conflict; democratic politics peacefully processes, but does not cancel, conflict.

44. Given the high level of generality at which I placed myself in this paper, I cannot go further in the present discussion. In each country the possibilities as well as the modalities of the eventual emergence of such a coalition will be contingent on the preexisting political allegiances of the popular and middle sectors and on the configuration of the respective party systems.

REFERENCES

Acuña, Carlos H., and William C. Smith. 1994. The Political Economy of Structural Adjustment: The Logic of Support and Opposition to Neoliberal Reform. In *Latin American Political Economy in the Age of Neoliberal Reform: Theoretical and Comparative Perspectives for the 1990s*, edited by William C. Smith, Carlos H. Acuña, and Eduardo A. Gamarra. London: Transaction Publishers.

Altimir, Oscar. 1990. Development, Crisis and Equity. *CEPAL Review* no. 41 (August): 7–27.

———. 1993. *Income Distribution and Poverty through Crisis and Adjustment*. ECLAC/United Nations Working Paper no. 15 (September). Santiago: ECLAC.

———. 1994a. Cambios en la Desigualdad y la Pobreza en la América Latina. *El Trimestre Económico* 241 (January–March): 85–134.

———. 1994b. Distribución del Ingreso e Incidencia de la Pobreza a lo Largo del Ajuste. *Revista de la CEPAL* no. 52 (April).

Banco Interamericano de Desarrollo. 1993. *Reforma Social y Pobreza. Hacia una Agenda Integrada de Desarrollo*. Washington, D.C.: UNDP.

Borón, Atilio. 1992. La Pobreza de las Naciones: La Economía Política del Neoliberalismo en la Argentina. EURAL (Centro Europa-America Latina), Buenos Aires.

Bradford, Jr., Colin I., ed. 1994. *Redefining the State in Latin America*. Paris: OECD.

Brandão Lopes, Juarez R. 1994. Brazil, 1989: A *Socioeconomic Study of Indigence and Urban Poverty*. Democracy and Social Policy Series Working Paper no. 7 (spring). Notre Dame: Kellogg Institute.

Burki, Javed Shahid, and Sebastián Edwards. 1995. Consolidating Economic Reforms in Latin America and the Caribbean. *Finance and Development* 32 (March), no. 1: 6–9.

Caldeira, Teresa Pires do Rio. 1992. City of Walls: Crime, Segregation, and Citizenship in São Paulo. Ph.D. diss., Department of Anthropology, University of California, Berkeley.

Cardoso, Eliana, and Ann Helwege. 1992. Below the Line: Poverty in Latin America. *World Development* 20 (January), no. 1: 19–37.
Cominetti, Rosella. 1994. Gasto Social y Ajuste Fiscal en América Latina. In *Proyecto Regional de Política Pública*. Santiago: ECLAC.
Conaghan, Catherine, and James Malloy. 1994. *Unsettling Statecraft: Democracy and Neoliberalism in the Central Andes*. Pittsburgh: University of Pittsburgh Press.
Conaghan, Catherine, Bruce Kay, and David Scott Palmer. 1995. Articles on the 1995 Peruvian election. LASA Forum 26 (summer), no. 2: 9–20.
Crummett, María de los Angeles, and Marya Buvinic. 1994. *Symposium on Women and the Transition to Democracy: The Impact of Political and Economic Reform in Latin America*. Latin American Program Working Paper no. 211. Washington, D.C.: Woodrow Wilson International Center for Scholars.
Danzinger, Sheldon, and Peter Gottschalk, eds. 1993. *Uneven Tides: Rising Inequality in America*. New York: Russell Sage Foundation.
Dasgupta, Partha. 1993. *An Inquiry into Well-Being and Destitution*. Oxford: Clarendon Press.
Davis, Diane. 1994. With Capital, Labor, or on Their Own? Middle Classes in the Economic Development of Latin America and East Asia. Graduate Faculty of Political and Social Science, New School for Social Research.
Díaz, Alvaro. 1994. Tendencias en la Reestructuración Económica y Social en América Latina. *Revista Mexicana de Sociología* 6 (October-December), no. 4: 3–35.
Draibe, Sonia M., Maria Helena Guimarães de Castro, and Beatriz Azeredo. 1995. *The System of Social Protection in Brazil*. Democracy and Social Policy Series Working Paper no. 3 (spring). Notre Dame: Kellogg Institute.
ECLAC (Economic Commission for Latin America and the Caribbean). 1994. *Panorama Social de América Latina 1994*. Santiago de Chile: ECLAC.
———. 1995. *Informe de la Comisión Latinoamericana y del Caribe sobre el Desarrollo Social*. Santiago: IDB, ECLAC, UNPD.
Emmerij, Louis. 1994. Social Tensions and Social Reform in Latin America. IDB (Inter-American Development Bank) Working Paper. Washington, D.C.
Esping-Andersen, Gosta. 1994. *After the Golden Age: The Future of the Welfare State in the New Global Area*. Occasional Paper no. 7. Geneva: UNRISD (United Nations Research Institute for Social Development).
Evans, Peter. 1995. *Embedded Autonomy: States and Industrial Transformation*. Princeton: Princeton University Press.
Faría, Vilmar. 1994. *The Current Social Situation in Brazil: Dilemmas and Perspectives*. Democracy and Social Policy Series Working Paper no. 1 (spring). Notre Dame: Kellogg Institute.
Feres, Juan Carlos, and Arturo León. 1990. The Magnitude of Poverty in Latin America. *CEPAL Review* no. 41 (August): 133–51.
Filgueira, Carlos. 1993. América Latina: Tendencias e Incertidumbres del Desarrollo Social. CIESU (Centro de Informaciones y Estudios del Uruguay), Montevideo.

———. 1994. *Heterogeneity and Urban Poverty in Uruguay*. Democracy and Social Policy Series Working Paper no. 9 (winter). Notre Dame: Kellogg Institute.

Filgueira, Fernando. 1995. *A Century of Social Welfare in Uruguay: Growth to the Limit of the Battlista Social State*. Democracy and Social Policy Series Working Paper no. 5 (spring). Notre Dame: Kellogg Institute.

Fishlow, Albert. 1989. Latin American Failure against the Backdrop of Asian Success. *The Annals of the American Academy* 505 (September): 117–28.

Fishlow, Albert, Catherine Gwin, Stephan Haggard, Dani Rodrik, and Robert Wade. 1994. *Miracle or Design? Lessons from the East Asian Experience*. Washington, D.C.: Overseas Development Council.

Fox, Jonathan. 1994. The Difficult Transition from Clientelism to Citizenship. *World Politics* 46 (January), no. 2: 151–84.

Golbert, Laura, and Emilio Tenti Fanfani. 1994. *Poverty and Social Structure in Argentina: Outlook for the 1990s*. Democracy and Social Policy Series Working Paper no. 6 (spring). Notre Dame: Kellogg Institute.

Hewitt de Alcántara, Cynthia, ed. 1993. *Real Markets: Social and Political Issues of Food Policy Reform*. Geneva: UNRISD.

Hirschman, Albert O. 1963. *Journeys toward Progress: Studies of Economic Policy-Making in Latin America*. New York: Twentieth-Century Fund.

———. 1970. *Exit, Voice, and Loyalty: Responses to Decline in Firms, Organizations, and States*. Cambridge, Mass.: Harvard University Press.

———. 1991. *The Rhetoric of Reaction*. Cambridge: The Belknap Press of Harvard University Press.

———. 1993. The Rhetoric of Reaction—Two Years Later. *Government and Opposition* 28 (summer), no. 3: 292–314.

ILO (International Labor Organization). 1995. *World Employment 1995*. Geneva: ILO.

Jaquette, Jane, ed. 1994. *The Women's Movement in Latin America: Participation and Democracy*, 2d ed. Boulder: Westview Press.

Johnson, John J. 1958. *Political Change in Latin America: The Emergence of the Middle Sectors*. Stanford: Stanford University Press.

León Batista, Arturo. 1994. *Urban Poverty in Chile: Its Extent and Diversity*. Democracy and Social Policy Series Working Paper no. 8 (summer). Notre Dame: Kellogg Institute.

Lipsky, Michael. 1980. *Street-Level Bureaucracy: Dilemmas of the Individual in Public Services*. New York: Russell Sage Foundation.

Lo Vuolo, Rubén M. 1995. *The Welfare State in Contemporary Argentina: An Overview*. Democracy and Social Policy Series Working Paper no. 2 (spring). Notre Dame: Kellogg Institute.

Lo Vuolo, Rubén M., and Alberto C. Barbeito. 1993. *La Nueva Oscuridad de la Política Social: Del Estado Populista al Neoconservador*. Buenos Aires: Miño y Dávila.

Lustig, Nora. 1992. *Poverty and Inequality in Latin America: Facts, Issues, and Dilemmas*. Washington, D.C.: Inter-American Dialogue.

———. 1994. *Coping with Austerity: Poverty and Inequality in Latin America.* Washington, D.C.: Brookings Institution.
Marshall, Adriana, ed. 1990. *El Empleo Público Frente a la Crisis.* Geneva: Instituto International de Estudios Laborales.
Mesa-Lago, Carmelo. 1978. *Social Security in Latin America: Pressure Groups, Stratification, and Inequality.* Pittsburgh: University of Pittsburgh Press.
———. 1989. *Ascent to Bankruptcy: Financing Social Security in Latin America.* Pittsburgh: University of Pittsburgh Press.
———. 1990. *La Seguridad Social y el Sector Informal.* Santiago: ILO.
———. 1991. *Social Security and Prospects for Equity in Latin America.* World Bank Discussion Paper no. 140. Washington, D.C.: The World Bank.
———. 1992. *Health Care for the Poor in Latin America and the Caribbean.* Washington, D.C.: PAHO (Panamerican Health Organization).
Morley, Samuel. 1994. *Poverty and Inequality in Latin America: Past Evidence, Future Prospects.* Washington, D.C.: Overseas Development Council.
Muller, Edward N. 1988. Democracy, Economic Development, and Income Inequality. *American Sociological Review* 53 (February), no. 1: 50–68.
Muller, Edward N. and Mitchell A. Seligson. 1994. Civic Culture and Democracy: The Question of Causal Relations. *American Political Science Review* 88 (September), no. 3: 635–52.
Naim, Moisés. 1994. Latin America: The Second Stage of Reform. *Journal of Democracy* 5 (October), no. 4: 33–48.
Nelson, Joan. 1992. Poverty, Equity, and the Politics of Adjustment. In *Politics of Economic Adjustment,* edited by Stephan Haggard and Robert R. Kaufman. Princeton: Princeton University Press.
Nelson, Joan, John Waterbury, Stephan Haggard, et al. 1989. *Fragile Coalitions: The Politics of Economic Adjustment.* New Brunswick: Transaction Books.
Nelson, Joan, ed. 1990. *Economic Crisis and Policy Choice: The Politics of Adjustment in the Third World.* Princeton: Princeton University Press.
O'Donnell, Guillermo. 1993. On the State, Democratization, and Some Conceptual Problems: A Latin American View with Glances at Some Postcommunist Countries. *World Development* 21 (August), no. 8: 1355–69.
Pinheiro, Paulo Sérgio, and Malak El-Chichini Poppovic. 1993. Poverty, Marginalization, Violence, and the Realization of Human Rights. Paper prepared for United Nations World Conference on Human Rights, April, Geneva.
Pinheiro, Paulo Sérgio, Malak El-Chichini Poppovic, and Túlio Kahn. 1994. Pobreza, Violência e Direitos Humanos. *Novos Estudos CEBRAP* 39 (July): 189–208.
Portes, Alejandro, and Richard Schauffler. 1993. The Informal Economy in Latin America. In *Work without Protections: Case Studies of the Informal Sector in Developing Countries.* Washington, D.C.: Bureau of International Labor Affairs, U.S. Department of Labor.
Przeworski, Adam and Fernando Limongi. 1994. *Modernization: Theories and Facts.* Chicago Center for Democracy Working Paper no. 4 (November). Chicago: University of Chicago.

Raczynski, Dagmar. 1994. *Social Policies in Chile: Origin, Transformation, and Perspectives.* Democracy and Social Policy Series Working Paper no. 4 (fall). Notre Dame: Kellogg Institute.
Rae, Douglas. 1981. *Equalities.* Cambridge: Harvard University Press.
Rakowski, Cathy A., ed. 1994. *Contrapunto: The Informal Sector Debate in Latin America.* Albany: New York University Press.
Reis, Elisa, and Zairo Cheibub. 1995. Valores Políticos das Elites e Consolidação Democrática. *Dados* 38 (1): 31–56.
Ros, Jaime, ed. 1993. *La Edad de Plomo del Desarrollo Latinoamericano.* Mexico: Instituto Latinoamericano de Estudios Transnacionales/Fondo de Cultura Económica.
Sawhill, Isabel V. 1988. Poverty in the U.S.: Why Is It So Persistent? *Journal of Economic Literature* 26 (September), no. 3: 1073–119.
Schumpeter, Joseph. 1975 [1942]. *Capitalism, Socialism and Democracy.* New York: Harper & Row.
Sen, Amartya. 1992. *Inequality Reexamined.* Cambridge, Mass.: Harvard University Press.
Soares de Lima, Maria Regina, and Renato R. Boschi. 1995. Democracia e Reforma Econômica: A Visão das Elites Brasileiras. *Dados* 38 (1): 7–30.
Stepan, Alfred. 1988. *Rethinking Military Politics: Brazil and the Southern Cone.* Princeton: Princeton University Press.
Streeten, Paul. 1994. *Strategies for Human Development.* Copenhagen: Handelshojkolens Forlag.
Taylor, Charles. 1985. *What's Wrong with Negative Liberty?* Philosophy and the Human Sciences Philosophical Papers no. 2. Cambridge: Cambridge University Press.
Tendler, Judith, and Sara Freedheim. 1994. Trust in a Rent-Seeking World: Health and Government Transformed in Northeast Brazil. *World Development* 22 (December), no. 12: 1771–91.
Tokman, Víctor E. 1989a. Policies for a Heterogeneous Informal Sector in Latin America. *World Development* 17 (July), no. 37: 1067–76.
———. 1989b. Economic Development and Labor Markets: Segmentation in the Latin American Periphery. *Journal of Interamerican Studies and World Affairs* 31: 23–47.
———. 1991. Pobreza y Homogenización Social: Tareas para los 90. *Pensamiento Iberoamericano* no. 19: 81–104.
———, ed. 1992. *Beyond Regulation: The Informal Economy in Latin America.* London: Lynne Rienner Publishers.
———. 1994. Informalidad y Pobreza: Progreso Social y Modernización Productiva. *El Trimestre Económico* 61 (January–March): 177–99.
———. 1995. Pobreza y Equidad. Dos Objetivas Relacionados. Lima: ILO.
Torrado, Susana. 1992. *Estructura Social de la Argentina 1945–1983.* Buenos Aires: Ediciones de la Flor.
UNICEF (United Nations Children's Fund). 1993. *The Progress of Nations: The Nations of the World Ranked according to Their Achievements in Health, Nu-*

trition, *Education, Family Planning, and Progress for Women.* New York: UNICEF.
UNRISD (United Nations Research Institute for Social Development). 1994. *The Crisis of Social Development in the 1990s: Preparing for the World Social Summit.* Geneva: UNRISD.
———. 1995. *States of Disarray: The Social Effects of Globalization.* London: UNRISD.
Williamson, John, ed. 1994. *The Political Economy of Policy Reform.* Washington, D.C.: Institute for International Economics.
Wilson, William Julius. 1987. *The Truly Disadvantaged: The Inner City, the Underclass, and Public Policy.* Chicago: University of Chicago Press.
———. 1991–92. Another Look at The Truly Disadvantaged. *Political Science Quarterly* 106 (4): 639–56.
World Bank. 1990. *World Development Report 1990. Poverty: World Development Indicators.* Washington, D.C.: Oxford University Press.
———. 1993a. *Social Indicators of Development 1993.* Baltimore and London: Johns Hopkins University Press.
———. 1993b. *The East Asian Miracle: Economic Growth and Public Policy.* New York: Oxford University Press.
———. 1994. *Social Indicators of Development 1994.* Baltimore: Johns Hopkins University Press.

Part II

Globalization and the Employment Issue

4 | Globalization and Job Creation

A Latin American Perspective

RENÉ CORTÁZAR

The globalization of the world economy has significantly changed the determinants of job creation and the effectiveness of different employment policies. In this chapter we discuss some of these changes from a Latin American perspective.

First, it must be recognized that job creation is a challenge for most countries in the region. Even though open unemployment rates are relatively low (see Table 4.1), good jobs are indispensable to combat widespread poverty and underemployment.

Second, most Latin American economies have become integrated into the globalized world economy. Tariffs have dropped to less than half, nontariff restrictions have been drastically reduced, and regional free trade agreements have been put in place. This has created a whole new set of conditions that influence the process of growth (see Table 4.2) and job creation, and determine the effectiveness of traditional employment policies.

The first section of this chapter discusses how the globalization process[1] has changed the workings of the economy, of the state, and of social organizations. The second section describes some of the agreements and disagreements with respect to the determinants of employment creation and analyzes how globalization has created the need for new rules (both formal and informal) in the labor market, for reforms in the educational system, and for new investment

Table 4.1 Unemployment Rates, Latin America, 1986–1994 (Average annual rates)

	1986–90	1990	1991	1992	1993	1994[a]
Argentina[b]	6.8	7.5	6.5	7.0	9.6	11.2
Brazil[c]	3.8	4.3	4.8	5.8	5.3	5.5
Chile[d]	9.0	6.5	7.3	4.9	4.0	6.2
Colombia[e]	10.8	10.2	10.2	10.2	8.7	9.3
Mexico[f]	3.3	2.7	2.7	2.8	3.4	3.7
Peru[g]	7.0	8.3	5.9	9.4	9.9	9.5
Uruguay[h]	9.1	9.3	8.9	9.0	8.4	9.0
Venezuela[i]	9.6	11.0	10.1	8.0	6.6	8.9

Source: ECLAC and ILO on the basis of official information.
[a] Preliminary figures.
[b] National urban.
[c] Metropolitan areas of Rio de Janeiro, São Paulo, Belo Horizonte, Porto Alegre, Salvador, and Recife; 1994 figure corresponds to the average for January to August.
[d] Metropolitan Santiago; 1994 figure corresponds to the average for January to October.
[e] Bogotá, Barranquilla, Medellín, Cali, Bucaramanga, Manizales, and Pasto; 1994 figure corresponds to the average for March, June, and September.
[f] Total urban; 1994 figure corresponds to the average of January to September.
[g] Metropolitan Lima.
[h] Montevideo; 1994 figure corresponds to the average for January to October.
[i] 1993–94, national; 1994 figure refers to first six months of the year.

Table 4.2 Growth of GDP, Latin America, 1980–1994 (Annual rates)

	1980–90	1990	1991	1992	1993[e]	1994[e]
Argentina	−1.0	−0.1	8.9	8.6	6.4	7.6
Brazil	1.5	−4.4	0.2	−0.8	4.4	5.7
Chile	3.0	3.3	7.3	11.0	6.3	4.3
Colombia	3.4	4.0	1.9	3.6	5.3	5.7
Mexico	1.5	4.4	3.6	2.8	0.8	3.5
Peru	−1.0	−5.6	2.6	2.3	6.5	13.0
Uruguay	0.4	0.9	3.2	7.7	0.8	n.a.
Venezuela	1.0	6.8	9.7	5.8	−1.0	−3.3

Source: ECLAC.
[e] Estimated.

in "social capital." The way these new rules and policies affect job creation and influence employment policies is also discussed.

What Has Changed with Globalization?

Globalization has changed the workings of the economy, the state, and social organizations. Let us review some of the main trends.

The Economy

To talk about job creation we must start with the labor market, and specifically with the demand for labor. In an open economy, the demand for labor in the modern sector depends crucially on the stock of capital,[2] technology, and other factors that affect productivity.[3] Given these parameters, the number of workers employed will depend on the cost of labor and its relation to productivity. When the cost of labor drops, firms in the modern sector are willing to hire workers whose productivity is lower.[4]

Wages and productivity are closely connected in open economies. This was different in the more closed economies that characterized most of the countries in the region from the 1930s to the early 1970s. In a closed economy, employment levels are more strictly related to aggregate demand levels. When aggregate demand is insufficient, firms do not employ all the workers whose productivity is higher than the cost of labor. On the other hand, in the modern sector, when wages grow at a faster pace than productivity, governments can raise tariffs or increase the prices controlled by the authority[5] so as to guarantee an adequate rate of return to firms. In that setting, wages can differ from productivity, at least in the short run.

Globalization has an impact both on the determinants of the level and on the variance of the demand for labor. In a rapidly changing world economy, firms have to adapt to change to stay competitive. Flexibility of the rules of the game (both formal and informal rules) crucially affects the demand for labor. This contrasts with the more stable and predictable demand for labor experienced during the import-substitution period.

The reality of the traditional or informal sector differs from that of the modern sector. Take the case of the self-employed in retail trade. Even if the level of sales does not increase, an "ease of entry" permits new workers to find a job at the cost of reducing the average income of those who are already working in that sector. More vendors at the main square will increase employment, at the cost of reducing the income that each one receives. This informal sector does not comply with much of the labor legislation and is the means of survival available to those who fail to find a job in the modern sector.[6]

Globalization also affects the supply of labor. In this changing economy, education and training must prepare workers to adapt to different jobs and to jobs that involve many different tasks. New technologies are replacing the simple tasks of the past with more creative activities. The fast rate of change means that education and training must be an ongoing process.

The State

This section will highlight only two points. On the one hand, governments in the region are showing considerable fiscal discipline. Whereas in the past most countries ran huge fiscal deficits, a significant part of the region now shows balanced budgets and even fiscal surpluses (see Table 4.3). This is partly owing to the need to reduce inflation (see Table 4.4). It is also attributable to the fact that capital now crosses borders ever more rapidly, despite the best efforts of some national governments to control it. A new discipline has thus been created for the governments in the region as they have realized that the only way to attract foreign and domestic capital is through a stable macroeconomic environment.

The impact of globalization on the state goes beyond fiscal discipline. It is widely recognized that the productivity of an economy requires both productive firms and an effective state. Not only firms compete in the world economy but also tax systems, infrastructure (roads, ports), and the judiciary system. Hence, in most Latin American countries globalization is pushing toward a smaller, more effective state.

Social Organizations

The process of globalization has affected the preferences as well as the constraints and incentives that influence the behavior of social organizations. Preferences in a global society are strongly influenced by the information people receive through the mass media. For example, what is perceived as the "Chilean success story" has affected the perceptions, the arguments of the debate, and hence the preferences of the social and political actors in other countries in the region. Waves of common views that simultaneously affect several countries in the region are not new. But what *is* new is the intensity and the velocity of the process induced by the globalization of the mass media. The debates on social security reform, on strategies to promote exports, and on social and macroeconomic policies now take place with explicit references to the experience of other countries in the region.

The constraints and incentives faced by the different social organizations also have been changed by globalization. For example, the fact that in an open economy wages must be closely linked to productivity makes government interventions in the area of wage determination less effective than in the past. Many countries have privatized at least part of their social security system as

Table 4.3 Fiscal Balance, Latin America, 1987–1994 (Percentage of GDP)

	1987–90	1990	1991	1992	1993	1994
Argentina	−4.6	−3.8	−1.6	0.4	1.1	0.1
Brazil	−4.1	1.2	1.4	−2.1	0.3	0.3
Chile	1.3	0.8	1.5	2.2	1.9	1.7
Colombia	−0.8	−0.3	0.1	−0.3	0.2	–
Mexico	−9.4	−4.0	−0.4	1.6	0.7	0.4
Peru	−3.7	−2.5	−1.6	−1.7	−1.4	–
Uruguay	−4.3	−2.5	–	0.5	−1.0	−2.5
Venezuela	−3.4	1.0	0.6	−5.8	−3.5	−7.0

Source: ECLAC.

Table 4.4 Inflation, Latin America, 1980–1994 (Annual rates)

	1980–90	1990	1991	1992	1993	1994
Argentina	650	1343.9	84.0	17.6	7.7	3.9
Brazil	450	1584.6	475.8	1149.1	2489.1	929.3
Chile	21	27.3	18.7	12.7	12.2	8.9
Colombia	23	32.4	26.8	25.2	22.6	22.6
Mexico	70	29.9	18.9	11.9	8.0	7.1
Peru	1000+	7649.9	139.2	56.7	39.5	15.4
Uruguay	57	129.0	81.3	59.0	52.9	44.1
Venezuela	26	36.5	31.0	31.9	45.9	70.8

Source: ECLAC.

well as their training institutions. This has changed the type of possible relationships between the state and social organizations and, hence, the incentives and constraints they face in defining their strategies.

Employment Policies: Agreements and Disagreements

Some Agreements

One of the most important agreements regarding job creation is the recognition that most of the action in this area does not take place in the labor market. If we consider the large swings in the employment levels of the 1980s we can see that they were closely linked to macroeconomic events (external debt crises, devaluations, rising interest rates) rather than to the workings of the labor markets. Indeed most of the Latin American countries, despite the wide variance in labor institutions and labor policies among them, were affected by the swings.

It is also a matter of agreement that one of the main determinants of employment is investment and that investment is determined by the rate of return and by "country risk," neither of which is solely affected by the labor market as such. That is to say, employment creation is the outcome of the workings of the economy and, more broadly, of society; the labor market is but one aspect to be taken into account.

Another point on which there is widespread agreement is that the choice of an open economy and the existing degree of competitiveness in the world economy have created a tight link between wages and labor productivity, which is a decisive factor when it comes to setting wages and determining the level of employment. Most countries in the region, with their considerably heterogeneous productive structures, also have a very heterogeneous structure of labor productivity. Hence, in order to connect remunerations to productivity, so as to remain competitive and make job creation possible, wage determination has to take place at a rather decentralized level. This allows the market and collective bargaining to play more significant roles, while the role of government intervention in this area becomes less important.[7]

Main Disagreements

Together with these broad agreements there are many disagreements that turn labor policy and labor reforms into hot topics of debate in most Latin American countries. The disagreements can be organized into three views: "old consensus," "neoconservative," and "growth with equity."[8] While none of these three views is held in its pure form by any of the social or political actors, many actors come close to one or another in their "preferences."

The old consensus refers to the approach that prevailed throughout most of Latin America from the crisis of the 1930s up to the early 1970s. This consensus assigned a leading role to state intervention in labor issues. As the Director General of the International Labor Organization (ILO) pointed out in his Annual Report to the 1992 American Regional Conference, to talk of labor policy during this period was to refer to "the preeminence of the state as regulator and guarantor of the goals of employment, wages, and work conditions; this without paying much attention to the market, and, in most cases, with only token participation by social partners" (Hansenne 1992).

The neoconservative view, on the other hand, asserts that the state should intervene as little as possible so as to not interfere with the workings of the market. In this view social organizations such as unions are impediments to the development of "well-behaved" labor markets; unions are monopolies that press for higher wages for their affiliates at the expense of less job creation. On a national level, social concertation is generally catalogued as the participation of corporatist interests that tend to distort the policy agenda. Thus, social organizations are seen as a threat to development. A weaker state and a weaker society foster a stronger economy.

The growth-with-equity view reserves a more important role for government intervention in the labor market than the neoconservative view, but a less predominant role for the state compared to the old consensus. Probably the main difference between this view and the other two lies in the desired role for social organizations, which are seen as an opportunity for rather than as a threat to development. At the company level, productivity is viewed as being strongly influenced by the social climate prevailing in the firm. Creative and productive work and the firm's capacity to adapt to change may be enhanced by the role of unions which provide a "voice" to company workers (Freeman and Medoff 1984). On the national level, social agreements can contribute to consensus building. Stronger consensus reduces the variance of future policy shifts, diminishing the "country risk" and thereby favoring investment. Basic consensus also promotes social peace which feeds back into the development process through higher productivity growth. A stronger society may foster the construction of a stronger economy and a stronger state.[9]

A further debate centers around the issue of whether to protect versus what and how to protect. The neoconservative view, in its more radical form, questions the need to protect workers through either public policies or collective agreements. The market determines wages and working conditions that reflect the productivity of labor. Why interfere with those results? Exceptions are sometimes made for income transfers to the very poor.

In contrast, the old consensus and the growth-with-equity views share the perception that there is a need to protect workers (especially lower-income ones). They answer positively to the question of whether to protect but quarrel about what to protect and how to do it.

The two views maintain important differences about what should be protected. For example, the old consensus tends to favor the protection of job security and a more homogeneous wage structure across firms, while the growth-with-equity view favors the protection of job mobility and wages that reflect productivity.

How should protection be provided? The old consensus said: Leave it to the state. The growth-with-equity perspective says: Let the state determine the basic rules of the game, but let labor and business determine most of the conditions and norms that will define their relationship, through collective bargaining or even individual bargaining. Let social autonomy characterize the process of creating norms. Whereas the neoconservative view holds that most of the needed protection comes from the market and the old consensus asserted that it should be provided by the state, growth-with-equity proponents argue that social organizations play a crucial role in providing protection.

Employment Policies: Within and Beyond the Labor Market

Employment policies can take the form of labor policies, policies in other markets, or even policies that go beyond the economy.

New Rules for the Labor Market

The most important labor policies are related to the creation and enforcement of the rules of the game, both formal and informal. These rules create the incentives and constraints that affect the behavior of workers and business[10] in the labor market. The globalization process has significantly changed the effectiveness of the different rules of the game in the labor market.

Labor legislation
The fact that firms are competing in a highly variable world economy makes strong job security a questionable objective. There is growing recognition of the need to move from strong job security in the modern sector,[11] guaranteed by high severance payments, to protection for job mobility through some form of unemployment insurance.[12] In recent years Argentina, Brazil, and Chile have moved in this direction.

The fact that a country is highly integrated into the world economy implies that, to maintain full employment, wage increases must be tightly linked to the growth of productivity.[13] This has created a trend to decentralize collective bargaining, for in a very heterogeneous productive structure productivity can only be measured at the firm level. In recent years several countries, including Argentina, Brazil, and Chile, have moved or are moving toward greater decentralization.

A shift is also occurring away from the view that we only need homogeneous and general rules of the game, determined by law, and common to all firms in the economy or to those of a given industry. In the emerging view, the rules of the game should also be adapted to the reality of different industries and firms and be determined by direct bargaining between workers and business.

In all these changes, the debate on whether protection is necessary is being replaced by the recognition that, with globalization, the *what* and *how* to protect must be revisited.

Enforcement

Globalization has affected the degree and type of enforcement of labor legislation in several ways. The new fiscal discipline has limited the amount of resources devoted to enforcement, requiring a more effective use of resources. There is less emphasis in having a strong "labor police" who raid firms to impose fines. The emerging view emphasizes prevention through the creation of social norms and incentives to ensure compliance. This is undertaken through mass media campaigns, the active participation of business and labor and a more effective labor legislation.[14] Trade agreements like the North American Free Trade Agreement (NAFTA), which have established rules for strict enforcement of legislation for member countries, will affect this process.

The new view on these issues takes into account that when labor legislation has not been adapted to the new economic reality, its strict enforcement among the weakest firms of the modern sector may induce a shift of those productive activities into the informal part of the economy.

Social security reform

Several countries in the region have reformed the old pay-as-you-go social security systems—Chile (1981), Peru (1992), Argentina (1993), and Colombia (1993). In most of these countries the old system will coexist with the new ones in the future. The new systems are based on capitalization and managed by the private sector. The fact that the funds are privately managed opens up the possibility for social organizations to create their own pension funds. These reforms were induced in part as a means to reduce the deficits of the old social security system. Recall that globalization has favored a tighter fiscal discipline. The reforms are also aimed at reducing social security taxes, which distort labor market equilibria. Additionally, they are a means to increase savings and deepen capital markets. The show case was the Chilean social security reform which reduced social security taxes to 20% (including contributions for pensions and health care). Total savings in the new system have reached over 40% of GDP and by the end of the decade they will probably reach 80% of GDP.

The reform of the social security system could help create jobs mainly through three mechanisms. First, by reducing social security taxes it could foster an increase in employment and in take-home pay. Second, by increasing savings and investment it should raise the demand for labor by increasing the capital stock. Third, it should also increase the efficiency of capital, thanks to deeper capital markets which, in turn, expand the demand for labor (Cortázar 1995; Diamond and Valdés 1994).[15]

Training

Globalization has increased the rate of technological and economic change, thereby inducing a larger variation in the demand for labor in the different productive sectors and the different types of skills. The rate of change has created new information requirements on the specific skills and competences required. It is difficult for centralized government agencies to anticipate these changes, and the equipment required for training purposes must be upgraded more frequently. This is, obviously, very costly for the training institutes. Hence these changes have produced reforms in training policies that are gradually being applied on the basis of three principles:

- Decentralization: training should be offered by numerous institutions that compete for government funds. The type of training that firms require can only be determinated at a local level. Information cannot be generated at a centralized level;
- Privatization: the private sector should participate actively in the supply of training courses (there is no reason why training should be supplied solely by public institutions). When we refer to the private sector we do not only refer to traditional private firms. Social organizations, and specifically unions, have a potential role to play in providing training;
- Closer link with the productive structure: the definition of the specific competences and skills that are required must be done through rules that link training programs to the needs of firms. One way this is being done in several Latin American countries is by developing dual systems in which workers get their practical training as trainees in firms. Before resources are allocated to training institutions, the institutions must prove that firms are willing to receive their students as trainees. The assumption is that firms generally do not accept trainees in areas in which they have no intention of hiring in the future. This is then a practical manner of linking the expected demand for labor with the content and design of courses.[16] It also allows the use of the equipment of the firms for training purposes, saving significant resources for training institutes.

Wage policies
As we have argued above, one of the most important corollaries of the globalization process for the workings of the labor market is the need for wage changes to be strictly linked to the evolution of labor productivity.[17] Only then will it be possible to guarantee the process of job creation. The fact that wages may grow at the same rate as productivity is good news for workers in several Latin American countries that have already implemented basic economic reforms and show high rates of productivity growth.[18]

This corollary is important for discussing wage policies, the adjustment of minimum wages, and salaries paid to public sector workers. The debate on the adjustment of minimum wages normally considers two aspects: the real adjustment that is pursued and the amount of adjustment needed to maintain the purchasing power of wages owing to inflation.

In a context of strong deceleration of inflation, as is the case throughout most of Latin America (Table 4.4), the second part of the discussion is normally more crucial than the first. It is essential to build an understanding among social and political actors regarding the fact that, to maintain the purchasing power of wages, they must grow according to expected inflation during the period in which the new nominal wage is to be effective and not only the past inflation registered since the last adjustment took place. We are referring here to the need to build informal rules that are as important for the workings of the labor market as formal rules expressed, for example, by labor legislation.

Regarding wage adjustments for public sector workers, besides the importance of considering expected inflation, wage determination mechanisms that are consistent with the need to modernize the state must be established. The quality of the policies and services provided by the state are essential for the productivity that is required at this stage. As previously mentioned, in the world economy, countries—not only firms—compete with their infrastructure, tax systems, judiciary system, labor legislation, and the rest of the formal and informal rules that condition the behavior of the different actors.

To have an effective state, public sector wages should not lag significantly behind those paid by the private sector. Moreover, remunerations should be used to reflect productivity and to enhance it. Very little has been done in this area; a highly traditional system of labor relations exists in the public sector. Wage determination is normally an inorganic process, triggered by pressures exerted by public sector workers. Conflicts are centralized and normally highly political, which leaves little room to discuss productivity and its links to the wage structure.

Government intervention in social conflicts
The fact that wages must reflect productivity is an argument for decentralization and for bipartism in collective bargaining and labor relations within firms.[19] On the other hand, for a bipartite system to work, there must be a strong policy rule precluding all government intervention in collective bargaining.[20] Labor and business know that if they sit at a table with a government authority they will be hard-pressed to reach an intermediate solution. The government official, who knows little about the specific situation of the firm but wants to solve the problem, will try to moderate the position of both parties so as to reach an agreement. In such a situation both parties have an incentive to exaggerate their positions before they are called upon by the authorities, so they can reach a reasonable result when they are asked by the government official to moderate their demands. By contrast, a policy of nonintervention in collective

bargaining induces both parties to moderate their positions. Because no one is going to come to the rescue, labor and business are encouraged to try to overcome their differences from the very first day.

The fact that collective bargaining in this globalized economy should primarily be a bipartite affair does not imply a passive role for the government in labor policy. Government interventions may remain significant at the policy level: social concertation, reforms and enforcement of labor legislation, social security, and training.

The new "mix"
In the policies described above we observe the emergence of a new mix of roles played by the market, the state, and social organizations (or civil society). The state is responsible, at least in part, for social security, training, and creating and enforcing labor legislation. In many cases, however, these "goods" are provided by the private sector or by social organizations. That is certainly the case with the reformed social security and training systems. Thus, a trend is emerging to change the mix that characterized the old consensus by placing more emphasis on the market and civil society. Within this general trend, the new mix will take different forms, with larger proportions of market forces, state, or civil society, depending on the relative prevalence of neoconservative or growth-with-equity views.

Beyond the Labor Market

As previously established, there is widespread agreement that job creation is closely linked to the general workings of the economy and not only to the behavior of labor markets. In this respect, maintaining basic macroeconomic equilibria is probably the most effective employment policy. When inflation, fiscal deficits, or current account deficits get out of hand, big swings in output and employment take place.

On the other hand, employment is crucially affected by the growth of productive capacity, induced by investment. Like job creation, investment is affected not only by events that take place in the labor market but also by events in the rest of the economy and society. Rather than solely analyzing the relationship between job creation and employment policies, it is more useful to study the relationship between job creation and different economic and social policies. Employment should be a goal of all economic and social policies, rather than a goal toward which a set of very specific labor policies are geared.

One of the impacts of globalization on these other markets has been the reduction of the tolerance for "errors" in economic policy. In a closed economy a departure from a sound economic policy only gradually affected investment, growth, and stability. But in a highly integrated world economy an increase in "country risk" can induce instantaneous capital flights which may affect the path of growth and stability in a matter of weeks.

Beyond the Economy

Job creation is affected by productivity growth which, in turn, is conditioned by variables that go beyond the workings of the economy. Let us highlight two of them: the reform of the educational system and investment in "social capital."

The reform of the educational system
One of the greatest contrasts that arises when one compares the success stories of Latin America with those of East Asia is the difference in the rate of investment in education and particularly in basic education.[21] Undoubtedly the quality of the educational system is one of the clues to productivity growth today. The difference between the educational systems of both regions is probably related to the fact that income distribution is much more equitable in East Asia. Today most Latin American countries are attempting gradual reforms to their educational systems.

Investing in social capital
Finally, a topic less mentioned in the literature and in political debates is the connection between job creation and investment in social capital. We define social capital as including three aspects: the degree of trust in society, both at the firm and at the sectorial and national level; the prevailing social norms; and the relations and networks that exist among different social and political actors (Putnam 1993). Voluntary cooperation is easier in a community that has a substantial stock of social capital.

We have argued that job creation in a globalized economy is closely linked to productivity growth. Productivity growth, in turn, is influenced by the quality of labor relations and the rate of investment. Both of them are positively affected by investment in social capital. Cooperation between labor and business at the firm and at the national level is certainly a source of creativity and a way to enhance the capacity of firms to adapt to change and is therefore a cause for productivity growth.

These same factors positively affect the investment rate, through their impact on the rate of return but mainly through their impact on the country risk. Country risk diminishes when the variance of policy shifts is reduced. For that to occur in an open polity, basic social and political consensuses are needed. Strong social capital—a high degree of cooperation and trust, strong shared social norms, and strong networks among social and political actors—helps produce the basic social and political consensuses and is a source of higher growth in investment and employment. These basic consensuses also permit more social peace and, hence, higher productivity levels and development.

NOTES

Basic research for this paper was part of a research program of the Corporación de Investigaciones Económicas para Latinoamérica (CIEPLAN), supported by the Ford Foundation. Comments by Albert Berry, Rolando Cordera, and Azizur Rahman Kahn are gratefully acknowledged. The usual caveats apply.

1. The term "globalization" will be used to signify the integration of most Latin American countries into the global economy.

2. The stock of capital, in turn, is the result of the investment process in a highly integrated capital market. A small increase in the "country risk" of an economy can have a big impact on investment and employment creation.

3. Since productivity is crucially determined by the creativity of work and the capacity of firms to adapt to change, it is affected by the education and training of the labor force, the quality of labor relations and, more generally, by the degree of cooperation within a given firm.

4. The demand for labor coincides with the marginal productivity of the labor curve. According to the "efficiency wage" hypothesis, the cost of labor, and specifically wages, also influences productivity. So the relation between productivity and wages works both ways.

5. A closed economy enhances the possibility of price controls.

6. That is partly the reason why open unemployment rates are so low in many of these countries. Because of the lack of adequate unemployment insurance, together with the possibility of finding a job in the informal sector, the excess supply of labor in the modern sector translates more into an increase in underemployment than an increase of open unemployment.

7. In a more closed economy oriented toward import substitution, employment is more dependent on aggregate demand. Fiscal, monetary and wage policies are mechanisms through which the government can affect aggregate spending and employment. In an open economy there is much less that the government can do to affect employment levels in the short run.

8. This latter view has different names in different countries. In some of them it is called a "sustainable human development" approach.

9. To put forth the potential contributions that social organizations can make to strengthen the economy and/or the state does not mean that the potential negative effects of unions, when they act as a monopoly or when they accumulate too much power and end up distorting the agenda, should be overlooked. Such negative effects, however, are not the necessary outcome of social participation.

10. Many people, among them Douglas North (1990), have argued about the importance of institutions, the rules of the game, not only for the results in the labor market

but also for the development process. The difference between those countries that have "made it" in the development process and those that have not apparently lies, in great measure, in their rules of the game, both formal and informal, which create the structure of incentives that conditions the actions of people and organizations.

11. In the informal sector, severance payments and job security are normally lacking.

12. This does not imply that severance payments should disappear but that they should lose importance in favor of better protection for the unemployed and for job mobility.

13. Although wages are not the only factor that affects competitiveness (infrastructure, institutions and, more generally, the effectiveness of the state and society also matter), globalization undoubtedly creates a new and tighter link between wages and productivity levels.

14. Sanctions, and specifically fines, continue to play a role but are not viewed as the only instrument to attain enforcement of labor legislation.

15. Some of the weak points of the new social security systems are their high administrative costs and the possible concentration of wealth that may arise. Other positive aspects besides the impact on job creation relate to the political economy of the new system: the new pension system makes it more difficult to tax the pension fund; regressive redistributions are more unlikely; it adapts to demographic and economic changes automatically through market forces and not through traumatic episodes in the political process; and it assigns a more crucial role to the private sector and civil society (Cortázar 1995).

16. Since firms, in general, try not to hire trainees from low-quality institutions, they also provide valuable information in this respect for training programs.

17. At least in the case of the traded goods sector.

18. Productivity grows at over 3% to 4% a year in several countries in Latin America.

19. How could the government know about productivity levels in each firm?

20. We refer to collective bargaining in the private sector and not in the public sector where the government is the employer.

21. The success stories in both regions are characterized by macroeconomic equilibria and a high degree of integration in the world economy.

REFERENCES

Cortázar, R. 1995. The New Chilean Pension System: Lessons after 15 Years. Paper presented at the United Nations Seminar on Social Security Policy, April, Lisbon.

Diamond, P., and S. Valdés. 1994. Social Security Reforms. In *The Chilean Economy*, edited by B. Bosworth, R. Dornbush, and R. Labán. Washington D.C.: The Brookings Institution.

Freeman, R., and J. Medoff. 1984. *What Do Unions Do?* New York: Basic Books.
Hansenne, M. 1992. Memoria del Director General. Speech delivered by the Director General at the Thirteenth Conference of the American Member States, ILO (International Labor Organization), Caracas.
Márquez, G. 1994. The 'Employment Problem' in Latin America. In *Social Tensions, Job Creation and Economic Policy in Latin America*, edited by D. Turnham, C. Foy, and G. Larraín. Paris: OECD.
North, D. 1990. *Institutions, Institutional Change and Economic Performance.* New York: Cambridge University Press.
Putnam, R. 1993. *Making Democracy Work*. Princeton: Princeton University Press.
World Economic Forum and IMD (International Institute for Management Development). 1995. *The World Competitiveness Report*. Switzerland: IMD.

5 | Restructuring, Education, and Training

MARÍA ANTONIA GALLART

The process of restructuring production includes a series of changes. In the labor market these include a different distribution of the work force among economic sectors, variations in its stratification, and new qualifications and working conditions; among enterprises, firms must adapt and compete in a new environment, which requires them to modify their structure and processes. The state changes its role toward both enterprises and individuals; thus, new demands appear for social services such as education and training. The education and training systems of Latin America, which have a long history and have developed particular institutions in response to past demands, today must rethink their organization and activities in order to face the new challenges.

The specific characteristics of the restructuring process that are of interest for education and training policies are presented in this paper. Their consequences for the qualifications and employability of workers will be explored. Comments on the present status and existing trends of education and training will precede some reflections on possible policy alternatives for answering the challenges for education and training arising from the need to increase productivity and competitiveness and, at the same time, enhance equity. Particular attention will be given to at-risk groups, especially those in poverty sectors. The roles of employers, workers, and institutions in the implementation of those policies will be examined.

Changes in the Labor Market

During the last decades a production restructuring process has taken place in Latin America as part of a global trend but taking particular characteristics in the region. This trend has three main components: public sector adjustment, including reforms in the public services and the privatization of public enterprises; liberalization and deregulation, which produce changes in the rules of competition and survival of firms; and technological change and organizational restructuring. Although the relative importance and timing for each of these components varies from country to country, they are all present in each.

The early expansion of the urban labor market took place during the import substitution process. Even though the magnitude of the industrial sector within this expansion was different in each country, in the most advanced countries an important part of the labor force worked in factories and a large service sector developed in cities throughout the region. Beginning in the 1970s, urban jobs began to dominate the labor market.

The public sector and the informal sector were the most dynamic sectors in terms of employment. In terms of particular kinds of jobs, this situation meant a strong demand for blue-collar skilled workers, white-collar employees in routine jobs, and a sizable group of college professionals. But the formal sector could not absorb the surplus of labor created by demographic growth and rural-urban migration. Thus, a large informal sector of microenterprises and self-employed workers grew steadily, with low productivity and scarce capital, incorporating unskilled workers, and attracting artisans and small entrepreneurs. This very heterogeneous sector was composed of workers in low-productivity jobs on subsistence income levels, as well as skilled self-employed workers and entrepreneurs who discovered niches of production and services to clienteles in the formal sector. In such a world, the demands for qualifications were clear: literacy and skilled training for the formal industrial sector, middle-level and higher education for skilled labor in the services sector, and basic literacy and specific skills for the informal sector—in the latter case, accompanying an income generation strategy. There was an implicit hope that the expansion of the urban labor market could absorb the supply of labor. The role of training was to accompany this process by helping to place workers in the labor market and enhancing their chances of increasing earnings.

The "lost decade" of the 1980s changed the whole picture. The debt crisis, structural adjustment, high inflation in some countries and stagnation in most of them undermined that hope. The structural adjustment stopped growth and diminished employment in the public sector. Furthermore, several countries privatized public services, which employ fewer people. Liberalization, including deregulation of markets, and increased competition among firms in a global marketplace accelerated the process of restructuring the productive sector. (See Table 5.1, end of chapter.)

The production restructuring process created a different organization of the firm and a different relationship among firms. The Fordist style of organization, based on the chain production of a series of identical products, best exemplified by the automobile factories, was work intensive and took place in large plants with a standardized production process. The work was specialized and the occupational structure hierarchical. In the new Japanese factory model, flexible production is stressed and a horizontal mode of organization, based on productive cells, is responsible for standards of production and quality. In this model workers need to possess multiple competences. Thus, networking of firms of different sizes ensures competitiveness, and the variation of products responds to a differentiated demand from the global market. These changes affect the structure of the labor force, the hierarchy and nature of qualifications, and the management of human resources, both at the firm level and within countries (Carrillo 1994; Gitahy 1994).

Some observations on these transformations which must be taken into account include technological change, particularly the introduction of microelectronic automated technologies and enhanced communications, and fierce competition for markets which initiate the restructuring process. But the diffusion of the new production model depends on the conditions of the political and economic environment and the strategy of firms. Generally speaking, there is a unique restructuring process of production in each country, where firms in different stages of the modernization process coexist. Moreover there are differences among economic sectors, some of them sticking to the old organization, others tending to disappear, destroyed by foreign competition. Generalizing across a region with such varied forms of production is a difficult task, but some discernible common trends do emerge. Several islands of modernity surface, signaling changes in the industrial fabric. Large firms begin to subcontract many tasks to smaller ones and tend to acquire international standards of quality (Gitahy 1994; Rachid 1995).

The consequences of these changes for the labor force and its qualifications are three-fold:

Changes in the structure of the labor force
Because the diffusion of capital intensive technologies implied by the new model limits the capacity of labor absorption by the secondary sector, subcontracting transfers many activities (such as security, transportation, personnel selection, and maintenance) to firms in the tertiary sector. The composition of the labor force changes with relatively fewer industrial workers. Better communications and new technologies permit the growth of small productive units

situated in locations distant from the larger urban concentrations, thus diminishing the concentration of workers in factories with negative consequences for the labor unions. Flexibility appears as a necessary condition for restructuring, which means frequent contracting and dismissal of workers and also frequent changes of tasks within the factory. Thus, individual firms can increase and diversify their production while employing fewer workers.

The hierarchy and nature of qualifications
Taylorism[1] permitted clearly classified qualifications associated with specific jobs to which corresponding salaries could be assigned by means of collective bargaining between firms and unions. Although this was not the operative system for the majority of the labor force in many countries, it was clearly a reference model to which social reform was directed. Labor regulations, training institutions, and social policies took this hierarchical organization for granted, in which the underlying concept was of a working career, as an unskilled or skilled worker or a supervisor, within a permanent occupation in one or few firms. This trajectory changed, however, and the need for broader competences increased the demand for more educated workers, capable of performing a variety of tasks, setting working standards, and upgrading their skills in response to technological changes. Because these workers are expected to change firms and jobs many times during their active life, qualifications are less structured, less hierarchical, and less specialized. The subject of qualification is no longer the job but the worker.

The management of human resources is crucial in the new model
It is no longer sufficient to select able workers; further training, participatory management, and the workers' compliance and motivation are needed to increase productivity (Leite 1994; Mercado 1994).

These characteristics of the modern production model may be valid as a paradigm since real firms, in fact, have mixed characteristics of the old and the new models. Nevertheless this paradigm influences the whole organization of work. Therefore, two kinds of questions emerge: First, what happens with the rest of the labor force? What kind of work will be available for the youth entering the world of work? The other question concerns the restructuring process with regards to exclusion and unemployment.

The need for firms—and countries—to increase productivity to compete with each other, in the context of technological and organizational changes, constitutes a demand for a relatively small number of workers (in terms of the total labor force) with higher educational standards than those of earlier skilled workers. The new requirements for workers with multiple competences are not fulfilled by short training courses but by years of formal education (Castro 1988). Hence, there is a large supply of workers, either unskilled or trained in traditional routine trades, and a restricted demand for highly skilled workers with a different kind of training. Firms choose the best workers, give them specific training, and leave the rest of the labor supply to compete in a tough market. Unskilled workers and people with low educational levels are perennial losers in this labor market and are overrepresented at the poverty levels.

The heterogeneity of the informal sector poses a special challenge for education and training. Small enterprises, artisans, and self-employed skilled workers have complex interlinkages with the integrated sector. In some countries they join forces in cooperative actions to gain access to foreign markets. Management skills are crucial in this context. Traditional ways of providing training programs for poverty sectors are questionable since trade training and apprenticeship without basic literacy and mathematical skills, and income earning programs without managerial and marketing skills do not help in such a market.

Qualifications and Competences

Qualifications can be defined in three ways: a) as an individual characteristic, i.e., the human capital skills and knowledge applied to work that a person possesses; b) as the abilities needed to adequately perform a particular job, depending on the complexity and skills required for that particular position; and c) as the characteristics of the tasks to be accomplished by a particular occupational level in an organizational structure. The third definition is a hierarchical one, often subject to collective bargaining (Carrillo 1994). The last two definitions were predominant for a long time in both organizational theory and training.

Nowadays, qualifications tend to be defined by entrepreneurs' policies for selecting, training, and promoting personnel. This is dealt with through internal labor markets and labor markets in general. In a flexible labor market, where firms with updated technology and organization compete, the first definition of qualifications tends to prevail; continuous learning and retraining are necessary and easier if workers have a stock of human capital to begin with. In terms of equity, this poses serious problems; it hinders salary agreements because one of the requirements of the new qualifications is the ability to fulfill different occupational roles. Consequently salary is based on capacities, not occupations, requiring that work conditions and salaries be negotiated more flexibly. Because access to professional careers within firms depends on knowledge and skills acquired through education and training or through previous experience, access is restricted to the elite sector of the work force, excluding the uneducated.

The problem then is not merely one of making specific training for particular occupations available to persons from all walks of life. There is a prior consideration—employability i.e., are these persons fit to be hired for work? The answer to this question is formulated in terms of competences.

An irreversible change has occurred from the old qualifications based on the mastery of manual and operational skills and a variable degree of autonomy from supervision in performing tasks towards new competences. This implies a higher degree of intellectual comprehension, the ability to deal with uncertainty and make decisions, and an aptitude for team work. Education and training involve the twofold challenge of updating the qualifications of traditionally trained workers and providing education and training for new workers. To be employable requires basic skills: written and oral communication; applied mathematics for problem solving; and cognitive abilities to abstract general characteristics from problems, make decisions, and learn from experience. Such competences require systematic and gradual learning.

Some authors add other competences to the fundamental ones previously presented: a) competences related to the use of resources (staff, money, time, materials, and equipment) in order to attain objectives; b) interpersonal competences (ability for teamwork, to teach and learn, lead, negotiate, serve customers, manage cultural diversity); c) information competences (ability to identify, acquire, and evaluate information and communicate it to others); d) systemic competences (ability to approach reality in its complexity of relations and not as isolated facts); and e) technological competences (knowledge and use of current technologies) (U.S. Department of Labor 1991).

Training builds on this base of competences, which are largely acquired through formal schooling and experience. Yet training should additionally be focused on specific families of occupations in the world of work, integrating the competences with practical skills necessary to perform occupational tasks, with the use of equipment and technology, and with the organizational learning of firms and markets as they adapt to new circumstances.

One possible objection to this approach is that only a minority of persons will get jobs in the modern, integrated sector. Therefore one must think of the particular qualifications needed in the informal sector, where most of the workers from poor backgrounds will find work. Research results suggest that several competences (basic skills, resource management, and interpersonal skills) are useful to progress in microenterprises and trades. Specific technical training and small scale marketing are also helpful (Gallart, Moreno, and Cerrutti 1991).

The State of Education

It is useful to compare the challenges of the labor market and the actual state of education and training in the region in order to evaluate the lifelong chances of employability for a majority of the population who lack competences.

Educational enrollment has had a steady growth in Latin America. Basic education coverage is close to universal, and secondary education reaches more than half the age group in most countries. Nevertheless, striking differences exist among countries. Generally speaking, growth in enrollment has coexisted with serious problems within Latin American educational systems, namely repeated grades and drop-out rates. The differences between gross and net enrollment rates point to many students older than the normal age for the particular grade they are studying. Census data show a constant loss of students, particularly in secondary education where about half the students beginning the level do not finish it.

A number of factors are at play in these problems. In some countries child labor is common and disturbs schooling. Great differences in enrollment rates also exist between rural and urban populations. In terms of equity of results, there are striking differences in achievement between urban and rural schools, elite and marginal schools, and among students of different family backgrounds. Educational decentralization policies were implemented in most countries, with somewhat contradictory results. While policies permitted local control of schools, they perpetuated large differences in resources and technical assistance between rich and poor districts. Two trends appear clearly in the change of the educational systems, resulting in decentralization and modifications in the relationship between technical-vocational and academic education.

The first trend is a tendency to avoid early choice of different tracks in particular vocational fields which are isolated from general academic education and taught in different premises. This tends to lengthen compulsory basic education to nine or ten years and delay the choice of specialization until the end of this cycle.

The second regards the need to improve basic skills. Educational quality tests point to a deficit in achievement. Basic education does not guarantee proficiency in basic skills, and a plurality of students at the secondary level have serious problems in comprehensive reading and applied math. (ECLAC-UNESCO 1992). Studies of secondary education in several countries of the region show a very heterogeneous system, containing elite schools that reach international standards of excellency and others that do not attain the minimum standards of competency. A clear stratification of quality, however, between academic and technical vocational schools, usually found in other regions, is not evident here. In some Latin American countries technical schools have high levels of achievement, particularly in mathematics. The segmentation of the educational system is related to the socioeconomic background of students and to decentralization effects rather than to type of education—general/academic or technical.

This assessment of the quality of education in Latin America indicates that a large share of the population, and particularly youth in poverty sectors, lacks the competences needed to be employable. Young people are more educated than their parents, having spent more years at school, but their credentials do not ensure the mastery of basic intellectual skills.

Strong educational organizations focused on education for work have developed in Latin America. These are technical vocational schools, which have a larger share of secondary enrollment than similar schools in other regions (Middleton et al. 1993). The National Training Agencies (NTAs) are another kind of educational institution in the gray area between formal and nonformal education.

The original curriculum of technical schools was a mixture of technological knowledge and technical skills directed toward diverse occupations and industrial sectors. Later on, trade schools (originally vocational schools for skilled occupations) gradually incorporated more theoretical content, the final result being a hybrid of technological and vocational education. The first organizations specializing in out-of-school training for work were established in the 1940s. The NTA model, born in Brazil (SENAI and SENAC), was transferred to most Latin American countries.

Originally the Latin American pattern of education for work was planned both as a formal technical education to train mid-level technicians and as training courses (*formación profesional*) to prepare skilled workers with only basic education (complete and incomplete primary education). Then parallel systems of vocational training developed, targeted to groups of different social origins. Secondary technical education was aimed at students from the lower strata of the middle class and manual workers' children, who were attaining postprimary education. Training agencies, on the other hand, directed vocational training at workers (many of them from rural backgrounds) entering the new urban jobs.

This model developed and grew during the 1960s and 1970s, but the expected demand by the industrial sector for skilled and technical workers stagnated after the initial growth of the industrial labor force in each country. Training targeted towards skilled occupations in the import substitution industry needed to be updated when these occupations changed and diminished owing to the restructuring process. The increase in the urban population and, consequently, the extended access to schooling, permitted a selection of better schooled candidates for vocational training. Training institutions thus raised their entry qualifications and tended to increase the length of courses. In many cases the programs became formalized with school-like centers and theoretical-practical syllabi similar to those of technical schools, and they trained middle-level technicians (Gallart 1993). These national educational institutions (the Technical Education and the National Training Agencies) were publicly funded (mostly by taxes on workers' earnings) and became very important in size and political power. They were the core of the education and training social policies.

In the 1980s a strong current of studies questioned this model (Psacharoupoulos and Loxley 1985). Researchers found technical education to be expensive and technologically outdated; they concluded that early specialization was unproductive; and they questioned the applicability of the special fields taught to occupational demand. The vocational training agencies had stronger links with firms and thus incorporated patterns of change adjusting to demand (Cinterfor 1990). At the same time, these large bureaucratic organizations (NTAs) tended to perpetuate old training modes due to organizational inertia and resistance to change.

The criticisms of this model can be summarized in several broad points: a) It is virtually impossible for large bureaucratic organizations to follow the pace of technological and occupational change. Therefore the contents of curricula and training tend to be defined from the point of view of institutions and are detached from the changing world of work. b) Paying for training with tax money removes the incentive to adapt to changing demand. In a period of adjustment of public budgets scarce resources are wasted. c) The target populations of education and training programs have changed. Technical students come from the middle class and expect to continue in higher education. Thus, vocational and technical education programs select their trainees from relatively privileged populations and do not reach the unemployed in the poorest sectors. d) Last but not least, the change in qualifications stresses the need for general education as a foundation for training. This is not present in the early specialization curricula of many vocational education and training programs. (See Table 5.4).

The response to these criticisms posits an alternative model that stresses a transformation from supply-driven vocational education and training to demand-driven training programs. These programs must answer demands from the productive sector with flexibility. No public funding for specific programs should be allocated if no jobs are available for the skills taught. Implementation should be left to small training organizations, often from the private sector, which must be linked to the labor market in order to survive.

In this alternative model, formal secondary education changes from a diversified academic and technical vocational education to a foundational formal education that prepares students for a field of work or advanced studies. This foundational stage is relatively narrower than the general stage of education that precedes it but not as specific as specialized training for particular occupations (OECD 1989).

Public funds are transferred from programs for undefined customers to financing programs targeted to specific users (students and firms). Students would be selected from groups that are in need of training to compete in the labor market: youth from underprivileged backgrounds, persons who have been unemployed for a long time, workers displaced by technological change, and unskilled women looking for work. The programs should be tailored to the needs of these groups, assessing their portfolio of competences and training them in the skills they lack. Selected firms are those in sectors that have possibilities to expand in the new markets but do not have the knowhow to train their human resources. In this case funding should be shared by the firm.

Training programs following this model were recently implemented in several countries of the region with support from the Inter-American Development Bank (IDB) and The World Bank. Chile initiated the process, followed by Argentina, Mexico, and Colombia. The programs, targeted toward populations at risk, include various components aimed at integrating the unemployed into the labor market. These include short courses with practice in enterprises, retraining for displaced workers, basic skills training for rural migrants, and employment agencies to facilitate links between demand and supply. The target groups are youth from poverty sectors, displaced workers, self-employed workers in the informal sector, etc.

The relationship between these programs and the traditional organization of training varies among countries. In some cases they are managed by the Ministry of Labor, independent from the NTAs; in others, they have become part of NTA programs. Furthermore, NTAs are undergoing a restructuring process, combining decentralization by sector and region, and increasing links with firms.

The traditional model of technical education taught in different schools and with an organization parallel to academic education is also in question and undergoing changes in a plurality of countries. In this case the organizational trends are not yet clear, but the central point is to promote general education with technological contents targeted at the mastery of competences, avoiding an early segmentation (ECLAC-UNESCO 1992; De Ibarrola and Gallart 1994).

Competitiveness and Equity: A Dilemma for Education and Training Policies?

The Bottlenecks of the Labor Market

Bottlenecks in the labor market are frequent in developing countries during periods of economic growth. This is owing to an excess supply of unskilled workers and an unsatisfied increased demand for workers with adequate skills for modern production. Because education and training are long-term processes, they cannot be tied to the short-term stop-go upturns and downturns of the economy. Most of the newly industrialized countries, as exemplified by those in South East Asia, have had active training policies and have benefited from a labor force with a large supply of skilled workers (Castro 1995). It is important to have as large a group as possible of workers with basic competences and flexible skills who can be trained in specific abilities in a relatively short time span. This diminishes the costs of adjustment to the changing demand of global markets, facilitates specific training in firms, and reduces the social costs by lowering hard-core unemployment. Also, if training is strictly tied to the present state of demand, there is a danger that it will not fulfill its role of fostering transference of technology, which has been crucial in the past (Castro 1995).

The Vicious Circle of Poverty, Education, Training, and Employment

An analysis of life histories reveals the trajectories that combine formal education, training, and learning on the job. There is no predetermined, or best way to reach and adequately perform a particular skilled occupation. Each life history embodies a different mix of basic and general education, usually acquired in formal education and learning on the job and often complemented by vocational training. These trajectories are influenced by socioeconomic background (migrants from poor regions or persons born in poor neighborhoods attend marginal schools, leave formal education early, enter unskilled jobs often in the informal sector, and have fewer opportunities to participate in technical vocational training) and family survival strategies (poor children leave school at an early age to enter the work force or help in family small business). These tend to be family conditions and decisions rather than individual options. Another factor is school quality, which is often segmented by location; schools in poor neighborhoods have fewer options and less equipment than those in middle-class neighborhoods. Finally, social connections are very important for youths seeking their first job; when family and friends lack connections in the formal economic sector, it is very difficult to have access to good jobs.

The competences needed in the a modern labor market are very difficult to acquire in the context we have just described. Employability requires basic skills of expression and practical math and social competences, for access to skilled training (on the job or in specific vocational programs) depends on the capacity to fulfill the requirements of training programs and/or social capital (connections to get a job). Workers in slums, particularly the young, lack both (Gallart et al. 1992; Jacinto 1995; Jacinto and Suárez 1994).

If social policies ignore these conditions and fail to include other basic provisions (for example, adequate nutrition and healthcare), the effects of specific narrow training programs will be limited. Focusing on specific populations, training programs must be designed (in terms of duration, contents, methodology) to achieve a balance between the competences acquired and the handicaps to be overcome. The training delivery should take into account the actual life conditions of the target populations—their attention span (modular methodology), motivation, and ability to reach the training locations, etc. The professional skills attained through training programs must include learning skills not acquired during schooling, work experience and discipline, and social connections. The objective is not merely to place workers in short-term jobs but to give them the abilities to develop skills and be retrained in a changing labor market.

Education and Training Policies for Productivity and Equity

If equity and productivity standards are the aims of education and training policies, those objectives should be fixed at two levels: a) to improve the competitiveness of firms, particularly of labor-intensive small enterprises, and b) to achieve reasonable standards of equal opportunity in the labor market for the whole population. The consequence should be to diminish the present segmentation between an integrated sector of firms and workers and a large group of the population reduced to exclusion and poverty. (See Table 5.5)

As stated in the preceding sections of this chapter, workers obtain their competences and skills from schools in the formal educational system, generally financed by the state and managed by public or private institutions. Schooling provides the foundation for specific technical and vocational training obtained either in training courses or on-the-job learning. There is a continuum in this process, from generality to specificity. Organizational differences make schools adequate to teach broad competences and nonformal education more suited for apprenticeship of specific skills to be applied on the job. In the educational realm, schools and society are responsible for the process of forming citizens; in the labor arena, the locus of work is to be found in the productive organization. As changes and new needs develop in the economy, firms have an irreplaceable role in defining the specific characteristics of training. This does not mean that enterprises should take charge of all training. The rationality of a productive firm is cost efficiency; training individual workers takes time and diverts resources from production.

Unlike Germany, where the private productive sector assumes the task of training as a social duty and a majority of youth pass through the dual system of alternating theoretical learning in schools with practical work in the productive sector, Latin America does not have a tradition of apprenticeship. Apprenticeship programs account for a small share of training enrollment in most Latin American countries. Enterprises generally assume only the costs of the technological and organizational training pertaining specifically to them, which cannot be transferred to other firms. Firms ask either the state or the worker to pay for the more general technical training which becomes part of the worker's skills and can be sold by the worker to a competing firm (Becker 1964). Therefore, private firms will not on their own create the pool of skilled workers with competences and flexible training needed to avoid bottlenecks. For this, there is extensive experience of collaborative training between the state and the private sector (CINTERFOR 1990).

On-the-job learning is a key way to acquire skills. If persons have no access to jobs, they cannot maintain or upgrade their skills. Therefore a training policy must take into account the access to real occupations for the trainees.

To reach the objectives of equity and productivity, formal education and training should be articulated and reach the target firms and individuals presented here. Large firms in the integrated sector have the political weight and critical size to demand and organize the training they need. Small firms that have difficulties defining their needs will benefit from policies that promote cooperation among such firms, as well as links with schools and training institutions, in order to implement adequate training.

In terms of the workers, policies should attempt to break the vicious circle of education and training deficits that contribute to unemployment. In order to break this vicious circle, several programs have been implemented with support of the multilateral banks. Some aim at diminishing educational segmentation by improving elementary schools that serve the poorer sectors. Chile's primary school program is one example. Other programs offer small enterprises comprehensive support, including credit, management and marketing training, and evaluation of experiences.

Education and training policies must take into account the differences among countries on crucial aspects:

The supply of education and training
Countries like Chile, Uruguay, and Argentina, with a large coverage of formal education, need policies to improve the quality and relevance of training for the world of work. Other countries must increase the supply of education by teaching basic skills to all age groups. In countries with well-grounded national training institutions (for example, Colombia and Costa Rica), the challenge is to update these institutions to avoid supply-driven programs and to increase their links with the productive sector. In countries where training programs are implemented by a plurality of institutions (Argentina, Mexico, Chile) policies are needed to guide these institutions in defining objectives and targets, to avoid unnecessary duplication. Technical assistance and financing are the tools used by the state in these cases.

The dynamism of the modern sector and the size
of the population in poverty levels
This modifies the relative importance of different target groups for training. The groups of first priority should include persons at risk of exclusion: populations in poverty levels, workers displaced by restructuring production, young people seeking their first jobs, and unskilled women entering the labor market.

Another relevant target group is composed of workers with outdated skills in modernizing enterprises, who must acquire new skills for a new organization of work and state-of-the-art technologies.

The characteristics of the programs will vary for each target group:

Populations at poverty levels
Evidence suggests that these groups are helped by community-based programs, with support from training agencies and implemented by NGOs and community groups in broadly based programs, including other social services (for example, health). Training programs integrate training in basic skills and social competences with vocational training for occupations in attainable sectors (construction, commerce). It is important to link the trainees to the possible sources of jobs, social capital being one of the basic needs of these groups (Jacinto 1995; Leite 1995). The pressing need to generate earnings contributes to the high attrition seen in the training programs for poor youth. This need forces trainees to seek any job, leaving training programs when they find low paid, unskilled, unstable jobs. Therefore, several programs funded by the IDB include a small sum awarded to the trainees for living expenses.

Workers displaced by restructuring
These are active workers who must be retrained to adapt to new demands. It is important to begin by evaluating workers' competences and skills and then tailor the training programs to their needs. Great Britain and France provide interesting antecedents in this respect. Techniques for searching for niches in the labor market and managing skills for self-employment should complement training. Effective employment agencies are needed to place these workers and avoid unemployment for long periods of time.

Young persons seeking jobs
The needs for training young persons will vary depending on the educational level attained. Some kind of compensatory basic skills teaching programs must be considered for uneducated youth. When they have mastered basic skills, vocational training linked to real occupations should be combined with practical work experience in firms.

Women
Women have special needs because of their two-fold reproductive role in the family and productive role in the world of work; many are principal household providers. The preceding policy proposals are valid for women in poverty, either young or displaced, but additional gender-based elements must be added. For example, flexible schedules for work and training will facilitate

the double roles women must combine. Occupational training will help women avoid employment in domestic service, which offers no opportunity for advancement. A large share of the region's working women work in other families' homes.

Retraining of workers in modernizing industrial branches
This is the group that now receives most attention through many programs, jointly implemented by training agencies and firms, to upgrade workers' skills. The programs of the Serviço Nacional de Aprendizado Indústria (SENAI), an NTA managed by the Brazilian employers association, are a good example of this. The firms can allot part of their taxes to these programs and SENAI gives technical assistance in the planning and execution of training. Between 1980 and 1992 the number of firms in the São Paulo area that participated in these shared training programs increased from two to 338 (Leite 1994).

Throughout Latin America there are now numerous programs that focus on all or most of these target groups. Following are brief descriptions of some of the best known programs.

The Mexican Labor Markets Modernization Project (PMMT), implemented by the Employment Directorate in the Labor Department, consists of four strategies: promoting participation by social actors in the state employment services; improving information on labor markets and promoting alternative employment; increasing efficiency of the employment services; and training. Several programs comprise the training strategy: a) basic training for incorporation in production, focused on uneducated rural migrants, including basic literacy and mathematical skills and technical instruction; b) initial, basic technical training for first job seekers with no previous work experience; c) retraining and reconversion for displaced workers; and d) training for self-employment. The PMMT encourages programs contracted with firms in which part of the training takes place at the enterprise. The firms pay for inputs and instructors and the state pays subsistence money to the trainees. Firms also agree to hire some of the trainees.

Chile has implemented a comprehensive training program with four components. Training in firms (CEL), aimed at helping youths master semiskilled trades for salaried work, provides 200 hours of training for youths seeking to learn a trade or occupation needing basic qualifications. Youths take the course in training institutions and then practice for three months in an enterprise. The training institution must obtain the enterprise's consent in order to qualify for course funding. This program has trained approximately 70,000 youths. Alternating training (AA) combines schoolwork in an educational institution and work in a firm, within the framework of an apprenticeship contract with an experienced worker guiding the apprentice. This program lasts a maximum of 12 months and has trained 3,500 youths. A third component involves training for self-employment. It offers the management and technical training needed for working independently. Future plans include a complementary network of technical assistance and credit for self-employed workers and small entrepreneurs. The fourth component, formation and training (FCJ), targets disadvantaged youths. The FCJ curriculum stresses personal development, self-esteem, basic cognitive skills and social abilities, and vocational training for semiskilled jobs. The program requires 420 hours including labor practice, which can take place in a firm or a workshop.

The main characteristic of these programs is that they are funded by the state but resources are allocated competitively to training agencies that present their training design, ensure training quality, obtain commitment from firms to accept the trainees for practice, and ask for reasonable prices. The state also gives support for equipment, training of trainers, and technical assistance to the training agencies. This mechanism is expected to directly link the supply of training to the needs of firms (if there is no practical work there will be no courses). Administratively it is designed to avoid bureaucratization and to be cost effective.

Evaluations of the Chilean program—the first to be implemented—are positive, particularly in terms of job placement of the trainees. Nevertheless, two general areas of concern have been noted. One stresses the limitations of short-term courses in overcoming the handicaps of poor youth. The other concerns the need for further institutional support for tasks that cannot be accomplished by the individual subcontracting institutions, such as curriculum development, training of instructors, and development of teaching materials. Both criticisms are being taken into account, as reflected in changes being implemented in the present stage of the program.

In Brazil SENAI has implemented training for poverty sectors called community assistance programs, which take three different modes: programs for initial training of minors, targeted at teenagers (PIPM); community training programs for youth over sixteen (PCFP), which have two levels—initial training for those entering the labor force and general training; and industrial training (TI) for community groups and institutions. The objectives of these programs are to initiate and train youth and adults for work; to create conditions of personal fulfillment and social mobility; to retrain unemployed workers; to extend SENAI action to regions not previously served; and to meet the demand from firms. The target group is slum dwellers. Many are unemployed and ask for training to enter the labor market. Others earn a salary or generate products and services for their household. Most have no access to the usual training programs because of distance or lack of schooling or money.

In 1991 SENAI–São Paulo trained 65,000 people in these programs. SENAI-SP implements these programs through agreements with agencies such as municipalities, religious institutions, community organizations, and trade unions. SENAI provides technical assistance, trains instructors, transfers funds to pay trainers, buys inputs, and monitors the implementation of each program. The local agency provides the premises, equipment, program management, and practice. In 1993 agreements were reached with around 400 local institutions in 300 districts of the São Paulo state (Leite 1995). U.S.$ 4.6 million of the SENAI-SP budget was allocated to these programs, representing 4% of SENAI-SP expenses for that year.

Several aspects of the aforementioned programs in Mexico, Chile, and Brazil respond to the needs of the target populations and to a changing economic context: the programs include basic literacy and mathematical skills, management training for self-employed workers, linkages to real occupations and firms in the labor market, agreements with local institutions and/or firms, and interest in avoiding supply-driven training. Successful programs require the support of various social actors who are in positions to put training on the social agenda: Ministries of Labor, training agencies, local institutions, trade unions, and firms. Some of these firms, for example, play a primary role; others, such as trade unions and small-scale private and public agencies, are only involved in certain programs. Because the interlinkage among these actors is different in each of the three national examples discussed here, a comparative study of differences and results would be welcome.

The Problems of Training and the Difficult Task of Evaluation

This section briefly addresses some remaining problems related to training, particularly when it is targeted toward groups at risk of exclusion. First, what is the best way to coordinate state and private action? In all cases most of the funds for training come from the state, although the programs can be implemented by state agencies, by public or private institutions competing in the training market, by agreement between the state and private firms or training institutions, or by an NTA which is privately managed but publicly funded. It would be interesting to evaluate the positive and negative consequences of each of these arrangements.

The second problem is how to identify and motivate the target population to participate in training. However good a program may be, it will fail in its stated purpose if it does not attract the right clients. Some programs screen the applicants, looking for characteristics of the target population. Others prefer to advertise the program's conditions in such a way that permits self-selection by the trainees themselves. Locating programs in poor neighborhoods and actively involving local organizations helps attract clients from these areas.

A third problem is how to modernize labor-intensive small and micro-enterprises, thereby increasing their demand for skilled workers. Local networks of firms and mechanisms of collaboration and competition could help, but this is a relatively unexplored field.

A fourth problem is who must pay for training—the firms, the trainees, or the state. Firms are often reluctant to cover the entire cost of training that can be used by competitors, but they are willing to share costs in the case of scarce skills. Middle-class students attending short and inexpensive white-collar courses can pay for their training. But working-class and poor youth seeking skilled technical training, which needs costly equipment and trained instructors, will find good quality training out of their reach. For these reasons, state support is clearly necessary, but it must be administered in cost-efficient ways that reach the proposed target groups, and evaluation mechanisms must be put in place (Castro 1995).

This brings us to the problem of evaluation in a universe of training that is highly heterogeneous, ranging from home economics to mechatronics. Most funding agencies use tracer studies of graduates as a first approach. They ask several questions about the trainees and about what happened to them in the labor market: Did the trainees belong to the target group? Did the program fulfill the expected results? Was the trainee's performance in the labor market improved by participation in the program? The most sophisticated approaches use rate-of-return methodologies to ascertain whether the difference in earnings between the trainees and the control group justifies the costs of training. Some authors say that this presumes a perfect market for skills which is not the case in most countries. They also point to externalities, such as transference of technology and training of future trainers, which are not measured by the rate of return analysis (Castro 1995). It is obvious that cost-efficiency control and follow-up studies of trainees are necessary, but they do not sufficiently evaluate training.

A complete evaluation must take a thorough look at education and training, the motivation of teachers and trainees, their social background and its consequences, the process of training and the specific way in which the skills are transmitted, and the interlinkage between training firms and actual work. Evaluation must also include a closer look at the labor market. Why are some trainees hired while others are not? What are the real conditions required to be employable in a particular labor market? Are there differences in the hiring practices of small and large enterprises? Answers to these questions will likely deal with concepts like cultural and social capital, generally not taken into account by training programs. This calls for a qualitative approach to evaluation, to complement the usual quantitative approach. The results of quantitative evaluations must be interpreted from the point of view of the actors within the training process, of the different strategies of enterprises, and of the specific objectives and characteristics of each program, in order to improve the training programs in general, and particularly those for groups at risk.

Final Comments

The process of restructuring production and the growth of poverty challenge educational and training systems, demanding flexibility, quality, and the ability to respond to the often-times conflicting needs of firms and (actual and prospective) workers. Meeting these demands is no easy task in a system of schools and training agencies riddled with serious flaws.

The educational mainstream in Latin America has traditionally stayed at a distance from the world of work, leaving the task of preparing youth for the labor market to special vocational training institutions such as technical schools or training agencies which reach only a minority of young people. Nowadays, the changes in the labor market and in the technology and organization of firms require the integration of knowledge learned in schools with practical experience in the work world. The competences that result from applying knowledge to the concrete challenges of real life are a vital part of a nation's human resources. The state and civil society, schools and firms, formal education and experiential training must join forces to provide more equitable access to the labor market across the whole population and to contribute to increasing national competitiveness in a global economic environment.

Table 5.1 Urban Unemployment Rates,* Total Population and
15–24 Age Group, 1992

Country	Total Population	15–24 Age Group
Argentina (B.A. Metropolitan Area)	6.6	12.6
Bolivia	5.5	8.6
Chile	6.0	14.3
Colombia (8 main cities)	9.1	18.7
Costa Rica	4.2	9.0
Honduras	5.1	6.9
Mexico	4.3	9.9
Panama (1991)	18.6	35.1
Paraguay (Asunción)	5.0	9.7
Uruguay	8.4	21.8
Venezuela	7.3	14.2

* The unemployment rates correspond to the reference period of each survey and not to the annual average.

Source: National Households Surveys; data from *Panorama Social de América Latina*. ECLAC-United Nations (1994, 144).

Table 5.2 Estimated Population, Total and 15–24 Age Group, 1994
(Thousands of persons, at midyear)

Country	Total	Age Group 15–24	%
Argentina	34,180	5,970	17.5
Bolivia	7,238	1,446	20.0
Brazil	159,147	30,449	19.1
Chile	13,994	2,441	17.4
Colombia	34,546	6,740	19.5
Costa Rica	3,347	611	18.3
Cuba	10,960	1,937	17.7
Dominican Republic	7,684	1,544	20.1
Ecuador	11,221	2,303	20.5
El Salvador	5,642	1,258	22.3
Guatemala	10,322	2,051	19.9
Haiti	7,035	1,374	19.5
Honduras	5,494	1,112	20.2
Mexico	89,571	19,749	22.0
Nicaragua	4,278	853	19.9
Panama	2,585	510	19.7
Paraguay	4,830	898	18.6
Peru	23,333	4,827	20.7
Uruguay	3,168	526	16.6
Venezuela	21,377	4,120	19.3
TOTAL	459,952	90,719	19.7

Source: Composed with data from ECLAC, *Statistical Yearbook for Latin America and the Caribbean*. ECLAC (1994, 176).

Note: These figures correspond to the recommended projection, which involves the use of an average fertility hypothesis.

Table 5.3 Educational Enrollment Rates by Age Groups (6–11; 12–17) and Sex, 1980 and 1990 (Specific rates)

	1980						1990					
	Age Group 6–11			Age Group 12–17			Age Group 6–11			Age Group 12–17		
Country	Total	Male	Female	Total	Male	Female	Total	Male	Female	Total	Male	Female
Argentina	95.3	95.1	95.5	67.7	65.2	70.3	97.2	97.3	97.0	79.4	76.4	82.5
Bolivia	86.6	91.0	82.2	37.2	42.4	32.1	87.9	90.1	85.7	54.2	60.1	48.3
Brazil	73.2	74.8	71.6	61.7	62.6	60.8	77.9	79.9	75.8	74.9	77.1	72.6
Chile	89.6	89.1	90.0	80.0	80.2	79.8	90.5	91.5	89.5	91.2	91.7	90.8
Colombia	82.9	81.3	84.5	58.7	57.6	59.8	80.4	79.2	81.6	71.1	70.3	71.9
Costa Rica	90.1	89.3	90.8	52.5	51.1	54.0	87.1	86.7	87.6	47.7	47.8	47.7
Cuba	99.7	99.8	99.7	80.6	81.1	80.0	97.4	97.6	97.3	80.2	79.7	80.8
Dominican Republic	83.4	81.4	85.5	62.6	61.3	64.0	...	...	...	...	...	...
Ecuador	87.8	88.1	87.5	62.2	63.7	60.6	92.2	91.5	92.8	75.5	77.0	73.9
El Salvador	65.0	64.2	65.8	50.0	50.9	49.0	70.8	69.7	72.0	53.8	52.6	55.0
Guatemala	49.4	52.4	46.4	36.6	40.7	32.5	56.9	59.3	54.3	43.4	47.6	38.9
Haiti	36.5	37.0	36.0	43.6	49.4	37.7	59.7	60.7	58.7	55.0	57.8	52.3
Honduras	66.1	65.2	67.1	48.1	47.9	48.2	82.3	80.9	83.7	55.2	53.2	57.2
Mexico	92.6	92.5	92.8	63.8	66.6	61.0	100.0	100.0	100.0	68.1	69.9	66.3
Nicaragua	63.2	61.8	64.7	59.1	55.8	62.5	72.0	69.8	74.2	51.8	43.0	60.8
Panama	89.2	89.0	89.4	64.9	64.4	65.4	91.6	91.8	91.4	66.3	66.4	66.3
Paraguay	78.6	78.5	78.6	46.8	50.1	43.3	80.1	79.8	80.4	50.2	53.0	47.3
Peru	87.1	89.1	85.0	71.8	76.0	67.5	98.9	100.0	97.5	81.0	83.6	78.3
Uruguay	83.6	82.8	84.5	72.5	72.3	72.6	94.6	95.5	93.7	80.0	78.2	81.9
Venezuela	85.9	84.1	87.9	59.2	57.3	61.8	91.0	90.7	91.3	64.8	61.1	68.6

Source: Composed with data from ECLAC, *Statistical Yearbook for Latin America and the Caribbean.* ECLAC (1994, 65–66).
Note: UNESCO estimates.

Table 5.4 National Training Agencies (NTA) Enrollment, 1980 and 1987

NTA	Total Enrollment 1980	1987	Increase	(%)	Decrease	(%)
SENAI (Brazil)	569,453	975,779	406,326	(71.4)		
SENAC (Brazil)	967,342	1,154,689	187,347	(19.4)		
CONET* (Argentina)	230,858	289,540	58,682	(25.4)		
SECAP (Ecuador)	20,210	43,410	23,200	(114.8)		
SENATI (Peru)	23,818	43,939	20,121	(84.5)		
UTU (Uruguay)	42,284	52,766	10,482	(24.8)		
SENCICO (Peru)		9,370	9,370			
INFOTEP (Dominican Republic)		8,190	8,190			
SENAR (Brazil)	190,077	83,229			106,848	(56.2)
SENA (Colombia)	663,183	580,113			83,070	(12.5)
INACAP (Chile)	58,858	39,568			19,290	(32.8)
INA (Costa Rica)	57,409	44,470			12,939	(22.5)
Total	2,823,492	3,325,063	501,571	(24.8)		

* Formal technical education

Source: NTA Publications (1980); CINTERFOR Survey (1987); composed with data from *La formación profesional en el Umbral de los 90*, Vol. 1 CINTERFOR/OIT (1990, 37).

Table 5.5 Distribution of Income in Urban Households by Poorest and Richest Quintiles* (Percentages)

		Quintile 1 (poorest)		Quintile 5 (richest)	
Country	Year	Decile 1	Decile 2	Decile 9	Decile 10
Argentina**	1992	2.30	3.56	15.87	31.60
Bolivia	1992	1.50	2.91	14.66	40.04
Brazil	1990	1.08	2.00	17.96	41.67
Chile	1992	1.91	3.29	15.02	38.25
Colombia	1992	1.25	2.89	16.86	34.54
Costa Rica	1992	1.75	3.86	15.59	26.92
Guatemala**	1990	1.73	3.04	16.06	37.12
Honduras	1992	1.53	2.99	17.40	35.44
Mexico	1992	2.69	3.75	15.60	34.79
Panama	1991	1.06	2.80	16.26	34.19
Paraguay**	1992	2.03	3.69	16.40	29.24
Uruguay	1992	3.77	5.20	14.63	25.88
Venezuela	1992	1.82	3.92	16.78	28.06

* Classified according to per capita income.
** Refers to the metropolitan area.

Source: National Household Surveys data from ECLAC, *Statistical Yearbook for Latin America and the Caribbean*. ECLAC (1994, 45).

NOTE

1. Frederick Winslow Taylor (1856–1917) was an engineer who created a system of shop management published under the title of "Scientific Management." This system is based on systematic observation and measurement of work processes to discover the most efficient methods of performing the job. "He considers that the work of a typical factory foreman is composed of a number of different functions . . . and he believes that these could be separated out and performed by different specialists who would each be responsible for controlling different aspects of the work and the workers" (Pugh, Hickson, and Hinings 1973, 100).

REFERENCES

Becker, Gary. 1964. *Human Capital: A Theoretical and Empirical Analysis with Special Reference to Education*. New York: National Bureau of Economic Research, Columbia University Press.

Carrillo, Jorge. 1994. Flexibilidad y Calificación en la Nueva Encrucijada Industrial. In *Reestructuración Productiva, Trabajo y Educación en América Latiná*, edited by L. Gitahy. Campinas, Buenos Aires: Red Latino Americana de Educación y Trabajo CIID-CENEP, CINTERFOR-OIT, IG-UNICAMP, UNESCO-PREALC.

Castro, Claudio de Moura. 1995. *Training Policies for the End of the Century*. Paris: International Institute of Educational Planning.

Castro, Claudio de Moura, and Ruy de Quadros Carvalho. 1988. La automatización en Brasil: Quién le teme a los circuitos digitales. In *Modernización, un Desafío para la Educación*, compiled by Marianela Cerri, Luis Eduardo González, and Gordon West. Santiago: UNESCO-PREALC, Cooperative Program CIDE-PIIE-OISE.

ECLAC-UNESCO. 1992. *Educación y Conocimiento: Eje de la Transformación Productiva con Equidad*. Santiago: United Nations.

CINTERFOR (Centro Interamericano de Investigación y Documentación sobre Formación Profesional). 1990. *La Formación Profesional en el Umbral de los 90*. Montevideo: CINTERFOR.

De Ibarrola, María, and María Antonia Gallart, compilers. 1994. *Democracia y Productividad, Desafíos de una Nueva Educación Media en América Latina*. Buenos Aires, Mexico City, Santiago: Red Latinoamericana de Educación y Trabajo CIID-CENEP, UNESCO-PREALC.

Gallart, María Antonia. 1993. Latin America: Articulation of Education, Training and Work. In *International Encyclopedia of Education*. London: Pergamon Press.

———, ed. 1995. *La Formación para el Trabajo en el Final de Siglo: Entre la Reconversión Productiva y la Exclusión Social*. Buenos Aires, Santiago: Red Latinoamericana de Educación y Trabajo CIID-CENEP, UNESCO-PREALC.

Gallart, María Antonia, Martín Moreno, and Marcela Cerrutti. 1991. *Los Trabajadores por Cuenta Propia del Gran Buenos Aires: Sus Estrategias Educativas y Ocupacionales*. Buenos Aires: CENEP.

Gallart, María Antonia, Martín Moreno, Marcela Cerrutti, and Ana L. Suárez. 1992. *Las Trabajadoras de Villas: Familia, Educación y Trabajo*. Buenos Aires: CENEP.

Gitahy, Leda, ed. 1994. *Reestructuración Productiva, Trabajo y Educación en América Latina*. Campinas, Buenos Aires: Red Latinoamericana de Educación y Trabajo CIID-CENEP, CINTERFOR-OIT, IG-UNICAMP, UNESCO-PREALC.

Jacinto, Claudia. 1995. Formación profesional y empleabilidad de jóvenes de bajos niveles educativos. Una articulación posible? In *La Formación para el Trabajo en el Final de Siglo: Entre la Reconversión Productiva y la Exclusión Social*. Buenos Aires, Santiago: Red Latinoamericana de Educación y Trabajo CIID-CENEP, UNESCO-PREALC.

Jacinto, Claudia and Ana Lourdes Suárez. 1994. Juventud, Pobreza y Formación Profesional. *Educación y Trabajo* yr. 5, no. 1.

Leite, Elenice. 1994. Trabalho e Qualifição: A classe operaria vai a escola. In *Reestructuración Productiva, Trabajo y Educación en América Latina*. Campinas, Buenos Aires: Red Latinoamericana de Educación y Trabajo CIID-CENEP, CINTERFOR-OIT, IG-UNICAMP, UNESCO-PREALC.

———. 1995. La Función Social del SENAI: Evolución de la Atención a la Comunidad. In *La Formación para el Trabajo en el Final de Siglo: Entre la Reconversión Productiva y la Exclusión Social*. Buenos Aires, Santiago: Red Latinoamericana de Educación y Trabajo CIID-CENEP, UNESCO-PREALC.

Mercado, Alfonso. 1994. Cambio Tecnológico, Calificación y Capacitación en un Contexto de Integración Económica. In *Reestructuración Productiva, Trabajo y Educación en América Latina*. Campinas, Buenos Aires: Red Latinoamericana de Educación y Trabajo CIID-CENEP, CINTERFOR-OIT, IG-UNICAMP, UNESCO-PREALC.

Middleton, John, Adrian Ziderman, and Arvil Van Adams. 1993. *Skills for Productivity. Vocational Education and Training in Developing Countries*. Washington, D.C.: The World Bank and Oxford University Press.

OECD (Organization for Economic Cooperation and Development). 1989. *Pathways for Learning: Education and Training from 16 to 19*. Paris: OECD.

Psacharopoulos, George, and William Loxley. 1985. *Diversified Secondary Education and Development: Evidence from Colombia and Tanzania*. Washington, D.C.: The World Bank and Johns Hopkins University Press.

Pugh, D. S., Hickson, D. J., and Hinnings, C. R. 1973. *Writers on Organizations*. London: Penguin Education.

Rachid, Alessandra. 1995. Nuevos sistemas de calidad en la industria de autopartes y sus efectos sobre la calificación de la mano de obra. In *La Formación para el*

Trabajo en el Final de Siglo. Buenos Aires, Santiago: Red Latinoamericana de Educación y Trabajo CIID-CENEP, UNESCO-PREAIS.

U.S. Department of Labor. 1991. *What Work Requires of Schools: A SCANS Report for America 2000*. Washington, D.C.: SCANS (Secretary's Commission on Achieving Necessary Skills).

Part III

Emerging Responses for Facing Poverty and Vulnerability

6 | Welfare and Citizenship

Old and New Vulnerabilities

CARLOS H. FILGUEIRA

Throughout the 1930s an accelerated process of industrialization and productive modernization began in Latin America, especially in the Southern Cone. These processes triggered and became part of a broader domestically oriented development model which assigned a central role to the state, both as a market regulator and as a provider of goods, services, and employment.

This was both a worldwide and regional trend. After a long period of expansion of capitalism and unregulated markets on both a domestic and international level, the state took on a very active role in the areas of production, distribution, and social reproduction. It is not totally accurate to say that before the 1930s the state had no presence as a regulating body aside from its minimal functions of external defense, public order, and defense of private property. The expansion of the state's fiscal capacity and the introduction of minimal social programs began gradually just a few years after the first industrial revolution. Nevertheless, the growth of state regulation and especially the increased presence of the "welfare state" took a dramatic upward turn in the 1930s and in the postwar period.

There has been a good deal of scholarly investigation into the reasons for the expanded role of the welfare state in domestic societies and markets. In Polanyi's (1957) classic work, this expansion of the state was, to a great extent, a set of defensive strategies against the destructive power of the market over community life. For other scholars, state regulation is one of the requirements of a new phase of capital accumulation (O'Connor 1973). Another point of view suggests that the state limits the market as a means of preventing intolerable levels of social conflict (Piven and Cloward 1971). In other interpretations, the emergence of a participatory state is more closely connected with societal and class pressure and also with distributive struggles among classes (Esping-Andersen 1990). Yet another version argues that the state has taken on roles that were formerly the purview of the family and of small rural communities. Some recent points of view place more emphasis on the role that the state itself has played in its own expansion. They argue that the bureaucracy's own interests and the appearance of a political class with its own political agenda (as distinct from the economic elite) are the primary driving forces behind the expansion of the state's participation fields (Heclo 1974). With direct reference to social programs in Latin America, two explanations are dominant: one is based on a pluralistic view that stresses the role of pressure groups (Mesa-Lago 1985); the other emphasizes the significance of political elites and the machinery of the state (Malloy 1985; Papadópulos 1992). Peter Flora (1987) has attempted to integrate these divergent views by applying the concept of the macro constellation. He finds that the appearance and subsequent expansion of the modern welfare state spring from a causal hexagon in which six interconnected processes contain and give form and meaning to social policy. On one hand, we have major transformations in the international system and in demographic aspects (i.e., family structure) and, on the other, the processes of the expansion of capitalism and industrialization. In addition, we have the consolidation of national states and mass democracy. The international system, the patterns of demographic evolution, capitalism, industrialism, the nation-state, and democracy define the macro constellation within which the welfare state emerged and expanded (roughly from the late nineteenth century to the 1980s).

Nevertheless, whatever functions one attributes to the modern welfare state and to the factors explaining its growth, there is a general consensus that the primary purpose of the state is to guarantee the security of members of society by transferring resources, goods, and services and by using general and sectorial regulatory policies. Such guarantees, to the extent that they are transformed into legislation stipulating rights of given categories of individuals, define an additional order of citizenship—social citizenship, which differs from civil and political citizenship. T.H. Marshall (1950) referred to social citizenship as the result of a kind of state activity intentionally directed and socially legitimized in the direction of providing social security and basic shared standards of welfare. Offe (1992, 61) similarly suggests such citizenship as:

> Positive *legal obligations and entitlements* [which are handed over to different] *categories of people* pertaining to *conditions*, risks and contingencies which are

recognized as requiring public regulation, transfers or services. If a person belongs to category X and meets conditions a, b, c . . . then he or she is entitled to services and transfers P. The working of these three components (categories, conditions and entitlements) is then supposed to implement the values of security and welfare. [Offe's italics]

Those sectors referred to as "at risk" during the 1970s and as "vulnerable" in the present are precisely those falling into categories requiring either positive action from the state or certain entitlements. If this is the case, the question remains: What kind of positive action should be taken by the state, and what is its relationship to social citizenship? Philanthropy does not bestow entitlements; it may be more or less beneficial to the groups to whom it is directed, but it is not a legal right unless it is mandated by the state. Neither are policies of assistance nor private programs intended to correct conditions found in vulnerable sectors. For this reason, it would appear that a principle of universality needs to be linked to the basic notion of social citizenship upon which the modern welfare state is based. Yet such a principle of universality does not mean that all members of society receive the same benefits and services. Rather, a given set of rights is shared by all individuals as long as they fall within similar categories (e.g., old age), share similar conditions (e.g., families with children), and/or risk similar contingencies (e.g., sickness or death of a spouse).

At this point it would seem advisable to pause and consider some complex problems that result from the concept of social vulnerability. First, basic needs, shortages, and risks or elements of insecurity that should or should not be covered by social security are all highly subjective in their determination and, therefore, constitute contested issues. The identification of given sectors as "at risk" or as "vulnerable" normally leads to social policy or at least to issues that in turn become part of the political agenda. To the extent that the basic function of the welfare state is to guarantee certain levels of security and protection through the offering of services, goods, and regulatory policies in such diverse areas as health, education, old age support, and so on, the identification of the areas of risk becomes a necessary and continuous activity. Second, who are the agents in charge of defining and identifying the vulnerable sectors and areas? How does a society arrive at a consensus as to what these sectors are? How does this become policy? How and why do society's perception vary regarding what constitutes legitimate structures of vulnerability?

The definition of the areas of vulnerability that a society identifies, prioritizes, and elevates to the level of policy should be understood as a social and political construct. A certain level of consensus among actors is required in order to determine the depth and level of coverage of the systems of security. For example, decisions must be made as to which categories of people deserve special treatment, what possible consequences might result from lack of coverage, and what should be the level of generosity or the limitations placed on the contributions. The consensus can be more or less stable, but in any case it is formed and transformed in the political and social arena, starting with values and social attitudes, power and interests, institutional mechanisms that serve to process and negotiate demands, in addition to more or less reliable information from which prejudices and stereotypes of reality cannot be excluded.

Although one should not be so naïve as to believe that policy is purely defined by informational inputs, the cognitive level remains an extremely important part in the formation of the aforementioned consensus. The setting up of systems of indicators of economic and social development and the contribution made by different disciplines to their construction and analysis are responsible to a large extent for the creation of shared beliefs concerning the most important areas of social vulnerability. In addition, information thus produced and analyzed plays a legitimizing or delegitimizing role in social policy options and in the welfare systems favored by one group or another; there is nothing neutral about the information, whether it is produced and analyzed by various international, domestic, and regional agencies or generated through academic research. The debate on policy options and choices is composed of the selection and prioritization of given areas of concentration of information and its analysis (e.g., poverty maps), together with the aggregation of indicators in complex measurement systems (e.g., indices and typologies of poverty, the index of human development, the human development diamond).[1]

Finally, areas of vulnerability change just as their evaluation and prioritization are changed by social and political actors. Change can be gradual, as indicated by certain secular trends operating in the family (e.g., fertility or marriage rates), or it can be abrupt and profound. The first type of change does not generally affect the basic matrix used by societies to guarantee the security of its members in the face of risks and other contingencies. In this case, the transformations of social policies and regulatory systems operate within a dominant paradigm. Innovation occurs on the edges of the system with no changes in the main organizational principles. Society deals with gradual changes in a context of vulnerability through new forms of regulation and social policies that are considered "normal." The process is adaptive, gradual, and continuous.

The "Moral Economy Approach"

In the presence of profound and rapid structural changes, however, the very societal matrix that guarantees protection to its members is at stake. The debate over the "moral economy approach" provides an example. A long tradition of scholarship has argued that the modern era, through the expansion of the markets, the intrusion of capitalist relationships, and the formation of the nation-state, has triggered processes that have destroyed traditional forms of community life and of subsistence economies.[2] The idea of the moral economy encompassed notions of social integration and solidarity of the local community, organized around principles of security. The liberal state was interpreted as a disruptive element that undermined the identities, commitments, and feelings of attachment that had been formed within the local community. For the scholar of current social policies, some terms of the moral economy approach are surprisingly modern: "The village is the key institution that provides the peasant with security in precapitalist society. It is a collectivity which typically operates to assure a 'minimum income' (Scott 1976) to its inhabitants; in Wolf's (1957) conception, [the idea] is to 'equalize the life chances and life risks of its members.' For Joel Migdal (1974), because peasants are so close to the [poverty] line, 'they developed community mechanisms to maximize security for the household'" (Popkin 1979, 10).

With reference to these ideas, the origins of the modern welfare state can be interpreted as a defensive policy of integration and civilization in the face of the changes and threats produced by the double processes of deterioration of patterns of precapitalist security and the rise of industrialization. The parallels between the moral economy vision and current changes become rather obvious with a slight modification of the terminology: globalization (the growing integration of international markets, services, and capital) recalls the former expansion of the market; the diminishing importance of the nation-state recalls the former destruction or weakening of the local community and of the organizational and regulatory principles of risk coverage; and uncertainty and insecurity in the modern welfare state recall the crisis of precapitalist protection systems. Of course, these are only parallels. They do not imply that history is repeating itself or that similar results are expected. Nor do we accept all the premises and suppositions of the moral economy approach.[3] However, the exercise of comparing "the great transformation" of the past with the profound changes of globalization in the present is useful in identifying processes and problem areas that appear to have a common nature in both of these historical experiences.

This introduction and the preceding comparative sketch are an attempt to create a frame of reference in which to locate the problems of social vulnerability. The term "vulnerability" has recently entered the discourse surrounding the problems of poverty and social policies. This concept attempts to create analytical instruments with which to identify populations and sectors at risk.

Poverty and Vulnerability: Progress and Challenges

In Latin America the 1970s and 1980s were times of economic adjustment and, in many cases, severe political repression. These decades marked the end of ECLAC's import substitution model of development and the beginning of new export models with unregulated markets and diminished states. According to some international organizations, after twenty years of neoliberal experiments, the countries of the Southern Cone and other parts of the region have either accrued a large "social debt" or have shown disregard for development "with a human face."

The economic crises, the stop-and-go economic cycles, and the process of structural adjustment have left debatable economic benefits but clearly negative social results. This has been the subject of the debate on questions of social policies emanating from academic, political, and governmental circles as well as multilateral agencies since the early 1980s. The debate has occurred at the theoretical, methodological, and policy levels. At the theoretical and methodological levels, great efforts have been made throughout the continent in the last decade to gather and systematize information about poverty and satisfy basic needs and to devise more sophisticated operational concepts and definitions of poverty and indigence. The most successful agency in this area has been the UN Economic Commission for Latin America and the Caribbean (ECLAC). More recently the Inter-American Development Bank and the World Bank have improved and refined their human and social development indices. Even the International Monetary Fund, usually not concerned with social issues, has started to generate new indicators and propose social policies.

The most noteworthy products of the aforementioned undertakings include: the achievement of regional comparability in the measurement of poverty (through the poverty line), the development and sophistication of the Index of Unsatisfied Basic Needs, the construction of the CEMIT index,[4] and a definition of a poverty typology that combines the poverty line with unsatisfied basic needs. All this has served to improve the understanding of the multifaceted phenomenon of poverty, providing better and more informed inputs for the design and implementation of public policy.

In its 1994 report on the social panorama of Latin America, ECLAC adds an innovation to the battery of measurements and concepts that deal with inequality and poverty. This new measurement attempts to identify the social groups that seem more likely to reach the poverty line during recessions or crises. ECLAC simplified the identification of vulnerable sectors by defining them as those households that fall between 0.9 and 1.25 of the poverty line. The reason for settling on these figures is that in almost all countries of the region 10–15% of households fall between them. Using this methodology in Argentina (1991–92), researchers noted that from among the total population, 6.5% of the nonimpoverished sectors closest to the poverty line had actually fallen below the line, and 9.4% were able to get out of the situation. This definition has the advantage of simplicity and reliance on a generally accepted measurement. Using this method, ECLAC has been able to examine the nucleus of the population most at risk of falling into poverty.

By defining "vulnerability" operationally in this sense, ECLAC has added a new horizontal cross section to the already established criteria in this subject matter. Perhaps the most interesting opportunity offered by the concept of vulnerability is the possibility of generating a vertical cross section of the structure of society in which vulnerability is defined by attributes that are specific not merely to a given position at a given level of the social structure but that cut across these levels. This way it is possible to define a given population (e.g., people located in the first quartile of income or those found between poverty lines one and three) and then study the configurations showing greater vulnerability. Within these categories areas of vulnerability can be studied, for example, by ethnic group, gender, or type of occupation or industrial sector.

Studying vulnerability in nonpoor social sectors is undoubtedly more complex. Data are less available, and the conditions, risks, and contingencies underpinning vulnerability in the middle and working classes are extremely diverse. Recent structural changes brought about by globalization have had drastic and unpredicted effects on the traditionally "integrated" sectors. Skilled and semi-skilled workers, professionals, white-collar workers, and service industry employees are having to deal with conditions that have changed the level and perception of their security.[5]

If proximity to the poverty line is too much of a simplification, what then would constitute a more complex but still manageable notion of vulnerability? Vulnerability, like many frequently used concepts, was developed intuitively and casuistically, through the enumeration and compilation of structural conditions, individual characteristics, and contingencies. Vulnerability may be defined as a predisposition to descend from a given level of welfare owing to a negative configuration of attributes acting against the achievement of material (e.g., income, goods, patrimony) and symbolic (e.g., status, recognition, shared identities) returns. By extension, vulnerability is also a predisposition to *not* escape from negative conditions of welfare. Thus certain attributes such as work situation, occupation, ethnic group, age, or a combination of these will be an indicator of various types and degrees of vulnerability.

Social vulnerability is not synonymous with downward mobility, but downward mobility is a probable consequence of the conditions of vulnerability. The very notion of vulnerability indicates risk triggered by some event or process. Not all downward mobility, however, is connected to conditions of vulnerability. If this were the case, the concept would be meaningless. Ex post facto we might conclude that all individuals of a given society experiencing downward mobility did so because they were vulnerable. It would be true, and trivial, if one accepts a purely atheoretical definition of vulnerability which approaches a specific object through a definitional criterion that looks at the probable effect of the condition but not at the factors that constitute the object. Such a definition, however, removes all specificity from the concept. The concept of vulnerability includes individuals but it mainly refers to groups or categories of individuals. In any society certain structures of inequality and dominant configurations of vulnerability exist. The greatest contribution that this concept can make toward the understanding of social inequities and their consequences is to identify sectors and social groups with shared situations.

Another aspect of the concept of vulnerability is its relationship between the ability (expressed as shared individual attributes) to mobilize resources and the structure of opportunities in society (expressed in structural terms). One way of representing this relationship is to imagine a nonquantitative quotient. The numerator stands for the possession, control, and management of material and symbolic resources that permit the individual to function in society. Work experience, family attributes, the development of various skills, the level of education, and the ability to understand the rationale that reigns in each of the different spheres of society work together to help improve the performance of the individual and enhance his or her possibility of upward mobility, or at least operate as a defense mechanism in situations of precipitous decline in his or her well-being.

The structures of opportunity that comprise the denominator in the equation are the market, the state, and society. Without dismissing other possible dimensions, the opportunity structure of the market refers basically to employment, income, and consumption. In addition to economic development, long- or short-term changes in the economy, factors of production, and technological changes affect the structure of opportunities. Economic crisis or growth, recession, unemployment, changes in the patterns of distribution of income, technological change and productive transformation, etc., have a differential effect on the structural opportunities of different sectors and social categories. These can create or eliminate opportunities, make the structure more rigid or more permeable. An example of this is the close connection that exists between the percentage of poor households and variations in unemployment and real wages in Latin America.

In this discussion, the state should be understood in terms of policy not politics. In other words, it is a "welfare state," which includes public policies that have direct or indirect redistributive effects. The state role is that of a regulating and ordering institution, together with the market and society, yielding an ensemble of functions that profoundly affect the structure of opportunities in a society.

The structure of opportunity of society comprises two additional levels: the sociocultural and the political. The sociocultural level involves the presence (or lack) of associative community forms, organizations of collective action, extended family structures, communities based on ethnic solidarity, etc. Other things being equal, the presence of these structures increases opportunities through informal channels. In the same vein, culturally open societies (for example, those with low levels of prejudice and discrimination) offer more opportunities than do societies with ethnic divisions. Within the political realm, pluralistic systems, the exercise of power through voting, labor unions, or customer-based systems are examples of areas that play an important part in the structure of opportunities.

I have so far intentionally omitted any reference to the interrelationships among these levels in order to distinguish the structure of opportunities within the three basic institutions of social order. The "quotient of vulnerability" can be studied by successive incorporation of the structure of opportunities from each level so as to gradually make the analysis more sophisticated.

Assuming that high numerator values in the "coefficient of vulnerability" correspond to areas with the greatest lack of resources, the quotient will show a continuum from greater to lesser vulnerability. Given the necessary data and some expertise, it is possible to estimate the position and level of well-being of an individual or family unit within the stratified system. Age, education, occupational level, and income are not only attributes that allow us to locate individuals on a scale of stratification, they are also material and symbolic resources that can be invested and utilized in order to maintain given levels of welfare. The opposite also holds true: from given values of the variables, we can deduce the propensity towards deterioration of welfare in individual cases.

Pensions, disability insurance, and life insurance for spouses are good examples of the mechanisms that a social order creates to protect individuals from losses or changes of welfare or status. Old age and a consequent diminished capacity pose fewer risks when a certain level of welfare is achieved through retirement pensions and other age-determined benefits. Similar protection exists for cases of incapacity or the loss of a breadwinner.

The more general notion of decommodification suggested by Esping-Andersen (1990) moves in the same direction. He argues that the social policies of the industrialized countries act as mechanisms that separate, at least partially, the fate of individuals from the fate or the ups and downs of the market. Such policies attach to individuals an additional to and different status from that of a commodity: social citizenship. These programs, as well as other forms of social protection, do not necessarily come from the state. They may be the response of communities to the uncertainty of industrial societies.

Note that the possibility of deteriorating welfare is connected with the rules of social production and reproduction in a given order. That is, the relationship between attributes (age, sex, education, occupation, etc.) and well-being is historically specific. If the order of production and social reproduction is modified, the situations of risk will in turn change. The effectiveness of systems of protection is relative to the specific context in which they are applied.

New and Old Vulnerabilities in Latin America

This section will address several issues: What transformations have recently occurred in the nature and content of social vulnerability? How can such vulnerability be identified and analyzed? What is the relationship between social vulnerability and social change at the macrolevel?

I begin with an examination of the difficulties involved with analyses of social vulnerability and its transformation within the context of complex processes of social change. I argue that the dichotomy of "old" and "new" vulnerabilities has limited relevance in its ability to effectively address the issues raised by this study. Old vulnerabilities have neither disappeared nor been replaced by new vulnerabilities. Rather, the old provide the basis upon which the new are generated. This combination of old and new engenders new structures of vulnerability. The section concludes with a discussion of the social trends underpinning these structures of vulnerability.

The current debate surrounding the crisis of the welfare state is closely associated with the increasingly accepted notion that the rapid emergence of new forms of vulnerability has undermined the ability of traditional mechanisms of society to guarantee its members protection against risk and uncertainty. There appear to be two main macrolevel changes:

A technological revolution which is currently in progress
The increased and accelerated flow of goods, services, and information among societies has brought the world closer together. The profundity of these changes has rendered states ever more limited in their ability to limit and control these exchanges.

A convergence of effects
Social manifestations of these transformations are similar in all societies. The impact of such macrolevel changes on structures of vulnerability creates demanding and potentially conflictive environments within which adequate responses must be framed and implemented.

The first of the aforementioned causes is widely accepted. The second assertion, however, is disputable. While a hard core of common traits can be derived from processes of globalization around the world, globalization neither implies nor produces similar impacts in all societies. It does not happen in a mechanical, unilinear form. Processes endogenous to each society mediate processes of globalization. The impacts and consequences of globalization are a function of the structural conditions and policy instruments available within each national system. Any analysis of the impact of globalization on vulnerabilities operating in Latin America would be erroneous without the recognition of this fact.

In comparison to Latin America, the more developed nations, despite the severe problems currently affecting them, display relatively open structures of opportunities and a higher capacity to mobilize individual resources. Such openness stems from the integration of capitalism with international markets, liberal democratic institutions, various forms of interest aggregation and articulation, and the development of well-institutionalized welfare states. Poverty in Latin America, as we will elaborate in the following section, stems from the inability of regional nations to incorporate significant sectors of the population into both the market and the sociopolitical system, causing marked deficits in capacities, skills, and policy instruments. Such factors further disadvantage and limit the responses adopted by the nations of Latin America to address problems of relative vulnerability.

Changes in the Structure of Vulnerability

Generic and simplistic explanations of changes in the structure of vulnerability attribute such change directly to processes of globalization and transnationalization. The identification of the causal relationships in structures of vulnerability, however, remains more difficult. The move from a macro- to microlevel of analysis suggests that no transformation in this structure can be reduced to or conceptualized exclusively in terms of the former level. The following analysis highlights several factors I consider to be fundamental to any discussion of old and new vulnerabilities as well as of the relation of both to macrolevel phenomena.

The Influence of Demographic and Familial Factors

Types of vulnerability associated with demographic and familial transformations do not specifically result from the globalization of the economy. However, it is possible that globalization may accelerate certain tendencies that have been taking place throughout this century. The demographic transition in Latin America, a long-term trend in the region, has been characterized by an increased aging of the population. Nevertheless, both extremes of the demographic scale—infants and the elderly—are expanding at a much faster rate than all other age groups. The manifestation and progression of this transition (via the differential reproduction of social strata) remains specific to each society, but in general the majority of births occur in the most vulnerable sectors, e.g., the poor and the lower classes. Approximately 60% of those children susceptible to new vulnerabilities belong to these sectors: poverty reproduces poverty. At first glance, it seems difficult to affirm that new vulnerabilities differ significantly and substantively from the old ones. Nevertheless, children who are born today will grow up in homes with less capacity to fulfill basic functions, in part a consequence of increasingly incomplete families owing to the weakening of the marriage tie, the growth of cohabitation, and the absence of the father figure in the home. Families without a father are not a new phenomenon, but the novelty lies in its determinants and consequences, e.g., divorce rates, disrupted family cycles, children's age, etc.

The identification of the consequences of vulnerability types associated with familial factors lacks precision. Above all, various trends currently observable in the developed world seem to also be part of the long-term trajectory in Latin America.[6] The combined effects of increased divorce rates, postponement of marriage, teenage pregnancy, single mothers, single-parent households, together with longer life expectancy have challenged the security traditionally provided by the family.

Determining the magnitude of these transitions remains difficult owing in part to variations in the rate of change within and among nations and to differences in their social structure. The transition currently operating in Latin America is arguably a mix, combining traditional and modern elements. Characteristics of the former include behaviors and values such as high fertility rates; those associated with the latter include the modern groups incorporated into and participating actively in their societies. The magnitude of change affecting intermediate sectors and middle classes, including integrated lower sectors, seems significant. It is characterized by a relatively new and ever more present type of vulnerability, which includes single-parent households headed by single mothers, high instability of the family, and increases in one-person households.

Changes in the Structure of Employment

One of the most important consequences of globalization is manifested in both the organization of employment and in the labor market. In more developed nations, profound changes have rendered labor less secure and permanent. New core technologies developed on the basis of information and robotization have reduced the number of highly specialized jobs. As a result, employment opportunities for several sectors of the working classes—blue and white collar, semiqualified and qualified—have become more limited. The rapid obsolescence of knowledge, combined with a growing demand for versatile workers and a redefinition of interenterprise relations (especially in industry), has altered the former Fordist model of labor organization. Especially in Europe, manifestations of these changes include high and relatively entrenched rates of unemployment and underemployment.[7] Concurrent changes in the organization and structure of labor have impaired the functioning of corresponding social security systems in most countries. The contributor/recipient relation has become increasingly unfavorable. The rise in unemployment and the aging of the population suggest that such systems are becoming overextended, paying out more than they take in, increasing the risk of fiscal crisis.

While such transformations have not reached the same proportions in Latin America, similar problems can be noted throughout the region. The majority of these are perpetuated and accentuated by policies of economic adjustment and reductions in public employment.[8]

Unemployment rates in the region have remained relatively stable. Average unemployment rates increased between 1980 and 1985 but fell to levels reminiscent of the 1970s by 1994. Such figures, however, are not homogeneous throughout the region. In Argentina unemployment rates increased nine-fold between 1980 and 1985, approaching 19% in May 1995. Similar increases have occurred in other countries: rates in Guatemala tripled; those in Panama increased by 60%; those in Paraguay by 30%; and in Uruguay, Mexico, and Venezuela by 40%. Unemployment in Chile, however, fell by 50%; reductions also occurred in Brazil and Costa Rica. Unemployment during this period affected some sectors (particularly youth and women) more than others.

Even though new employment opportunities have been generated by the aforementioned changes, PREALC (1993) found that such opportunities are generally of low quality and low productivity. Of 100 jobs created between 1990 and 1994, 81 were in the informal or small enterprise sector. Such a trend has been obvious since the 1980s, when large- and medium-size private enterprises and the public sector have absorbed only one in five new workers.

Reductions in public sector employment underpinned, in part, the expansion of small enterprise and informal sectors between 1990 and 1992. "State reform" and economic adjustment policies reduced employment opportunities in the public sector. Relative decreases in wages in the public as compared to the private sector accompanied the retraction of such opportunities and further reduced the traditional attractiveness of public sector employment. This situation shows signs of accelerating: between 1980 and 1992 the ratio of new jobs created in the public vs. the private sector stood at approximately 2 to 1. Between 1990 and 1992 this ratio decreased to 1 to 4.

As a result, from 1980 to 1992, the nonagricultural labor market registered important changes: employment in small enterprises increased from 15% to 22% and in the informal sector from 19% to 27% of the total Latin American work force. Together with domestic service (stagnant at 6.4%) these two sectors thus accounted for more than half of all nonagricultural employment. In the urban sector, formal employment in large and medium-size enterprises fell from 44% to 31%, and public employment declined from 15.7% to 13.6%. Unpublished PREALC estimates for the 1980–94 period indicate that in urban areas employment in informal activities more than doubled.

In 1994 the distribution of nonagricultural employment was as follows: 1) informal (33.2%); 2) small enterprise (22.5%); 3) large and medium enterprise

(30.8%); and 4) public (13.6%). The informal sector has remained the largest; the large and medium enterprise sector has been reduced by more than one-third; and the public sector is going through a slow reduction process.

Employment in the small enterprise sector is not exclusively within the informal economy. Several studies suggest that various modes of subcontracting and linking utilized by small enterprises are capitalist and, in some cases, technology-intensive. Large firms in Latin America seem to be following the strategy employed by large enterprises in more developed nations: out-sourcing activities not directly associated with their main patterns of production.[9] The growth of interenterprise exchange vis-à-vis intersector exchanges in the industrial sector provides a telling example of such strategies as well as an indicator of the flexibility and comparative advantages generated by new technology.

In the past, vulnerabilities associated with a segmented labor market were attributed to the system of late capitalism operating in the region. Such a system lacked the dynamism necessary to generate employment opportunities at a pace equal to that of demographic growth. Other factors (e.g., the transfer of capital-intensive technologies, low levels of investment, countercyclical adjustments, and massive rural-urban migration) perpetuated this lack of dynamism and generally coalesced along two dimensions: a) a dual labor market; and b) the formation and consolidation of large centers of urban poverty.[10]

At first glance, it would appear that recent processes of globalization and technological change have been neutral with regard to the aforementioned labor market vulnerabilities. The failure to create new job opportunities is also a characteristic endogenous to the new and internationalized models of labor organization. Furthermore, the inability of such models to create quality sources of employment is by no means endemic to the region; it is an international phenomenon. Under closer scrutiny, however, globalization heightens vulnerabilities by eliminating opportunities for life-long, permanent and/or full-time employment which is closely associated with the loss of personal security. This process operates across and within all occupational strata, affecting those traditionally vulnerable sectors (e.g., the poor, manual workers) and those who, in the past, considered themselves beyond the risks of market uncertainties (e.g., highly educated middle classes, professionals, higher-level bureaucrats, executives). This, in turn, bankrupts systems of social security, erodes social and cultural identities formed on the basis of employment, and weakens opportunities for collective action.

Poverty as Vulnerability and Constraint

Through the influence of international organizations and global agencies, the issue of poverty has acquired salience. The problem, however, is not new to the agendas of Latin American governments. Poverty has historically been a characteristic of the reality of the region. However, as shown in other chapters of this book, the three decades following World War II witnessed a slight improvement in indices of poverty. This improvement emerged as the product of economic growth, complemented by the expansion of urban employment and a decrease in unemployment and underemployment. The percentage of households falling below the poverty line decreased by 10% between 1970 and 1980. Absolute poverty, however, continued to rise.

Since the 1980s problems of chronic poverty and insecurity have worsened[11] and all indices of poverty have increased anew. It is important to note change in indices of poverty within urban and rural contexts. Presently, poverty in Latin America constitutes—for the first time—a predominantly urban phenomenon. In 1970, 37% of all incidence of poverty was urban in nature. By 1980 this figure had increased to 46%, and a mere six years later (1986) it had reached 55%. Such figures do not necessarily imply reductions in rural poverty. Indices of indigence still remain highest in rural areas, but indigence in urban areas increased from 36% in 1980 to 44% by 1986. If this trend is maintained, extreme deprivation will become a predominantly urban problem. This change is the consequence of rural-urban migration, perpetuated by demographic factors (especially high fertility rates) endemic to poor and immigrant populations. The manifestation of these factors in increased rates of urban poverty speak to the incapacity of urban structures to absorb new contingents of immigrants.

The Emergence of "New Poverty"

Another characteristic of the growing incidence of poverty refers not only to the volume of poor sectors but also to their condition. Sectors of the "new poor" in Latin America now include social groups who had achieved a certain degree of social, occupational, and educational integration. In spite of an accumulation of human capital, these groups have fallen below the poverty line. The existence of the new poverty contingents, coupled with the more traditional sectors of "chronic" and "structural" poor, attests to the sociocultural heterogeneity of poverty in Latin America.

Poverty has been accompanied by a plethora of other problems within the last few years such as lack of job training, social integration, and citizen participation in political arenas. Such problems suggest that poor sectors lack the sociocultural resources and psychological awareness necessary to perform the tasks associated with these realms.

In terms of social support, the processes of social integration of the rural poor are often more effective than the urban ones, but may also be more coercive and authoritarian. This is a function of the personalized nature of rural authority patterns, attachment to the community, and the predominance of the extended family and kinship as the basic social nucleus. These premodern and informal structures pose specific problems for the processes of familial socialization and personality development. From a sociological point of view, therefore, rural and urban poverty are different phenomena and so are the problems they generate. Above and beyond the greater social and political visibility of urban poverty, no operable framework exists where the problems of the urban poor can be located and addressed. The processes of urban poverty are currently taking place in a disjointed context. It encompasses cultural conflicts derived from tensions between personalized forms of social relations and a world guided by the logic of individualism and by formal organizational criteria rather than primary relationships. Urban poverty further differs from rural poverty in that the former places the individual in direct contact with the models and lifestyles of other social strata. The individual thus remains considerably more exposed to strong demonstration effects than in situations of rural poverty. Tensions derived from a world espousing strong values of achievement, consumerism, and social mobility inevitably arise.

Given this context, the social structure taking form within the region over the last few years faces challenges of anomie and social disintegration of an entirely new type.[12] Not all the poor are marginal, as cogently suggested by the literature on Latin American shantytowns. Arguably, however, the region is currently leaning toward the massive incorporation of new urban social groups in conditions of extreme poverty, clearly segmented from the rest of the "integrated" society. Socialization at an early stage in the lives of the majority of this new generation inevitably occurs within the context of a family that, as previously noted, is now less capable of performing its traditional integrating functions.

Current trends of poverty seem to confirm the most skeptical projections of the 1980s (Altimir 1981). Economic growth in most Latin American countries did not have the intended trickle-down effects on the poor sectors. Molina and Piñera (1979) estimated that if growth in real rates of income between 1974 and 1979 had been maintained, absolute poverty in Brazil would have been reduced to 10% in 33 years; in Mexico, in 45 years; and in Colombia, in 20 years. These rates of growth, however, were not maintained and more than 15 years later realistic projections suggest that the poverty reduction targets are increasingly out of reach.[13]

ECLAC (1994) studies substantiate the positive effects income growth have on the reduction of poverty. In spite of these effects two characteristics specific to the region emerge: 1) the persistence of highly unequal distributions of income; and 2) periods of growth and recession do not have a proportionate impact on the magnitude of poverty. Increases in income, employment, and/or real salaries slightly reduce the number of the poor, especially in postcrisis junctures. Effects of economic recession, however, fall disproportionately on poor sectors.

Poverty in Latin America thus does not strictly constitute a new type of social vulnerability. The exclusion of large segments of the population with little capacity to mobilize individual resources in the face of an increasingly narrow range of opportunities in all facets (market, state, and society) yields a structural characteristic of the region. What has changed is the constellation of factors underpinning poverty and the variation in its types. These changes are traceable, in part, to long-term trends affecting the structure of the family, demographic transition, and the geographic distribution of the population. The new vulnerabilities that do arise are a function of changes in the structure of labor and the organization of the labor market. The combination of these changes with macrolevel transformations further reduces the already narrow structure of opportunities open to poor sectors. The relation between economic growth and poverty thus remains complex: the former yields a determinant of the latter; the latter, in turn, constrains the former.

New Challenges Facing Welfare States

The instruments and mechanisms generated in the past by the welfare state to protect members of society from situations of risk and uncertainty are insufficient and inadequate today. The welfare state, crystallized in various versions of the Keynesian model, replaced traditional forms of social provision of pre-industrial communities. This change was neither rapid nor continuous but occurred as a long process of successive adaptations. Attempts to replicate the European welfare state in Latin America proved difficult; few countries were successful. Models excluding vast segments of the population have been maintained and remain the norm.[14]

The relation of the welfare state to society was built around several background factors. The middle class perceived the structure of vulnerabilities according to a stereotypical vision of the family and its relation to the social world[15] based on an integrated nuclear family with biological parents, and a marked division of labor. The male, as head of the household, constituted the sole bread winner, and domestic chores fell to the female. Unemployment—frictional or cyclical—was, in the worst case, an anomaly for which various forms of protection and transitory security existed. In those few cases where women worked outside the home, their labor remained contingent and served to complement family income.

Some stereotypes also underpinned notions of social stratification and mobility. A direct relationship existed between the ability to fulfill personal goals within the existing social structure and education: education yielded capabilities with which desired occupations could be obtained; these, in turn, generated a means with which income could be increased. Education occurred during one's youth and ended when one obtained employment. The entrance and exit from the work force operated in an abrupt and irreversible manner, with relatively structured patterns of deferred gratification delineating career patterns. Systems of social security operating within this context encouraged individual accomplishment and, when paths to social mobility failed or proved limited, these systems served to protect individuals against corresponding vulnerabilities. In the majority of the countries of the region, however, poor sectors remained outside of or marginalized from the protectionist mechanisms of the state.

These patterns, regardless of the extent to which they found concrete expression within society, provided the foundations upon which the structures of vulnerabilities associated with the welfare state in the past were based. Recent processes of change have questioned the validity of such notions and transformed the very core of the welfare state by weakening the once strong association between work and social security. Profound processes of social change in Latin America and around the world suggest that old forms of social security no longer suffice; new ones must be found.

Multilateral organizations and global agencies espouse programs containing new and different proposals (e.g., safety nets, work fare, minimum wage requirements), many of which wield or will wield significant influence on the future of welfare in the region. It is hoped that corresponding social policies will reengender the integrative and redistributive functions performed in the past by the welfare state rather than reproduce or deepen the segmented and exclusionary character of Latin American societies. It is thus necessary that the current debate about programmatic proposals be expanded. The current debate requires that active participation be extended beyond the circle of global agencies via the formation of an accountable political arena within and between countries (Deacon 1995). Latin American countries are increasingly unable to resolve their problems within the context of national policy. Social problems plaguing the region—and their solutions—have a crucial international component.

NOTES

1. The development diamond, based on four key indicators, shows the average level of development of a country compared to its income group, GNP per capita, life expectancy, gross primary enrollment, and access to safe water. See World Bank (1994).

2. The origins of this particular approach can be traced to the seminal work of Karl Polany (1957). Other examples can be found in James C. Scott (1976) and Eric Wolf (1969).

3. See Popkin (1979) for a critical perspective on this approach.

4. CEMIT index refers to gainfully employed persons who work more than 20 hours per week (monthly labor income capacity equivalent). It is computed by dividing

the monthly equivalent of hourly income by the per capita income at the poverty line. See ECLAC (1991, 1993, 1994).

5. The study by Minujin and Kessler (1995) is one of the few examples of a study of the middle sectors. The authors examine the concept of vulnerability as applied to the nonpoor, the middle classes, and the integrated working classes. The study describes and analyzes multiple paths of eroding well-being in certain social segments.

6. See ECLAC (1983, chapter 1).

7. Naturally, high rates of unemployment are not the only consequence of technological determinism; they also depend on policies and politics. The changing role of unemployment in welfare regimes is illustrative. In the past, for many welfare regimes, full employment was considered the necessary partner of the welfare state.

8. For a full discussion on the impact of technological change on employment in the textile and financial sectors, see Argenti and Filgueira (1985) and Filgueira and Argenti (1984).

9. See Portes (1950).

10. See Tokman (1982) and Moser (1978).

11. The issues addressed in this section build on the information and analyses contained in ECLAC (1991, 1993, 1994).

12. Differences in social and community organization extend beyond the urban-rural dichotomy. Mechanisms of solidarity and integration obviously operate within more specific circumstances. For a full discussion, see Perelman (1976).

13. Between 1970 and 1990 the percentage of urban households falling below the poverty line increased in Brazil from 35% to 39% and in Mexico from 20% to 30%. In Colombia, contrarily, this figure fell from 38% to 35%. Estimates of rural poverty remain less precise; in Brazil, such figures fell from 73% to 53%; no reliable estimates exist for the other countries of the region. More recently (1990–92), the percentage of poor households in urban areas increased by 3% in Colombia and fell by 4% in Mexico. See Altimir (1979) and ECLAC (1993).

14. At the beginning of the 1980s, in Bolivia, Ecuador, El Salvador, and Honduras, between 80% and 90% of the economically active population were not covered by social security; in Argentina and Uruguay one-third were not covered; the rest of the countries fell somewhere around the regional average of approximately 50%. For a full discussion, see Mesa-Lago (1985).

15. See Hicks (1995).

REFERENCES

Altimir, O. 1979. La dimensión de la pobreza en América Latina. *Cuadernos de la CEPAL* no. 27.

———. 1981. La pobreza en América Latina: Un examen de conceptos y datos. *Revista de CEPAL* no. 13.

Argenti, G., and C. Filgueira. 1985. Tecnología y sociedad: Algunas precisiones para el caso uruguayo. *Cuadernos de CIESU* no. 51.

Deacon, B. 1995. Global Institutions, Social Policy and Social Development. Paper presented at the Summit on Social Development, UNRISD (United Nations Research Institute for Social Development), Copenhagen.

ECLAC. 1983. *Cambios en el perfil de las familias: La experiencia regional.* Santiago de Chile: ECLAC.

———. 1990. *Transformación productiva con equidad.* Santiago de Chile: ECLAC.

———. 1991, 1993, 1994. *Panorama social de América Latina.* Santiago de Chile: ECLAC.

Esping-Andersen, G. 1990. *The Three Worlds of Welfare Capitalism.* Princeton: Princeton University Press.

Filgueira, C., and G. Argenti. 1984. Implicaciones del conflicto entre tecnología y sociedad. CIESU (Centro de Informaciones y Estudios del Uruguay) Documento de Trabajo no. 65. Montevideo: CIESU.

Flora, P. 1987. *Growth to Limits: The Western European Welfare State since World War II.* Berlin: Walter de Gruyter.

Heclo, H. 1974. *Modern Social Polities in Britain and Sweden.* New Haven: Yale University Press.

Hicks, P. 1995. Establishing an Effective Social Policy Agenda with Constrained Resources. In *Social Policy in a Global Society,* edited by D. Morales-Gómez and M. Torres. Ottawa: International Development Research Centre.

Malloy, J. M. 1985. Statecraft, Social Security Policy and Crisis: A Comparison of Latin America and United States. In *The Crisis of Social Security and Health Care,* edited by C. Mesa-Lago. Pittsburgh: University of Pittsburgh.

Marshall, T. H. 1950. *Citizenship and Social Class.* Cambridge: Cambridge University Press.

Mesa-Lago, C., ed. 1985. *The Crisis of Social Security and Health Care.* Pittsburgh: University of Pittsburgh.

Molina, S., and S. Piñera. 1979. *La pobreza en América Latina: Situación, evolución y orientaciones de políticas.* ECLAC Working Paper, E/CEPAL/PROY. Santiago: ECLAC.

Minujin, A., and G. Kessler. 1995. *La Nueva Pobreza en la Argentina.* Buenos Aires: Planeta.

Moser, C. 1978. Informal Sector or Petty Commodity Production: Dualism or Dependence in Urban Development. *World Development* 6 (September), no. 9/10: 1041–65.

Offe, C. 1992. Un diseño No-Productivista para las políticas sociales. In *Arguing for Basic Income: Ethical Foundations for a Radical Reform,* edited by Philippe van Parijs. London: Verso.

O'Connor, J. 1973. *The Fiscal Crisis of the State.* New York: St. Martin's Press.

Papadópulos, J. 1992. *Seguridad social y política en el Uruguay.* Montevideo: CIESU.

Perelman, J. 1976. *The Myth of Marginality: Urban Poverty and Politics in Rio de Janeiro.* Berkeley: University of California Press.

Piven, F. F., and R. A. Cloward. 1971. *Regulating the Poor.* New York: Vintage.

Polanyi, K. 1957. *The Great Transformation: The Political and Economic Origins of Our Time*. New York: Rinehart & Co.
Popkin, Samuel. 1979. *The Rational Peasant: The Political Economy of Rural Society in Vietnam*. Berkeley: University of California Press.
Portes, A. 1950. *En torno a la informalidad: Ensayos sobre la teoría y medición de la economía no regulada*. Mexico City: FLACSO.
PREALC. 1993. América Latina: Un crecimiento económico que genera más empleo, pero de menor calidad. *PREALC Bulletin* (September), no. 32.
Scott, James C. 1976. *The Moral Economy of the Peasant: Rebellion and Subsistence in Southeast Asia*. New Haven: Yale University Press.
Tokman, V. 1982. Unequal Development and the Absorption of Labor: Latin American Experiences, 1950–1980. *CEPAL Review* no. 17.
Wolf, Eric R. 1969. *Peasant Wars of the Twentieth Century*. New York: Harper & Row.
World Bank. 1994. *Social Indicators of Development*. Baltimore: Johns Hopkins University Press.

7 | The Crisis of Old Models of Social Protection in Latin America

New Alternatives for Dealing with Poverty

DAGMAR RACZYNSKI

Social policies and issues of social reform are increasingly on the political agenda of the countries of Latin America. The model of social policy that evolved during the twentieth century has been discredited. New orientations for social policies, most of them instrumental, are being proposed, diffused, and implemented.

This chapter starts with an overview of the "old system" of social policies, highlighting its achievements and problems. We then take up emergent trends centered on the redefinition of the roles of the state, the market, and community (civil society) and on proposals of decentralization, privatization, and targeting. The issue of social policy content and the challenge of designing public policy that responds to the diversity of poverty situations are central concerns throughout.

The content of the chapter is very much conditioned by the experience of Chile. Within Latin America, Chile, together with Uruguay, is a pioneer; in the 1920s it began to build a system of social policies that expanded steadily up into the 1970s, covering increasing proportions of the population. In the mid-1970s Chile again led the way in incorporating new orientations into its social policies—targeting, decentralization, privatization, incorporation of market mechanisms, and demand-driven subsidies. In the 1990s the design of social policies has shifted, centering on issues of equity, social integration, and participation. The results and impact of these innovations on poverty and inequity are under debate.

The "Old Model" of Social Protection in Latin America: Origins, Content, and Achievements

In the 1930s and 1940s Latin American countries initiated an economic strategy of import-substituting industrialization. The countries closed themselves to international trade, and the state encouraged and subsidized the growth of national industry and domestic markets for manufactured goods. The state played a leading role. It protected national industry through import tariffs, tax policies, and favorable prices. It invested directly in industry and infrastructure, and it assumed direct management of the main productive and financial activities. While enormous differences existed in the way individual countries implemented this development strategy and its outcomes, the Southern Cone countries were the first to adopt and adhere more closely to these orientations.

Within the framework of this economic strategy some countries of the region developed a system of social policies. This "old system" was significant in some countries (including Argentina, Brazil, Chile, Colombia, Costa Rica, and Mexico) while in others (for example, Bolivia, Ecuador, and Peru) it was weak or nonexistent. In the latter, social policies, with the exception of education, showed enormous discontinuity and did not build up a system of social services.

The beginning of public social policies in the region can be traced to the building of the nation-state and the first steps in the process of industrialization, the growth of cities, and the weakening of the traditional social order based on the *hacienda*. Accelerated urban and mining upheavals were influential in generating government and state involvement in social issues. Political elites, inspired by the emerging social legislation in Europe, influenced by the social encyclicals of the Catholic church, and guided by recommendations from international organizations (of which the International Labor Organization was probably the most important), pushed in that direction.

The growth of the system in the 1940s, 1950s, and 1960s responded principally to characteristics of the political representation system and its relation with the state and with the socioeconomic base. Garretón (1994, 243) poses a "classical sociopolitical matrix" where "the state has played a referential role for all collective action—development, social mobility and mobilization, redistribution of wealth and the integration of the grassroots sector—but it has had little autonomy with regard to society and is the target of all sorts of pressures and demands." Mesa-Lago (1978) has documented for several countries in the region how the organized segments of society (middle strata, industrial bourgeoisie, urban workers, and public employees) pressured the state, through their organizations and political parties, with demands for social security and health care.

Concepts such as *populismo*, *estado de compromiso*, and *estado nacional-popular* include references to this dynamic. The underlying traits of this system were an increased presence of the state throughout the whole of society, the central role of politics,[1] and a feeble presence of the actors of the socioeconomic base ("civil societies").[2] This "mobilizing state" embodied three types of objectives: national integration, economic growth, and redistribution of income. "It did not separate economic policy and social policy, modernization, and the strengthening of national unity; in fact it tried to combine them all in a single model that was designed by the state, not negotiated at a parliamentary level by the social partners themselves" (Touraine 1994, 46).

The realm of social policy included sectoral policies in education, health, social security, and housing; wage and labor regulations; and basic consumer price policies. In the 1960s some countries formulated policies to support social organization in urban and rural areas (promotion of urban neighborhood organizations, rural cooperatives, and labor unions). These were state-led, top-down policies. During the same period some countries, alleging social and poverty-combating aims, initiated structural reforms that affected the distribution of property (agrarian reform and nationalization of mining and industrial enterprises).

The system operated under the assumption that highly subsidized state services would benefit all population strata. Special poverty alleviation programs were rare. Those that existed were mainly public work programs to provide employment during periods of economic recession and rising unemployment and food distribution programs delivered autonomously or as part of other health or educational programs.

To varying degrees, the countries became equipped with social service infrastructures, and demand for such services grew (although significant disparities existed in regional and rural-urban distribution). Gross enrollment rates in primary education expanded, as did the proportion of the population covered by social security, health programs, and state-subsidized housing. The systems' coverage expanded, particularly in primary and secondary education and to a lesser degree in social security and health.

The process of economic development and the extension of social services to vast sectors of the urban population brought important transformations in the productive structure (technological development and expansion of the industrial base), growth rates that were among the most rapid in the developing world, and advances in traditional human development indicators (literacy, level of schooling, infant and child mortality, and life expectancy at birth). Improvements in overall welfare were more pronounced in countries that were able to build up a system of social policies with wide coverage: Chile, Costa Rica, and Uruguay were most outstanding.

The process of development, including social policies, yielded results that modified the profile of the problems and the sociocultural traits of the population: The poor are no longer illiterate; they avail themselves of health services; they have fewer children; and families are smaller. Old vulnerabilities became less acute while new ones emerged. The countries entered the intermediate and advanced stages of the demographic transition and began an epidemiological transition. Traditional health problems coexist with modern ones. The quantitative goal of basic education coverage has been phased out, while issues of equity and quality of education have moved to the forefront.

The population has become increasingly urban. Middle- and working-class strata expanded and benefited from economic and social development. The social structure showed symptoms of upward social mobility, mainly of the structural type—growth of middle strata, rural-urban migration, and urbanization. Poor families managed to meet some of their basic needs and invested in the education of their children. Poverty profiles have changed: poverty is more urban and the poor in the metropolitan areas live in a situation of increasing geographical segregation. Poverty is more heterogeneous than in the past. In the 1970s and 1980s, traditional poor population groups were joined by the "new poor," the "pauperized" middle strata expelled from the labor market because of economic recession and restructuring.

Institutional Arrangements and Benefits

As a consequence of a growth dynamic marked by pressure group politics, the system expanded by adding specific benefits to specific groups in an unorganized way. Coverage increased, but benefits were highly stratified and fragmented. Groups with stronger organizations and more power to influence the state got more and better benefits and/or contributed less to the financing of the system. The central stratification lines were drawn according to the size of the economic enterprise with which the individual was associated and his/her occupational position, type of economic activity, and rural vs. urban residence.

Multiple institutions developed, servicing different segments of the population with different rules and conditions and delivering benefits that differed in quantity and quality. Over time, some of the smaller fragmented institutions were amalgamated into larger ones. Service delivery became the responsibility of big, highly centralized institutions of national or federal (never local) character. Most of the institutions were state owned or owned jointly by the state and labor associations.

State expansion generally paralleled shrinking private, community, or labor association services. The space for a private market of social services was small with clients being reduced to elite population groups (higher social strata) who often used the highly subsidized public facilities (curative health, university education). The state simultaneously assumed policy design, service delivery, and financial functions. The evaluative and control functions were of an administrative-legal-financial type, managed in some situations by autonomous comptrollership entities. The social impact of policies and programs was unknown and unexamined until the end of the 1960s.

Sectoral organization predominated, leaving little space for multisectoral interventions. Each sector defined standardized products that were formally homogeneous for all public services of similar type and sometimes obligatory for the private sector (e.g., educational curricula). Programs and procedures were the same throughout a country, with little adaptation to unique regional or local conditions. Nevertheless, the quality of services rendered differed significantly according to the social sector being served, thus reproducing initial inequalities.

In addition, labor legislation had a protectionist character, centering on regulations to protect workers' rights (to associate and organize, to bargain collectively, to strike, not to be dismissed at will) and to establish minimum levels of compensation for work and basic standards for decent working conditions. As in social security and health, the regulations allowed different rules and benefits for different workers, leaving behind agriculture and traditional productive units (small enterprises and the informal sector). Severance pay (the right to compensation when laid off) was rarely included anywhere.

The system was highly "legal" in character; rules and regulations abounded. Many of them were rarely respected or followed, however, contributing to an enormous gap between legal regulations and actual practice and opening the door to discretionary decisions, clientelistic relationships in the allocation of resources, and corruption, though these problems were less acute in countries with a strong autonomous public comptrollership institution.

Local organization and social participation were nonissues, despite the fact that in many countries the responsibility for meeting social needs was in the hands of the family and community. Instead of creating programs to efficiently complement and encourage family and community action, the state's meddling in social matters often inhibited community initiatives. Even in countries where governments did support social organization, and "social promotion" activities took place, these measures were vertically imposed and left little space for local or community responses.

Public Spending: Financing and Distribution

The financing in labor, health, and social security initially came from tripartite mandatory contributions from workers, employers, and the state. Over time, financing was increasingly transferred to the state. Educational spending was financed by general revenues. Financing of social security and health and the tax system were inefficient; all showed high degrees of evasion. Financing of social security, a pay-as-you-go system, imposed significant taxes on the hiring of labor, which according to some interpretations had negative consequences on the creation of jobs in the formal sector and on social security affiliation and financing.

As benefits and coverage of the system expanded, public/fiscal spending grew, reaching figures that represented over 20% of gross national product in some countries. The growth in spending was seldom offset by increased revenues, creating budgetary imbalances and inflationary pressures. The conservation of basic macroeconomic balances was not seen as important. Attempts to brake expansion of public expenditure, if they existed at all, were unsuccessful. Social spending was procyclical, however, and negative variations in per capita expenditures followed economic downturns.

Social security tended to receive a concentrated share of the intersectoral distribution of public social spending—as much as 40–50% in the Southern Cone countries. While this percentage was lower in other countries of the region, age structure and the pressure of occupational groups and labor unions were important factors explaining the high level of participation.

Within the intrasectoral distribution of health and education expenditures, complex services were favored. Health delivery largely centered around curative care, with investments in hospitals, specialized medicine, and physicians, rather than on preventative, primary health care. There were some notable exceptions to this trend, however. Costa Rica, Chile, and Colombia implemented maternal and child health and nutrition programs with vast coverage. Spending in education became increasingly oriented toward the postsecondary area, mainly the university level. Public university education was free and, in some countries, even private universities were highly subsidized by the state. Clearly, educational expenditures at this level were (and continue to be) regressive. In all of this, the allocation of resources to services and programs was supply driven; subsidies were handed out to schools and universities, health establishments, and housing construction firms, giving them an incentive to spend. This resulted in a multiplication of activities that were not monitored for productivity results or achievements, a situation unlikely to lead to efficient solutions.

Around 1970 the overall distribution of public spending was regressive. Middle and higher strata got more and better benefits than the lower ones. Without exception, expenditures in social security, postsecondary education, and housing were regressive, though basic education and maternal and child health had a progressive distribution in most countries.

Crisis of the Old Model of Social Protection

Despite important achievements, the system of social policies that developed in the region accumulated problems. Various circumstances contributed to the crisis of the old model, including weaknessness and difficulties inherent in the system. Economic stagnation due to increasing difficulties in the import-substitution development strategy was an important factor. Additional situations, external to the system, inevitably brought change. The most significant were:

- The oil crisis of the 1970s and the debt crisis of the 1980s. Coupled with the limits of the import substitution development strategy and expansionary macroeconomic policies, these crises resulted in macroeconomic disequilibria, inflation, and external financial imbalances.
- Pressures from international and multilateral agencies to implement structural adjustment programs in which a central element was the reduction of social expenditures. This measure was accompanied by highly targeted, short-term, compensatory poverty alleviation programs (safety nets, social emergency funds), policies previously unknown in the region.
- The fiscal crisis of the European Welfare State and the diffusion of neoliberal ideology which generally discredits state services in favor of market-oriented models of private welfare and targeting schemes. The fall of socialism in Eastern Europe pushed in the same direction. At the same time the experience of Southeast Asia revealed that the state does matter and that state-supported expenditures on education, health, and nutrition, and investments in human capital are sine qua non conditions for economic growth and social equity.

Emerging Trends and New Policy Orientations

The Latin American experience has shown the limits of the import-substitution industrialization strategy and its nonviability in the global world of the 1990s. The region learned that it is an error to use expansionary macroeconomic policy to pursue social and redistributive goals. In every case (e.g., Allende in Chile, Alan García in Peru) the result was triple digit (or higher) annual inflation, with the poorest sectors suffering disproportionately. The region learned that social development and poverty reduction depend on steady economic growth and the creation of productive employment. However, economic growth is a necessary but not a sufficient condition to achieve these aims. Economic growth does not mechanically and homogeneously benefit the entire population. Trickle down effects are not always present and even when present they are rather slow in reaching the poorest population groups.

It is possible to identify growth paths that accelerate poverty reduction and others that are "immune" to poverty alleviation. For example, in Chile economic growth in the second half of the 1970s was "immune" while in the second half of the 1980s and in the 1990s it was highly favorable for poverty reduction. Empirical evidence indicates that the links between economic growth and poverty reduction (measured by income) are employment and the evolution of real salaries and wages. The data also suggest that some poor segments of the population are able to overcome poverty as the economy grows and jobs are created, while others are left behind. Growth may cause new segments of the population to fall into poverty (noncompetitive sectors, sectors undergoing significant technological innovation, or sectors affected by changes in the labor market). These dynamic aspects of poverty are rarely looked at, mainly for lack of data. Information on these aspects should be essential ingredients in the design of poverty programs.

Because economic growth by itself is not enough, social policies and programs are crucial. This is particularly true in the present context where market competition in the global international economy, coupled with rapid technological innovation and change, make education and knowledge the main productive factor. Furthermore, transformations in the organization of production and of labor markets create situations of labor flexibility, job mobility, and increased job instability. The mobility and speed of exchanges of information, news, people, goods, and services increase daily. Geographical barriers are easily transcended. Language (and to a lesser extent, cultural) barriers are weakening. International mobility and diminished cultural distance affect the middle and higher social strata more than the lower ones, increasing social distance within countries.[3] Social policies that aim at social integration are more necessary than ever.

The way of approaching social matters has changed, with the current emphasis on expenditure restrictions, efficiency, decentralization, privatization, targeting, cost recovery, demand-driven subsidies, and the introduction of market mechanisms into the functioning of the public sector. (Figure 7.1 compares the neoliberal model that prevailed in the 1980s and the emerging model of the 1990s.) Other issues under debate are the locus of poverty programs in the social policy realm; the conceptual definition of poverty that guides social policies; the advisability of adjusting poverty programs to meet the specific characteristics and determinants of diverse poverty situations; and the methods of monitoring social programs and evaluating their impact on the living conditions of the poor and on equity and social integration.

Various policy proposals are under discussion and in a state of flux. The adoption and implementation of recommendations have been very different from country to country, depending on economic and political conditions; the system of social policies that existed in the past; the characteristics of the social structure; the magnitude and profile of poverty; the capacity of effective state action; and the role of organizations, institutions, and actors of civil society. This social policies debate cannot be separated from the broader issues concerning development strategy and political transitions, particularly the redefinition of the role of the state in a context of a market economy and political democracy and the interrelationship between economic and social policies.

The sections that follow present the main positions on these questions and take up some of the challenges of the instrumental options that are being implemented.

The Relationship among the State, the Market, and Society

The redefinition of the role of the state has been approached from a quantitative and a qualitative point of view. The quantitative approach is represented by authors who support the neoliberal view that the market provides the best means of efficiently allocating resources. The role of the state should be as small as possible, limited to intervening only in areas with important externalities, assisting those segments of the population that do not have the means or resources to participate in the market, and guaranteeing external defense. In social matters this view translates into highly targeted social programs and the privatization of services that attend nonpoor strata.

For others the issue is not primarily the economic size of the state. What are at stake are the functions the state should play, the type of relationship it establishes with the economy and society, and its managerial capacity. Tomassini (1994) talks about the realignment of functions between the state and public society. Ozlak (1994) calls for a redefinition of the boundaries of what is public and what is private and of the interrelationships between both. Bradford (1994b, 23) compares the interventionist, inward-looking role of the state, identified with import-substitution industrialization of the postwar era in Latin America, and the minimalist role, identified with the trade and market liberalization of the neoliberal period in the 1980s "with a strategic or catalytic role of the state." The state assumes leadership in articulating a vision, mobilizing support and setting policy priorities and constructing flexible and innovative mechanisms to engage the state and civil society and the private sector. For Garretón (1994, 244) "the issue at hand is not to have the state play a lesser role, but rather to reform the state: modernize it, decentralize it, reorganize it in such a way as to make it participatory." He adds, "We must not expect the state to be a unifying agent for the life of society and the diversity of its actors, but we definitely need state intervention for the constitution of spaces and institutions within which actors can come forth who are autonomous with regard to the state, without being marginal" (1994, 245). Kliksberg (1994b) encourages the move from the formerly prevalent view of the state versus civil society to one that sees the state as facilitating and creating adequate conditions for private enterprise and civil society. He calls this view "state plus civil society."

It has become common to distinguish among a general policy-setting and regulative function, a financial and resource-allocation function, a program

Figure 7.1 Models of Social Protection in Latin America

Dimensions	Old model	Neoliberal model	Emergent model
Economic policy/ social policy	Weak relationship. Fiscal unbalance.	Social policy subordinated to economic policy. Fiscal balance attained mainly by cuts in expenditures.	Social policy integrated with and complementary to economic policy. Fiscal balance based on revenues and expenditures.
Goal/purpose/ function of social policies	Building of the nation-state; industrialization; social integration.	Poverty alleviation; satisfaction of basic needs of the poor.	Growth with equity; social integration; poverty reduction.
Policy content and orientation	Supply and coverage of social services (education, health, social security, housing). Standardized programs and procedures across a country. Little adaptation to regional or local conditions. Protective labor legislation. Price subsidies for basic consumer goods.	Supply of basic social services for the poor. Reach poverty pockets. Special poverty alleviation (safety net) programs. Standardized programs and procedures. Minimum of labor regulation. Maximum of flexibility for the firm. Privatization of social security and social services that attend the nonpoor population.	Equity and quality of education and health. Reach poverty pockets with programs that support capabilities and opportunities (youth training, urban and rural small productive activities, support to community organizations and social participation). Adaptation of program content and methodology to the diversity of poverty situations. Labor regulations that protect labor mobility.
Roles of the state, market, and civil society	State dominance (formulates, regulates, finances, delivers social services and programs). Little space for private markets and community initiatives.	State designs, regulates, and finances programs for the poor. Privatization of social services for the nonpoor and administration and delivery of state financed services for the poor by the private sector and local units of the state.	State designs, regulates, and evaluates social services and programs. It also contributes to the financing and may deliver services.

Figure 7.1 Continued

Dimensions	Old model	Neoliberal model	Emergent model
Centralization/ decentralization	Centralized.	Centralized national programs oriented toward the poor. Deconcentration of education and health services.	Decentralization.
Logic of decision-making	Bureaucratic. State dominance with heavy influence of corporate interests and groups. Centrality of political considerations. Top down decision-making.	Incorporation of technical-analytic and economic considerations. Top down decision-making.	Incorporation of technical-analytic and economic considerations. Development of instruments for regional and local decision-making, community participation, and public-private collaboration.
Financing 1. General orientation	General and specific taxes plus workers' and employers' mandatory social security and health contributions.	Taxes and workers' mandatory social security and health contributions. State finances only services for the poor. Cost recovery.	Taxes and workers' mandatory social security and health contributions. State finances basic social services for the population. Cost recovery.
2. Allocation of public resource	Supply-driven mechanisms. Historic allocation trends.	Introduction of demand-driven mechanisms. Allocation according to poverty indexes.	Combination of demand- and supply-driven mechanisms, which vary depending on the objectives of specific programs. Allocation according to poverty indexes in some programs.
3. Level and trends in public expenditures	Growing.	As low as possible, depending on the size of the poor population and fiscal balance.	No definite trend. Fiscal balance is central and can be obtained through less spending and more revenues.
Targeting	Little concern. Emphasis on nominally universal programs.	Strong concern to reach only the poor. Design and implementation of targeting tools. Preference for demand targeting.	Strong but not exclusive concern. Country requires investment in non-targeted programs. Combinations of various targeting mechanisms.

Source: Based on Raczynski (1995b) and ECLAC (1995).

implementation or service-delivery function, and a policy-monitoring and evaluation function. In the old model these functions were ill-defined, intermingled, and all in the hands of the state, which was segmented sectorally. What is proposed is a state that plays an active policy-setting and regulative role, assumes monitoring and evaluation functions, and participates in and regulates the financial function. Program implementation and service delivery should be transferred as much as possible to nonstate agents: civil society, the private sector, nongovernmental organization (NGOs), grassroots social organizations, labor organizations, and regional and local entities (Bradford 1994b, 42).

The transition that states in the region are expected to make is not easy. In order to assume an effective strategic or catalytic role in poverty and equity matters, it is necessary to support and develop its managerial capacities and technical skills. Innovations are difficult owing to strong inertial pressures to retain past conditions and decisions, the lack of coordination among sectoral ministries and among services, lack of political leadership skills in social matters, and the presence of corporate interests and political pressures that push toward initiatives that many times do not favor equity and/or the fight against poverty.

Economic Policy and Social Policy

That economic growth and macroeconomic balance are prerequisites for social development, equity, and poverty reduction is undisputed in the region. That social policies matter is not disputed either. Yet, for some, the sole aim of social policies is to protect the poor, while for others poverty alleviation and the satisfaction of basic needs of the poor is only one dimension of social development. The first group sees a trade-off between economic growth and social expenditures. For the latter, there are important complementary relationships between both.

Implementing targeted social programs and safety nets, historically nonexistent in most countries of the region, is the priority for the first group. They recognize the importance of investment in human capital (education, health) for economic growth, but they believe state-supported policies should benefit only the poorer strata of society, those who are unable to pay market prices for these services. Fiscal expenditures should be as small as possible because they conflict with economic growth. The financing of expenditures (taxes and other mandatory contributions) negatively affects investment, and social programs, if generous in benefits, will create state dependency, disincentives to work, and even family disintegration.

The second position holds the state responsible for providing opportunities for the integration of the poor into the economy and society and for strengthening their capabilities to take advantage of societal opportunities. A report by the UN Economic Commission on Latin American and the Caribbean contends that the challenge for Latin America is to integrate effectively economic and social policies, so that both become an integral part of the development strategy. It defines education and knowledge—human capital in a broad sense—as the main factor in an open economy for achieving simultaneous economic growth and equity. Productivity and investment in human capital have to go hand in hand. Basing economic competitiveness and growth on low wages, favorable exchange rates, and unregulated exploitation of natural resources is a false premise. The challenge is to achieve economic competitiveness with high wages and a healthy price system that incorporates the costs and benefits of social development, of natural resources exploitation, etc. (ECLAC 1990; ECLAC-UNESCO 1992). The aim is growth with equity. Economic policies and social policies are complementary and have to be formulated hand in hand. Notwithstanding important restrictions, public expenditures must not become minimalist. Tax reforms that increase resources without negatively affecting economic growth are possible and necessary; improving the state's technical and managerial skills will make programs and expenditures more cost/benefit efficient.

Decentralization and Participation

Both positions referred to above propose the deconcentration and decentralization of the state apparatus. Many countries of the region are transferring areas of responsibility and resources from the central or federal level of government to subnational levels, preferably to the local one. The idea is to bring services and programs closer to the people and pave the way for greater social participation. The driving arguments are efficiency to respond more rapidly and adequately to the needs of the poor and democracy (local citizenship).

Social policies in Latin America traditionally have been highly centralized, bureaucratic, and sectorially segmented, with nationally standardized provisions for education and health services by the state that did not respond to the demands of the diverse population segments. The decisions by countries to change from a centralized to a decentralized system have occurred in different political and economic moments and have taken different paths. All countries have encountered barriers and difficulties, among which the following stand out:

- The policy space actually open at the local (municipal) level is rather small. Economic and human resources, and the training necessary to manage social services and programs are feeble. At the same time, political processes at this level are often guided by partisan or corporate interests which generally do not favor equity and poverty aims.
- Resource allocation continues to follow a centralized and sectoral logic. National or federal decisions, as well as decisions of private investors, impinge

upon the local territory without providing local authorities with adequate information and/or decision-making power. The resources invested or taken away by these "external agents" surpass many times those of local government, altering and/or conflicting with local priorities and decisions.
- Decentralization measures are often equivocal. Regional, provincial, and local governments have been created without a clear definition of their legal and economic competence. Education and health delivery have been decentralized, but management of human resources remains centralized. Deconcentration is more frequent than decentralization because ministries and central state services do not put full trust in the capacity of the lower levels of the state.
- Decentralization so far has not been favorable to territorial equity. Regional and local inequities in social conditions are correlated with the availability of resources. Municipalities with greater concentrations of poverty dispose of significantly fewer resources. Although municipal legislation often authorizes the redistribution of resources between rich and poor areas, the policy tools created are ineffective in diminishing the enormous disparities. Private and market-oriented investments often conflict with the intended territorial redistribution of resources.

Decentralization will always be incomplete if it takes place only at the level of the state apparatus. For an effective process of decentralization two main elements must exist: a decentralized and efficient state apparatus and organized, informed, local groups that are motivated to participate in local government. The tendency in the region is to transfer responsibility for executing social programs or delivering social services that receive state subsidies either to lower levels of the state apparatus or to nongovernmental agents, community organizations, or private commercial and service delivery enterprises. The idea is to create a space where new actors (e.g, the organized community, nongovernmental organizations) manage their needs and demands, collaborating with local government and superseding old oppositionist relationships. The expected result is more efficient and effective management of services and programs.

Achieving this result is not easy. Historically, decisions and actions of the central or federal state tended to inhibit autonomous societal mobilization, while autonomous social organizations acted in opposition to the state or subnational authorities. The convergence of both requires clarity with respect to levels and forms of social participation and its instrumentation at the local level. Little is known on this issue. Empowerment and accountability are concepts that only recently have been "imported" to the region.

In Chile the new relationship between the state and society operates through private and public biddings. This modality works to the extent that there is a "market" of NGOs, community organizations, and training agencies and schools that are informed, trained, and motivated to participate and to provide quality services or projects. Presently, the expansion of some programs is limited by shortages in this market. A problematic link in this instrumentation is that projects often are small and of short duration, spelling uncertainty and discontinuity for the program-executing agencies, preventing them from accumulating experience. The model may also stifle or frustrate community initiatives because of uncertainty of the bidding result and discontinuity of projects. Moreover, "bidding funds" have multiplied over time and overlap in their content, duplicating efforts. Coordination and complementarity between project initiatives and sustainability of the impact generated are main challenges. A territorial approach to poverty and the strengthening of local governments seem to be sine qua non conditions for the success of bidding funds as are adequate community diagnosis and poverty assessments.

In sum, the present situation reflects maladjustments between the system that consolidated during most of this century—centralized, vertical, sectorially organized, with homogenous and standardized programs—and the requirements of a decentralized system that prioritizes collaboration between the public and the private sectors and social participation that opens the way for geographically and socially differentiated programs. Despite advances, the process of decentralization still has a long way to go. It is essential to strengthen regional and local governments and civil society and to evaluate the social impact and sustainability of projects implemented by intermediate agents (NGOs, social organizations, and others).

Privatization

Privatization in the social sector has taken different paths in the region: subcontracting or outsourcing of services to the private sector; incentives for creating subsidized private schools and health services for the poor population; and authorization and design of private health, education, and social security institutions that serve the middle and higher social strata, restricting fiscal or public subsidies to the poor population groups.

The attention in this section is on the last and most drastic expression of privatization. Chile has been a pioneer in these privatizations and its experience in social security is being exported to various countries. Its experience in health is under critical scrutiny.

The Chilean social security reform

Chile had a pay-as-you-go social security system that evolved more or less as described in section I, accumulating inequities and inefficiencies. By 1970 the system, mandatory for wage earners, covered around 70–75% of the labor force, excluding self-employed workers, workers in small enterprises, and significant portions of rural workers. The main benefit of the old system was pensions.

Beginning in the 1980s, the military government replaced the old pay-as-you-go system, which was discredited and enormously problematic, with an individual capitalization system administered by the private sector. In the new system, which is also mandatory, the pension is the result of the accumulated lifelong contributions of the worker.

Administration of the contributions is in the hands of private corporations (Administradores de Fondos de Pensiones; AFPs) that take care of the funds operating in the financial market under regulations of the state. The state guarantees a minimum return based on the average return of the system in a given period. Each worker chooses the AFP he wants to affiliate with, having free choice at all times. Workers who participated in the old system had to choose whether to stay or transfer to the new system. In the latter case, a "seniority bond" was given for past contributions. A rapid and massive transfer of wage earners to the new system occurred, encouraged by economic incentives (an increase in net wages owing to the reduction of the mandatory social security contributions) and by the generalized discredit of the old system. The labor force covered by social security did not increase, however, as expected by the authors of the new system.

This system has both advantages and problems. Benefits are no longer tied to specific labor situations. Contributions and requirements are uniform, except for a lower retirement age for women.[4] Each affiliate accumulates for himself/herself so that, theoretically, strong incentives exist to contribute regularly and according to the real wage. The system eliminates the demographic impasse that pay-as-you-go systems inevitably face as the population ages. Administrative costs of the system are significant, owing to the commercial competition among AFPs to increase the number of their affiliates and to the right of the affiliate to change AFPs as many times and as often as desired.

The transfer of social security savings to private hands invigorated the Chilean financial market and through it, national and international investments. This transfer, however, resulted in a significant increase in the public sector deficit due to the transition from one system to the other. It is estimated that within 30 to 35 years, the state will have to allocate around 2% of GDP to social security, representing the expenditures of a state-guaranteed minimum pension for workers who, despite having made contributions for 20 years, do not have sufficient savings to finance a pension above the legally established minimum and of a welfare pension for the poor population over 65 years of age that contributed fewer than 20 years (or not at all) to social security.

From a poverty perspective, it is important to note that: (i) the system does not have social or intergenerational redistribution aims; (ii) it did not produce increased social security coverage, as expected by its authors; and (iii) the state guarantees a minimum pension and a social welfare pension, both defined annually by the Congress.

Growth and stability of the economy are at the heart of the system, for the returns to the funds accumulated in each individual account are tied to the behavior of the financial market. So far the average performance of this market has been favorable, but an economic crisis, like that of 1981, can destabilize the system. Currently the growth in AFPs is exceeding the capacity of the domestic market to absorb additional investments.

Another external factor that encroaches upon the system and on the future value of pensions is the situation of the labor market. Present trends in the Chilean labor market include more frequent temporal or seasonal contracts, implying a high percentage of irregular social security contributions. This will result in lower pensions and a likely increase in the future demand for state-guaranteed minimum pensions or welfare pensions.

The pensions paid so far under the new system are few in number. Rules, procedures, and options for becoming a pensioner are not simple and greater public information/education is needed.

The creation of private health insurance institutions
The other radical privatizing reform implemented in Chile was the creation of private for-profit organizations that operate with prepaid health insurance plans (Institutos de Salud Previsional; ISAPREs). Since 1981 social security affiliates have had the choice of placing their mandatory health payments (which previously went automatically to the public health fund) into an ISAPRE. The affiliate signs a private annual contract with an ISAPRE that specifies the monthly amount to be paid and the health care that is included, as well as maximum allowable charges and discounts. If the cost of the family health plan is higher than the mandatory contribution, the affiliate either pays the difference, looks for a cheaper health plan in the same or another ISAPRE, or stays in/returns to the state system. In the original design, if the cost of the health plan was less than the amount that corresponds to the mandatory health payment, the ISAPRE kept the balance; now the ISAPRE must save the difference for extraordinary health expenses of the affiliate.

The ISAPRE system expanded after receiving several special state supported incentives: (i) increases in the mandatory health contribution from 4% to 7% of taxable wages; (ii) elimination of ISAPRE responsibility to pay maternity leave to working mothers; and (iii) the option for employers to increase by 2% their payment to ISAPREs for workers who earned close to the minimum salary and to deduct that amount from their (the employers') taxes.

Presently around 25% of the population is affiliated with an ISAPRE. Affiliation is highly selective of higher and middle strata and the population with low health risks. This population gained greater freedom of choice in curative health care and lower copayment (out of pocket) costs. The health care costs for this segment of the population represent more than 50% of the total mandatory health contributions of the country.

The transfer of mandatory health contributions of these segments of the population to the ISAPREs stimulated the creation of medical infrastructure in high-income areas and contributed to an increasing emigration of professional resources from the public to the private sector. The private health sector, almost nonexistent in the past except for the *ejercicio liberal de la profesión* (physicians in private practice), is a new phenomenon in the country and represents a powerful new interest group. It has divided the unity of the national medical association and diminished its traditional commitment to social medicine.

A negative consequence of the creation of the private health system has been a decrease in resources for the public system which, nevertheless, continues to provide preventive health care for the entire population as well as serving 65–70% of the population with curative care.

The privatizing reform in the Chilean health sector clearly was socially regressive. Moreover, it probably stimulated health cost inflation and exacerbated longstanding administrative and organizational problems in the public health sector, which is in need of profound reforms. Partial and preliminary government proposals have provoked arduous debates and conflicts with the medical and paramedical professional associations and with the newly created private sector. Reform of the health sector and the definition of health policy are two of the most conflictive issues in the present Chilean public agenda.

Incorporating Market Mechanisms into the Operation of the Public Sector

Some Latin American countries have stimulated the incorporation of market mechanisms into the operation of the public sector. The main mechanism has been competition for clients and users among public establishments of similar type (schools, health clinics). This is expected to improve efficiency and the quality of services rendered. Another mechanism is cost recovery.

In Chile two resource allocation instruments have been developed. The first is a demand-driven subsidy (voucher) and the second is the transfer of resources to educational and health establishments according to indexes of school attendance or health services rendered. The implementation of both instruments has encountered difficulties, revealing the need for modification and/or requirements to ensure greater operational efficiency.

A demand-driven subsidy was adopted in housing. Poor families were able to make use of their vouchers only after interventions of the state that guaranteed: (i) an adequate supply of housing units for poor families; and (ii) a complementary financial market that would give credit to finance the difference between the value of the housing unit and that of the voucher plus the savings of the poor family (Vergara 1990).

In order to allocate resources to health services, prices were established for the services rendered. These prices were set administratively, without adequate information about real prices, and thus did not correspond to actual expenditures. Those in charge of the services rapidly learned which were the more profitable medical exams, consultations, or treatments and altered the supply of services accordingly. At the same time a tendency to segment health care into as many individual consultations as possible emerged. The amount of services rendered escalated and the system broke down. Since the change of government in 1990, resources at the primary level have been allocated according to population attended (per capita amount).

The financing mechanism applied in education was an educational subsidy paid according to the mean attendance of students in the previous month. This mechanism elevated administrative costs and introduced a series of distortions in the pedagogical practices. The latter were exacerbated by the fact that the per student subsidy lost purchasing power. These situations, combined with processes that negatively affected the labor situation of teachers, eroded the quality of primary and secondary education. After 1990 corrections were introduced in calculating the value of the per student subsidy, teachers' wages were improved, and a massive state program to improve the quality and equity of education (MECE) was implemented. Since 1993 the national educational test scores, which measure the extent to which students in specific schools have learned the school objectives expected for their level, have improved.

Thus the allocation of resources to poor families or to services for the poor requires a combination of supply and demand criteria. Information and accessibility to options are sine qua non conditions for demand to operate. If supply is inadequate or does not exist, the state must create incentives to increase it. Experience indicates that changes in the allocation of resources towards demand—without complementary measures on the supply side—do not necessarily translate into greater efficiency and/or better quality.

Two purposes have guided the incorporation of the cost recovery mechanism. One, as the term indicates, is to increase revenues through cost recovery. The other is targeting—to guarantee that the higher income strata do not benefit from public expenditures. Initial results in Chile have been mixed. In the area of public health, recovery of resources was rather low and targeting did not improve it. In education the introduction of fees at the university level has been positive from a distributive point of view. A new co-payment system has also been introduced at the secondary level of public education, but its outcome has not yet been evaluated.

Targeting

Chile was a pioneer in introducing targeting of social policies in Latin America. Targeting presumes that state action should only benefit the extremely poor—individuals or households who are unable to take care of their most urgent needs independently. It is based on the idea that it is possible to reduce public spending and balance the fiscal budget while also protecting the poorest segments of the population and reducing poverty. Focusing social spending only on the poor should save resources that otherwise would be captured by sectors able to pay and should thus enable more resources to be allocated to the poor. In this way, targeting would lead to higher efficiency in social spending.

The real world is not as simple. Targeted policies are not always more efficient and effective in reducing poverty (Besley and Kanbur 1988). Their efficiency and effectiveness often depend on the preexistence of universal programs, as the favorable evolution of infant mortality and nutrition indices, despite an increase in poverty, has shown. Universal mother and child health and nutrition programs supplemented by highly targeted actions for children and mothers at risk were a main factor that led to the gradual decrease in infant mortality in Chile (Raczynski 1995a). Thus, the relationship between targeted and universal programs is not necessarily a conflicting one. Both are needed, but for different situations.

Targeting can be inefficient from a political point of view. According to Bamberger:

> Programs geared exclusively to supplying the poor with benefits rarely have enough support to guarantee that the necessary resources for their uninterrupted operation will be available. Even though the necessary support is available to begin a program, in time this will be undermined, making it difficult to sustain the targeted programs (1993, 42–43).

An excessively targeted social program can produce undesired sociopolitical results, especially if middle strata who enjoyed benefits under pervious social policies are adversely affected. They are endowed with more political resources to mobilize against the government than poor sectors. If public policies do not partially meet the interests of these middle sectors, these policies can lead a fragile democracy to a stalemate (Nelson et al. 1989). Moreover, rigid targeting tends to cut off middle strata from public social services to which they have traditionally had access, which contributes to a dualization of society. The poor are served by targeted public services; the rich are served by private ones. The not-so-poor middle strata are attended by neither (Vergara 1990; Sojo 1990).

Achieving the benefits of targeting in social spending depends on overall public policy orientations, on macrosocial decisions, and on decisions taken at the level of specific programs. General policy orientations and budget allocations, in terms of the sectors and the level of care to which they are geared, are fundamental. Spending on primary education and primary health care in public establishments with wide population coverage tends to benefit the poor. However, exclusive allocation of resources to these levels has limits. As Raczynski and Oyarzo stated for the case of Chile:

The increase in maternal and child care, without an expansion of health expenditures, was made possible by a sharp reduction in public investment in health. In the medium term, this situation leads to a deterioration of facilities and equipment which has an adverse effect on the health care provided at the secondary and tertiary levels. The prevailing disease pattern in Chile since the mid-1970s shows that to improve the health indices of the whole population (not just children) these levels of health care need to be improved, in addition to primary health care (1981, 68).

Or, when educational coverage at the primary and secondary levels is wide, the demand is for support for postsecondary and technical-vocational training and for improving the quality and equity of basic education. Moreover, given the present international context where knowledge-intensive technology is the main productive factor, investments in research and technology cannot be neglected (ECLAC-UNESCO 1992).

In the case of specific programs it is necessary to decide whether targeting is appropriate and, if so, to choose among different targeting mechanisms. Generally, it is inappropriate to target programs to which the general population makes mandatory contributions and therefore has a rightful claim (e.g., social security). Nor is it appropriate to target the operating costs of free or subsidized basic education and health services. Universal coverage of these programs is fundamental to guarantee a minimum level of opportunities to the entire population (Crispi and Marcel 1993). To enhance equity, however, programs of universal coverage must be supplemented by specific programs targeted at the most vulnerable groups or at the most neglected services. Targeting is indispensable in programs geared to generating opportunities for the most deprived sectors to overcome the causes of poverty or vulnerability, as well as in welfare assistance programs.

The information required for efficient targeting decisions is not limited to identifying the poor population, as it is frequently understood to be. It should also include a diagnosis of the specific situations a program wants to modify, the most efficient mechanism for achieving the goal, the size of the destination group, and the most expeditious way of reaching it. Sometimes the best way to benefit people living in poverty is to work with nonpoor agents who can help generate opportunities for the poor. And sometimes working with socially heterogeneous groups, which integrate the poor with people from other economic levels, is a more effective approach to raising people out of poverty than highly targeted programs, which enclose the poor with each other, isolating them from the rest of society. (The field of education provides many cases in point.)

A variety of targeting mechanisms exist, and socioeconomic means testing is not necessarily the best. This mechanism, which discriminates the direct demand exerted by the population on a program or benefit, has considerable administrative and, frequently, psychosocial costs (social stigmatization, dependency on state programs, and stifling of the initiative and creativity of the users). At the same time, the error of inclusion (benefits filtering to nonpoor households) tends to be low and the error of exclusion (difference between the universe of the target group and the target population actually reached) high. Although the problem of inclusion is most frequently studied, the problem of exclusion is more important since the impact of a program on poverty likely depends more on its coverage of poor groups than on the spillover to nonpoor groups (Cornia and Stewart 1992), particularly in situations where targeting is politically ineffective.

Other targeting mechanisms include specifying territorial or geographical areas and selecting specific services (supply targeting). Each mechanism has its advantages and disadvantages. The suitability of one or the other, or of a combination of both, depends on the objectives and nature of the social programs concerned, the magnitude and characteristics of the country's poverty, institutional aspects, and the availability of timely and pertinent information (see Grosh 1992; Raczynski 1995a).

The preference for one or another type of targeting mechanism is related to political-conceptual perceptions of poverty and its determinants. If poverty is seen as an individual phenomenon causally associated with characteristics of the poor person or household, a demand-based targeting tool that screens the poor from the nonpoor will most likely be chosen. It assumes that direct transfers to the poor person or household will take him/her out of poverty. On the other hand, if poverty is understood as the result of the pattern of opportunities a household or a person faces and of the relationships of power in society, priority will be given to programs that act on the sociocultural and economic context in which the poor live. Programs will enhance local opportunities (e.g., productive resources, transportation, supply of services, social relationships) as well as individual and household capabilities. Under this approach geographic targeting and supply targeting will be preferred.

It is extremely important that countries accept targeting as a legitimate option, while recognizing that not all social programs should be targeted, that alternative ways of targeting exist, that universal and targeted programs are complementary, and that highly targeted programs are not necessarily the most efficient and effective ones from a political, social, or economic point of view. It is also essential to remember that targeting in no way guarantees the social impact of programs.

Conceptualization of Poverty and Social Policy Content

Poverty is certainly a priority, but it cannot constitute the sole objective of a country's social policy. Societies also need social security programs to protect the population from unemployment, illness, disability, and old age. And they need to support technological and scientific research and development, vocational training, higher education, etc. At the same time, combating poverty requires more than good social policies. Macro- and microeconomic policies, labor policies, and policies of infrastructure investments are as important, and often more important, than social policies that fight poverty.

In Latin America today poverty is approached primarily from an economic point of view. The issues under discussion center on revenues and the financing of social services and programs; on targeting and the economically efficient use of resources; and on how to protect the sectors negatively affected by structural adjustment, economic liberalization, and the opening of the economy to world markets. Only recently has the debate advanced to issues of policy content, examining the consistency between program designs and the diversity of poverty situations and its conditioning factors.

Definitions of poverty in the region follow a quantitative approach that identifies deficits and shortages and delimits absolute poverty. Poverty is measured by comparing family income with the cost of a basic food basket, combined at times with some measure of nonsatisfaction of basic needs, such as inadequate housing or low schooling. This way of looking at poverty is useful for some purposes: diagnosing the magnitude of the problem, its heterogeneity according to the specific combination of unsatisfied needs, and its geographical and rural-urban localization; and identifying poverty profiles (e.g., size and composition of household, sources of income, main activities of household members). Information on these topics contributes to the identification of geographical areas most in need and the estimation of shortages in income, housing, schooling, potable water, and so on, that need to be covered.

The usefulness of this information for elaborating the content and characteristics of specific poverty programs however, is limited, for it does not provide evidence on the conditioning factors of poverty nor on the process of poverty reproduction. It also ignores the cultural and psychological heterogeneity of the poor. It does not look at the potential, capabilities, and behavior of the population, social organization, and communities.

Twenty years ago a target group was defined as "a group of people who are not only all poor but also relatively homogeneous with respect to the effect that a given set of policy instruments might have upon them" (Bell and Duloy 1974, 91). The latter part of the definition has been forgotten. Among the poor, as many studies have revealed, there are different types of persons, households, and communities. The differences are associated not only with income level or the number and intensity of unsatisfied basic needs but also with the capabilities of the person, the household, and the community to discover and take advantage of opportunities. Some persons, households, and communities—the "active poor"—have high capabilities to solve their problems. Given an opportunity, they are able to supersede their situation. Another segment is "passive"; their capabilities latent. Solving their needs requires activating their capabilities and linking them to opportunities. A third segment represents the "refractory poor," those who have not been able to develop capabilities or whose abilities have been damaged. Poverty programs must recognize that these three segments will respond differently to specific policy instruments. The method of reaching the target population (the content and priority of a program and the methodology of social intervention) must be tailored to each case.

Social programs under the old model emphasized the generation of opportunities, understood as the supply of services, which in turn often generates capabilities, as in education. It was assumed that the poor would take advantage of these. In reality, the refractory poor and part of the passive poor did not use these services. Mechanisms had to be invented (school meals, food distribution at health posts) to attract these segments to the services. Combating poverty requires differentiated programs that simultaneously consider and link capabilities and opportunities. The active and latent capabilities of the poor emerge and are reinforced through local, participatory programs that address the needs identified by the target group.

The emerging trends in social policies—decentralization, locally based programs, social participation, and the new relationships among the state, market, and society—could open the way to flexible, innovative formulas that begin with the behavioral and cultural diversity of poverty situations, responding to and building on them. If this is so, a territorial approach to poverty will become prevalent. This approach hypothesizes that the place where one lives or works determines one's poverty history and opportunities; that a majority of the poor live in communities that concentrate poor people; and that to fight poverty it is important to address the characteristics of the places where the poor live or work, including the position and relationships of these places within the broader societal context. Empirical evidence in the region supports this approach.

Conclusion

The countries of Latin America are implementing a new generation of instrumental orientations in their social policies: decentralization, privatization, targeting, demand-driven subsidies, introduction of market mechanisms into the functioning of the public sector, public-private collaboration, and more flexible (less standardized) approaches to poverty.

In some countries these new approaches to social policy have coincided with a debate and measures to redefine the role of the state and to modernize its operation. In others the new instrumental orientations are implemented without touching the state apparatus; parallel structures, administered by the executive branch of government, have been created. In a few countries social policies and poverty programs are formulated as integral parts of a national development strategy, while in others the initiatives in the social area are isolated from measures taken in other dimensions of society and the economy.

This chapter has spelled out some of the complexities, tensions, and ambiguities in the proposals promulgated, providing specific examples from the Chilean experience. It is still too early to conclude from the available evidence whether a single model with national variations or several different models, are emerging.

The new orientations—decentralization, privatization, targeting, etc.—acquire different meanings depending on the political and economic context in which they take place, the stage of social development a country is in, and the characteristics of the state institutions and programs built up in the past. They further depend on the demographic size and ethnic and social composition of the population and on the development strategy each country is able to adopt and implement. Three dimensions of this strategy will mold the system of social policies of each country: (i) the role of the state and its relationship with the market and society/community; (ii) the interrelationship that is postulated and implemented between economic and social policy; and (iii) the political priority that governments and societies put on poverty and equity. Because of the different meanings and the variety of measures taken, often emphasizing different components, comparative studies are urgently needed to examine the objectives, meaning, and content of policies and to evaluate the results obtained from specific instruments.

We conclude that the interplay among the market, the state, and society in social matters depends on capabilities in the public and private sectors and at the community and family level—capabilities that differ among countries. Policies of decentralization often restrict themselves to deconcentrating the administration of activities without significantly affecting the decision-making space at the local and regional levels. It can be limited to the state apparatus without touching the relationship of the local level state with the community. Targeting can be done in different degrees and through various mechanisms without diminishing all universal programs; an adequate balance between both is needed.

We affirm that neither decentralization nor privatization per se ensure greater efficiency or equity. Privatization of social services presents difficulties from an equity and poverty perspective, as observed in the example of Chile's private health insurance institutions. The processes of decentralization are encountering multiple obstacles associated with inertia and characteristics of the state or administrative apparatuses, as well as with limits and weaknesses in the private sector, NGOs, and social organizations, which cast doubts on efficiency. At the same time, the impact of decentralization on equity depends strongly on state regulations and the definition of instruments that neutralize spatial and social inequities created by the market.

Increasing equity and reducing poverty are primarily political goals that require state will and leadership and a strong commitment from society. A nationally shared consensus on the priority of equity and poverty eradication and the political construction and legitimation of the measures taken (e.g., tax policies, formulation of programs, implementation of specific instruments), are both essential.

Increasing equity and poverty reduction are long-term tasks[5] that require good economic performance (sustained economic growth, creation of productive employment, fiscal balances), along with a national tradition of investment in basic social services (health, nutrition, education), policies designed to create opportunities for productive employment, and specific programs targeted to discrete geographical areas and/or social sectors that are especially vulnerable. The strategy must coordinate pertinent social programs, some universal and some targeted, that create opportunities for poor sectors; invest in human capital (quality of education, job training and retraining, basic health services); support small-scale productive units; and transfer information, social skills, and organization to the poor. Land redistribution, property ownership regulations (*saneamiento de títulos*), and clear legal definition of water rights are other important dimensions. Managerial capabilities to implement programs, solid work teams in local, regional, and national government and in the executing agencies (public or private), and skills for the technical handling of social policies are indispensable requirements for efficiency and effectiveness of social policies and programs.

Poverty programs must provide the poor with capabilities and tools and provide opportunities so that by their own effort they can become productively involved in the development process and gain access to the formal economic and social circuits.[6] Welfare and social assistance programs, such as emergency employment schemes, monetary transfers, and food distribution, should be the exception rather than the rule. Social investment and opportunities are the priority and the programs should be tailored to specific groups and sectors of the population, addressing their particular needs and incorporating their participation. Highly standardized national programs should be replaced by flexible ones that permit variations and adaptations to specific poverty situations, responding to the heterogeneity of the poor.

It is not enough, however, to implement programs only for the poor. Efforts must be made to create attitudes and behaviors in the nonpoor population that will prompt them to work with and for the poor, to diminish discrimination, and to raise equity and social justice to the position of primary national values.

NOTES

This chapter builds upon readings and research done over several years. My participation in the following three regional projects on poverty and social policies are fundamental inputs to the paper: "Social Policies for the Urban Poor in the Southern Cone of Latin America," coordinated by the Helen Kellogg Institute for International Studies; "Social Policy Research Priorities," coordinated by the International Development Research Centre (IDRC); and "Strategies to Combat Poverty in Latin America: Programs, Institutions and Resources," financed by the Inter-American Development Bank (IDB). I want to thank Víctor E. Tokman and Verónica Montecinos for their extensive comments on an earlier version of the chapter. Unfortunately I was not able to include all their important suggestions and comments; thus, the faults that remain are my own.

1. According to Garretón (1994, 243), politics were "more of the mobilizing than of the representative type" and with weak institutions of representation.
2. See Oxhorn (1995) and Garretón (1994).
3. Television could be an integrating mechanism, yet differing program preferences and initial cultural differences tend to diminish its social integration potential. Instead, television raises expectations that can seldom be fulfilled for the poorer sectors.
4. However women must contribute more in order to receive the same pension that men get (Arenas de Mesa and Montecinos 1995).
5. Equity and poverty reduction do not necessarily covary, as the Chilean experience indicates. Since 1985 the economy has grown on average around 6–7% annually. Head count indexes of poverty fell from 45% of the population in 1987 to 40% in 1990, 33% in 1992, and 28% in 1994. Inequities in the distribution of income, however, did not change significantly during this period.
6. The *Human Development Report 1994* stated that it is necessary "to create an economic and polical atmosphere in which people can enhance human capacity and use it appropriately" (UNDP 1994).

REFERENCES

Arenas de Mesa, A., and V. Montecinos. 1995. Reinforcing Discrimination against Women: The New Social Security System in Chile. Paper prepared for the XIX International Congress of the Latin American Studies Association (LASA), 28–30 September, Washington, D.C.

Bamberger, M. 1993. *La función del gasto público en la focalización de los servicios económicos y sociales para los pobres*. Economic Development Institute Working Paper (April). Washington, D.C.: The World Bank.

Bell, C. L. G., and J. H. Duloy. 1974. Formulating a Strategy. In *Redistribution with Growth*, edited by H. Chenery. London: The World Bank; Institute of Development Studies, Oxford University Press.

Besley, T., and R. Kanbur. 1988. *The Principles of Targeting*. Development Economic Research Centre Discussion Paper no. 85. Coventry: University of Warwick.
Bradford, Jr., C. I., ed. 1994a. *Redefining the State in Latin America*. Paris: OECD.
——. 1994b. Redefining the Role of the State: Political Processes, State Capacity and the New Agenda in Latin America. In *Redefining the State in Latin America*, edited by C. I. Bradford, Jr. Paris: OECD.
Cornia, G. A. 1994. *Macroeconomic Policy, Poverty Alleviation and Long-Term Development: Latin America in the 1990s*. Innocenti Occasional Papers, Economic Policy Series no. 40 (February). Florence: UNICEF International Child Development Centre.
Cornia, G. A., and F. Stewart. 1992. Two Errors of Targeting. Paper presented at conference on Public Expenditure and the Poor: Incidence and Targeting. Washington, D.C.: The World Bank.
Crispi, J., and M. Marcel. 1993. Aspectos cuantitativos de la política social en Chile 1987-93. Dirección de Presupuesto, Ministerio de Hacienda, Santiago.
ECLAC (Economic Commission on Latin America and the Caribbean). 1990. *Transformación productiva con equidad*. Santiago: ECLAC.
——. 1995. Modelos de desarrollo, papel del Estado y políticas sociales: Nuevas tendencias en América Latina. División de Desarrollo Social, LC/R.1575 (7 September). Santiago: ECLAC.
ECLAC-UNESCO (United Nations Education, Science, and Culture Organization). 1992. *Educación y conocimiento. Eje de la transformación productiva con equidad*. Santiago: UNESCO.
Garretón, M. A. 1994. New State-Society Relations in Latin America. In *Redefining the State in Latin America*, edited by C. I. Bradford, Jr. Paris: OECD.
Grosh, M. 1992. *From Platitude to Practice: Targeting Social Programs in Latin America*. Human Resources Division, Latin American and the Caribbean Technical Department, Regional Studies Program, Report no. 21 (September). Washington, D.C.: The World Bank.
Kliksberg, B., comp. 1994a. *El rediseño del estado. Una perspectiva internacional*. Mexico City: Instituto Nacional de Administración Pública, Fondo de Cultura Económica.
——. 1994b. El rediseño del estado para el desarrollo socioeconómico y el cambio. Una agenda estratégica para la discusión. In *El rediseño del estado*, edited by B. Kliksberg. Mexico City: Instituto Nacional de Administración Pública, Fondo de Cultura Económica.
Lustig, N., ed. 1995. *Coping with Austerity: Poverty and Inequality in Latin America*. Washington, D.C.: The Brookings Institution.
Mesa-Lago, C. 1978. *Social Security in Latin America: Pressure Groups, Stratification and Inequality*. Pittsburgh: University of Pittsburgh Press.
Nelson, J. M., John Waterbury, Stephan Haggard, et al. 1989. *Fragile Coalitions: The Politics of Economic Adjustment*. Washington, D.C.: Overseas Development Council.
Oxhorn, P. 1995. *Organizing Civil Society: Popular Organizations and the Struggle for Democracy in Chile*. University Park: Pennsylvania State University Press.

Ozlak, O. 1994. Estado y sociedad: Las nuevas fronteras. In *El rediseño del estado*, edited by B. Kliksberg. Mexico City: Instituto Nacional de Administración Pública, Fondo de Cultura Económica.

Raczynski, D. 1994. *Social Policies in Chile: Origin, Transformation, and Perspectives*. Democracy and Social Policy Series no. 4 (fall) Notre Dame: Kellogg Institute.

———. 1995a. Focalización de programas sociales: Lecciones de la experiencia chilena. In *Políticas económicas y sociales en el Chile democrático*, edited by C. Pizarro, D. Raczynski, and J. Vial. Santiago: CIEPLAN-UNICEF.

———, ed. 1995b. *Estrategias para combatir la pobreza en América Latina: Programas, instituciones y recursos*. Santiago: CIEPLAN, Red de Centros de Investigación Económica Aplicada, Inter-American Development Bank.

Raczynski, D., and C. Oyarzo. 1981. *Porqué cae la tasa de mortalidad infantil en Chile?* Colección Estudios CIEPLAN no. 6 (December). Santiago: CIEPLAN.

Sojo, A. 1990. Naturaleza y selectividad de la política social. *Revista de la CEPAL* no. 41 (August).

Tomassini, L. 1994. Relaciones entre estado y sociedad civil. In *¿Qué espera la sociedad del gobierno?* edited by L. Tomassini. Santiago: Centro de Análisis de Políticas Públicas y Asociación Chilena de Ciencia Política, Universidad de Chile.

Touraine, A. 1994. From the Mobilising State to Democratic Politics. In *Redefining the State in Latin America*, edited by C. I. Bradford, Jr. Paris: OECD.

UNDP (United Nations Development Program). 1994. *Human Development Report 1994*. New York: Oxford University Press.

Vergara, P. 1990. *Políticas hacia la extrema pobreza en Chile*. Santiago: FLACSO.

World Bank. 1993. *World Development Report 1993*. New York: Oxford University Press.

———. 1995. *World Development Report 1995*. New York: Oxford University Press.

8 Balancing State, Market, and Civil Society

NGOs for a New Development Consensus

CHARLES A. REILLY

Poor and desperate men
Invented four things that are useful at sea:
Sails, rudders, oars
And the fear of drowning.
   —Thomas McGrath, "Revisionist Poem: Machado"

Advisors from the Past

Suppose that, at the cusp of the twentieth and twenty-first centuries, we could call upon Machiavelli, Tocqueville, and Adam Smith to first help us build a new consensus on ways to check poverty and then recommend sensible paths to development. From his Italian civic perspective, Nicolo might observe that the prince should marshal *virtu* and bank on *fortuna* to counter those forces bent on undercutting the state. Alexis, depressed by the breakdown of aristocracy and rise of tyranny in nineteenth-century France, would find hope in his impressions of associational vigor and democracy in twentieth-century North America. Yet, while celebrating associational diversity and the vigor and self-help propensities of citizens in civil society, he would surely regret the diminishing "equality of conditions" taking place in Latin America during and after structural adjustment. At the same time, he would encourage Latin Americans to chronicle and celebrate the human rights they have already achieved and their determination to overcome inequality. Adam Smith, ahead of his time in rejecting a whisky import-substitution strategy for the Scottish highlands, would remind us that self-interest and profit motive spur the market forces that bake the bread, fill the barrels, and create the jobs required to break the chains of poverty.

Although unable to guide us in person, these philosophers have nonetheless bequeathed many of the ideas and perspectives that influence contemporary views on the roles and responsibilities of "princes," merchants, and citizens confronting peremptory change and poverty. States, markets, and civil society are constantly redefining themselves, each reshaping the others. Through push and pull, demand and supply, their contours—far from resembling those of the eighteenth and nineteenth centuries—no longer resemble those of even a short ten years ago, when development debate allegedly arrived at a "Washington Consensus."

Since the 1960s and 1970s, "popular" organizations and movements have multiplied throughout Latin America. Most of them originated from committed citizens in what we now call civil society—triggered by churches, by ethnic revival, by cooperatives, by charismatic leaders or displaced professionals, and sometimes by the availability of international funding. In settings where civil society emerged in frank opposition to an authoritarian state, adversarial overtones may linger on. Elsewhere, the civil society lineage traces to "popular participation" schemes or corporatist organizational models of democracies and dictatorships, *dictablanda* and *democradura*. Citizens emerged while formal and informal economies of the region grew increasingly intertwined, import substitution strategies yielded to the competitive pursuit of elusive global markets, corporatist labor organizations lost their clout, and structural adjustment and state downsizing led to dramatic declines in employment. Civil society has elbowed its way between state and market, receiving a wary welcome from both.

Five decades of development initiatives have followed a curious sequence: nearly three-and-one-half decades of emphasis on state building, about a decade-and-a-half concentrating on market forces, and a scant half-decade of enthusiastic rhetoric about the virtues of civil society. Development models and paradigms have come and gone. Spanish poet Antonio Machado penned an evocative phrase adopted by many people engaged in Latin American development:

> *Caminante, no hay camino: se hace camino al andar* (Walker, there is no path: the path is made by walking.)

We have been walking, trying different paths, but we have not gotten very far. There are more poor, and poorer poor. There is more flagrant inequality today

Figure 8.1

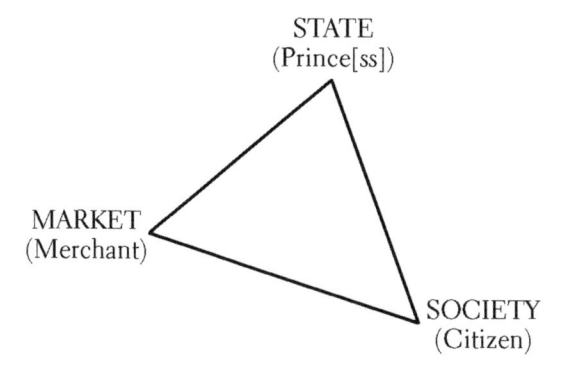

```
              STATE
           (Prince[ss])
              /\
             /  \
            /    \
    MARKET /      \
  (Merchant)      \
                   \ SOCIETY
                    (Citizen)
```

that challenges the development business to greater imagination. Desperation can spark creativity, a fact captured in nautical images by American poet Thomas McGrath in his "Revisionist Poem: Machado," quoted at the beginning of this chapter.

Although it is indeed time for invention, those in the development business are to a certain degree in the position of sailors on a frail craft: if too many rush to the side of civil society, they will swamp the boat. If the fear of drowning moves sailors to keep their balance (and learn to swim), such a fear should be equally useful in matters of state, markets, and civil society. Like sailors keeping the raft afloat, virtue works best when it remains somewhere in the middle.

Several decades of debt and structural adjustment, a new global trade environment, and always-reversible democratization (rendered less vulnerable by the emergence of organized citizens) have combined to transform the boundaries of state, market, and civil society.[1] Most observers agree that in Latin America today, state, market, and civil society are dynamic—changing internally and externally, rapidly modifying their relationships, reapportioning the division of labor and the mix of tasks falling to each. Today, the development establishment cannot choose among state, market, or civil society: no single sector nor any two have instruments to grapple effectively with poverty and the structures contributing to its growth. Equally, praise and dispraise must be shared by all three, if not in identical measure. Thus, it becomes a matter of balancing the claims, competences, and capacities of each while discovering ways to make them complementary. In this way the inevitable tension among them is channeled into paths beneficial to the majority, who are poor and becoming poorer.

Development: A Failure of Elites

While some analysts persist in attributing the failures of development to the poor, I am convinced that underdevelopment in Latin America flows far more from failures of elites, whether ensconced in the state, in markets, in civil society, or in the development business. Those of us whose livelihood comes from development must share the dispraise, for in our short-sightedness (and stubbornness) we have often failed to learn from our mistakes. In effect, Latin America's maldistribution of wealth stems more from "successes" of the wealthy than from failures of the poor. Think, for example, of the "new rich," i.e., the thousands who have personally, often spectacularly profited from privatization, appropriating public goods for private profit. Meanwhile, countless former members of the middle sector or "mesoi" began to slide into poverty during the past decade. These "new poor" wield a crucial swing vote in determining whether some elusive blend of a smaller but more effective state, expanding but better regulated markets, and civil society driven as much by citizen responsibilities as by their rights could prevail.

Economic, political, and social reform—an integrated approach to development—has once again appeared on the agendas of the development mainstream. While renewed attention to civil society is most welcome, I suspect that we in the development business should examine whether we welcome civil society as an end or civil society as a means: an instrument for our own designs or a value in and of itself. Are citizens in civil society socially viewed merely as political insurance to make adjustment policies sustainable, or will they be architects as well as beneficiaries of its programs? Will they become mere surrogates for a shrunken state or advocates of more accountable policy? Does the alleviation of poverty boil down simply to expanding consumer purchasing power, or will there be change in the distribution of social power? In the language of Catholic social thought, is the goal "to *have* or to *be* more"?

While ideologies persistently infiltrate our thinking, many of the old "isms" no longer prevail. Old ideologies fade, some "isms" becomes "wasms," and new recipes appear. Meanwhile, poverty grows, poverty understood not just in economic terms—lack of access to jobs, income, or goods—but in social and political terms as well. For the long-excluded poor, this means the absence of social organization, networks, financial resources and tools, information, skills, and adequate space and time. Within this context, "empowerment" means improving poor people's access to these many bases of social power. Like it or not, poverty reduction translates into power sharing, and power sharing provokes resistance.

Shifts from confrontation toward cooperation among state, market, and civil society has been uneven. In some Latin American countries civil society emerged in frank opposition to the authoritarian regimes of the 1960s and 1970s, and many of its spokespersons were suspicious of the "cruelty" of markets, especially those controlled by global corporations. The informal economy, by definition and praxis, emerged outside legal frameworks—frequently furnishing the only survival strategy and safety net available to the very poor. Citizen rapprochement with the state has been slow—with markets, even slower. Some political elites view civil society leaders as disloyal opposition, more ready to subvert than to support, to make demands rather than accept responsibility. Others offer more positive appraisals, echoing one public official who recently told me, "Some of the *clase política* view civil society leaders as unwelcome competitors for clientele, but those of us responsible for implementing social programs see them as partners for implementing more effective social policy" (Buenos Aires, 25 July 1996). Slowly but surely, antagonisms and stereotypes make way for negotiation and collaboration.

Hunches and Hypotheses

What is to be done? The challenge posed by a thinker at the last turn of the century, remains pertinent today as we wind down the twentieth and embark upon the twenty-first. Can state, market, and civil society in the countries of the Americas shift gears and enter the twenty-first century with relationships that are more equitable, productive, efficient, and civil? Can governability, civility, productivity, and efficiency learn to get along? Which are the more effective blends of public and private responsibility? Which macro policies will yield beneficial effects at the micro and meso-levels? Will the making and implementation of policy be opened up to those long excluded from any say in governance?

There are some promising signs within the region. Politics and economics (although perhaps reluctantly) have begun to yield space to civics. State, markets, and civil society are being redefined; the boundaries marking their spheres are shifting, solid lines become dotted lines instead, and many innovative dynamics unfold in the transition zones between them. Certainly, we still have a great deal to learn about understanding and managing these frontiers.

What we do know is that citizens' movements enliven democratization by taking on greater responsibility while exacting a more responsive state; regional trading blocks and the General Agreement on Tariffs and Trade (GATT), like structural adjustment and neoliberal economic policy, promise to transform local markets. I have a notion, somewhere between a hunch and a hypothesis, that our best hope for overcoming poverty, equalizing social justice, and enlarging opportunities for the poor majority lies in relationships emerging from

Figure 8.2

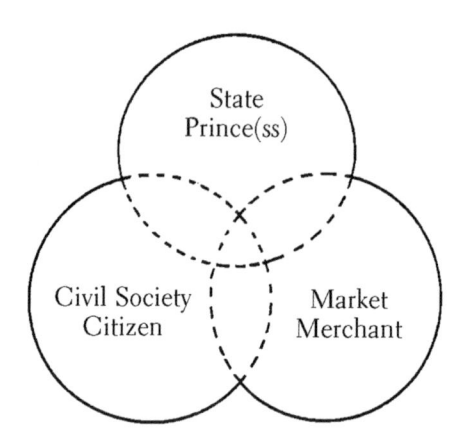

```
        State
       Prince(ss)

Civil Society    Market
  Citizen       Merchant
```

negotiations, encounters, disputes, and pacts among actors and managers working these borders. I sense that important changes occur in the gray zones, the frontiers, the spaces between dotted lines where civil society, state, and markets intersect. As public and private spheres mingle and merge, the commonweal and *res publica* require leadership of a different sort: social entrepreneurs emerging from civil society, public-sector "border managers" comfortable with newly articulate citizens, corporate philanthropists aware that private wealth has a public function.

Do we already catch glimpses of innovation in relationships at the margins between state, civil society, and the market? Bridges spanning the gorges and gaps dividing prince, merchant, and citizen? Are there new relationships—tentative, awkward, sometimes clumsy (much like adolescent courtship, in fact)—which engender trust and hope? And if so, how can they be multiplied? My answer to the first three questions is affirmative; the fourth gives purpose to this essay. The theoretical issues underlying relationships of economy, society, and polity are thoroughly practical; heuristic constructs translate readily into reality when merchants and corporations practice good citizenship, when citizens expand their self-provisioning rights and responsibilities, and when (and if) politicians, recognizing that the commonweal is their first task, risk transparency and accountability. When such events regularly take place, things will have changed.

Already, sturdy bridges connecting state, market, and civil society have arisen throughout the region. In many large cities, nongovernmental organizations (NGOs) and social movements complement the state by providing services for the poor. At the level of the "local" state—that is, municipal and regional governments—rapprochement is frequent and untrammeled, usually linked to problem solving and the provision of services (Reilly 1994). In Brazil a nationwide campaign of "solidarity and citizenship" has mobilized millions to do something specific for the hungry. In the words of campaign director Herbert de Souza (Betinho), "People have discovered that hunger is killed with rice and bread, not just theories" (Ford Foundation Report, summer 1994, 19). In El Salvador, Nicaragua, and Guatemala peace processes have gained strength from business interests as well as from human rights organizations and churches.

Throughout the continent, social investment funds have sometimes linked state and organized poor in novel, nonpaternalistic fashion; new incentives or regulations by governments make business carry a fairer share of social costs or provide favorable incentives for regulations and philanthropy; fax machines and E-mail democratize information flows to and from the poor of civil society; new marketing schemes connect isolated producers of organic coffee with alternative markets in the United States and Europe; and on it goes. Information and incentives seem to be working well at the boundaries.

Some Working Definitions

Let me offer some brief descriptive definitions and highlight some boundary issues regarding state, market, and civil society, recognizing the rich and often highly nuanced literature and controversy surrounding each concept that I will not explore here. (See the bibliography in Reilly 1995 for further commentary.) My purpose here is to devise manageable, operational categories attuned more to action than to contemplation. The calculus of responsibility for poverty reduction must deal largely in degrees rather than in definition. Living up to my North American stereotype, let me offer some pragmatic, operational concepts for the discussion.

State

The state (we *gringos* usually find this an awkward term and prefer to use "government") refers to the members of governing classes assembled in a governing body, or a politically organized body of people claiming sovereignty and occupying a defined territory. According to Weber, the state deals in "the authoritative allocation of values," and Gramsci reminds us that the state wields instruments of both coercion and consensus. If coercion, or the capacity for coercion, characterizes state exercise of power, most philosophical traditions agree that equity should serve as a key normative criterion of its efficacy. Lasswell's classic definition of politics, "who gets what, when, and how," is a deft summary of what goes on in the borderlands among state, civil society, and markets.

In recent years, advocates of privatization have insisted on the sale of government enterprises, arguing that the state has grown far too large and inefficient. Although attacks on the state have multiplied, in the words of Edmundo Jarquín, the state is:

> neither source of all the solutions nor cause of all the problems . . . The state is part of the solution, responsible for conciliating public and private interests and creating conditions for the development of private initiative . . . It sets rules for the functioning of markets and intervenes to correct its imperfections . . . As the state unloads responsibility for implementation and administration, it should pick up instruments of regulation, especially those which promote competition and equity, since there is little to be gained by shifting from inefficient state bureaucratic control to inefficient private monopoly. (1993, 148).

The best hope for a more responsible state, I firmly believe, lies in an organized, involved citizenry that insists on a more transparent and responsive state. As state responsibility changes, new issues arise for citizens. Some revolve around governability, state reform, and rearguard actions to preserve past "social conquests," such as social security or labor legislation won by labor unions and the organized poor. Decentralization and deconcentration potentially correlate well with democratization, but only to the degree that fiscal crises are dealt with creatively and local state impotence is overcome. What of the urban crisis throughout the region? How to manage cities, especially the megalopolises? What are the real prospects for state–civil society collaboration, especially with the local state? How profound is the disenchantment occasioned by transitions to democracy that yielded democratic practice falling far short of high expectations?

As we have seen, disappointment with government practice translates into increased discontent, anticorruption and anti-incumbent movements, a pervasive climate of indifference, hostility toward the "political class," in sum, pervasive antipolitics. Participation in community affairs is more easily preached than practiced. While many are indifferent and apathy is widespread, for the very poor participation may be a luxury. In the United States we hear negative generative words and prescriptive "sound-bites" daily: voter discontent, streamlining, downsizing, lean and mean, or reinventing government. In Latin America similar code words criticize corruption and call for reform through measures to ensure transparency and accountability. Under siege, both North and South, the state may yet gain relief through its association with countervailing forces that create a degree of balance—such as that arising from constructive collaboration among state, markets, and civil society.

Markets

If the state lay at the core of earlier development models, markets represent the magic word for many today. Regional trade blocs like the North American Free

Trade Agreement (NAFTA) and the South American Common Market (Mercosur) have begun to prove their worth, while the GATT debate has changed the terms of trade context considerably. More open trade regimes will supposedly attract higher levels of investment and will, one hopes, create more jobs and increase productivity. Stimulated productive potential and growth at the macrolevel must somehow relate to the microlevel subsistence and survival strategies that preoccupy and sustain the majority. The informal economy will need to be both revisited and revitalized, and the widespread assumptions that it can rescue the poor majority discarded. Regional trading blocks should indeed be energized and alternative markets identified. Many exciting possibilities may flow from "green" technologies and markets, for example.

Although there is cause for hope, contemporary economic setbacks in the North raise somber questions for the South. What, for example, are the implications for the South of growing unemployment and the rapid spread of service economies? Of rapid urbanization and population growth—the "urban apartheid" to which Brazilians often refer? What happens to families with the feminization of labor markets? What are the prospects for industrial reconversion and agricultural diversification, especially when technological advances, labor markets, gene sweeps, and intellectual property rights seem persistently skewed away from the South? And the region's distorted distribution of wealth raises yet another question: Why, among the Latin American super-rich, including recent profiteers from privatization, have there appeared so few philanthropists?

Increased levels of savings and investment are fundamental, as is the task of ensuring that pricing systems reflect normal market forces. Fiscal equilibrium, an appropriate blend of state deregulation and supervision, realistic interest rates, and efficient institutions of financial intermediation are all on the agenda. Innovation and entrepreneurial imagination must take rapidly changing technologies into account, yet link them to labor-intensive growth. Businesses must interact with educators to narrow the gap between human resource training and available jobs. The Latin American trade union movement must adapt to changing labor markets, sort out its response to the challenges of the "informal sector," and forge horizontal alliances with NGOs and other organizations of civil society. (Yet, inexplicably, the "Washington Consensus"[2] neglected to address human capital formation.) Experience in other areas of the world can be instructive as well: for example, when celebrating East Asian "tigers" it must be remembered that radical land reform, profound educational changes, and reliable safety nets preceded any miracles in that region—proof that equity and efficiency need not be antagonists.

Markets grow more global every day, whether buyers and sellers exchange commodities, goods, or services. Markets tend toward concentration, rely upon competition as their driving force, and operate according to efficiency criteria that are inherently cruel, if not exploitative (often despite the good will and ethical proclivities of their actors). Dividing lines between public and private no longer fit liberal, structuralist, nor Marxist expectations. Private initiative, entrepreneurial energy, and the first stirring of philanthropy indicate that many in Latin America are prepared to compete globally while adjusting locally. Yet old reflexes compel others to continue seeking subsidies, protection, inoculation from risky markets, or cushions from technology. Perhaps Adam Smith would have found it troublesome to enter global markets, but his grandnephews have mastered the marketing techniques that brought Johnny Walker, red and black, to the entire globe.

Civil Society
While Hegel referred to civil society as "everything between the family and the state," contemporary Latin American usage refers to multiple, self-limiting organizations of citizens publicly exercising their rights and responsibilities before the state. The concept embraces social organizations and movements of many sizes, shapes, and origins as well as individual citizens. In this paper I often refer to civil society organizations engaged in development action and reflection, especially development NGOs. If not necessarily the most representative cluster of civil society, NGOs have played an extremely important role in making development more participatory and in obtaining recognition of a "third sector" beyond markets and the state. Like democratizing states and globalizing markets, an expanding civil society, including development NGOs, social movements, and a plethora of associations for collective action, is now seen on cognitive maps and heard in social policy debate. Civil society emerged in Latin America as a concept and social construction during the struggle for democracy and against poverty and was energized, even legitimated, by Eastern European efforts.

Despite Tocqueville's celebration of associational life in North America, civil society is more generally perceived in the United States as a recent import from Latin America, Russia, and Eastern Europe. There is, of course, a civil society tradition among some U.S. political philosophers. In the words of John Courtney Murray, SJ, echoed recently by Robert Bellah, a relative degree of consensus on the rules of engagement characterizes societies that are civil, and *trust* is the fundamental ingredient: "We hold these truths, therefore we can argue" (Murray 1962; Bellah et al. 1991). Civil society is much less than "society" (since it is both organized and public), but far more than "political society," i.e., political parties and individuals bent on capturing power and occupying office.

Following Lester Salamon, North American authors tend to refer to the "nonprofit" or "third sector" more than the more comprehensive (and fuzzy) concept of civil society. The experience of welfare states of the North is distinct from that of the South, of course, but the parallels are many and profound. Associational activity is not monopolized by the North (and some observers fear it is decreasing there). Perhaps the Tocquevillian preconditions of fundamental equality and generalized political rights are but partially fulfilled, and distinct cultural contexts give different shape to citizen emergence, yet:

> A striking upsurge is under way around the globe in organized voluntary activity and the creation of private, nonprofit or nongovernmental organizations . . . The scope and scale of this phenomenon are immense. Indeed, we are in the midst of a global "associational revolution" that may prove to be as significant to the latter twentieth century as the rise of the nation-state was to the latter nineteenth. The upshot is a global third sector: a massive array of self-governing private organizations, not dedicated to distributing profits to shareholders or directors, pursuing public purposes outside the formal apparatus of the state. The proliferation of these groups may be permanently altering the relationship between states and citizens, with an impact extending far beyond the material services they provide.
>
> Ideological blinders have also obscured a clear assessment of the nonprofit sector's true scope and role. For much of the past 50 years, politicians on both the political right and the left have tended to downplay these institutions. The left has done so to justify the expansion of the welfare state; the right to justify attacks on the state as the destroyer of private "mediating institutions." The rise of the welfare state thus crowded out the nonprofit sector from both public discussion and scholarly inquiry even as the sector continued to grow. (Salamon 1994, 110)

While Salamon chronicles third sector emergence, other authors have engaged Robert Putnam's somber assessment of individualistic trends in contemporary American society, a study that follows on his equally provocative, if not pessimistic, examination of the origins of civic traditions in Italy (Putnam 1993). Civil society becomes manifest in the eruption of ethical and moral outrage in many Latin societies, which mobilized anticorruption campaigns, rewrote constitutions, even impeached presidents, or contemporary debates in the United States about morality and ethics in the public domain and the appropriate role of religious minorities or "moral majority" in public life. Should we, can we, define "civil society"? Some authors, like Salamon, opt to avoid the conceptual morass and focus rather on a "third" or "emerging sector" which embraces the many forms of not-for-profit associational activity that have quietly occupied broad roles and employ amazingly large numbers of people throughout North and South (Salamon and Anheirer 1993). Larry Diamond offers a definition inspired by the recent emergence of new social actors in Eastern Europe and Latin America:

> Civil Society is conceived here as the realm of organized social life that is voluntary, self-generating, (largely) self-supporting, autonomous from the state, and bound by a legal order or set of shared rules . . . it involves citizens acting collec-

tively in a public sphere . . . [it] not only restricts state power but legitimates state authority when that authority is based on the rule of law. (1994, 5)

Tocqueville would agree. The future of Latin American civil society revolves around how many citizens will have a voice in shaping the norms and values that sustain states and markets—and what form that voice will take. Like Columbus's discovery of America, discovering civil society may be an epochal event. But enthusiasm for its potential must first be tempered with realistic appraisals of the limitations of civil society and then focused upon developing its capacity. For example, civil capacity to absorb functions down-loaded from a shrinking state must be realistically assessed; the state cannot reasonably expect to assign the bulk of social services to for-profit businesses and NGOs, thereby leaving citizens on their own to try to weave sturdy enough social safety nets.

Changing relations among the spheres of market, state, and society need chronicling. Why does the state often provide research and development and shape regulatory contexts for private entrepreneurs? How and when do philanthropists find incentives? What happens to autonomous NGOs when they become contractors for the state? What new energies and innovation arise from people organized around gender, ethnicity, or class? Do religions act as mediators and build communities or do they exacerbate societal cleavages? Who will serve as advocates for generations yet to come, now that environment and development have been recognized as potentially compatible, and equity, both present and future, has been dealt into the distributional equation?

Evidently, no single member of the state-market-civil society trinity can exist without the others; a permanent tension exists among them. One hopes that the tension will be increasingly perceived as creative, with division of both labor and power proven feasible and efficacious. In the absence of perfectly competitive markets, the state must step in with regulatory capacity. But because states are imperfect themselves, they need civil society's accountability mechanisms. And because civil society is also imperfect and incomplete, both state and market must play a role in ensuring rights, channeling interests, and generating employment.

State Reforms

Already the Latin American state has been redefined by the transition to democracy, as well as its consolidation, and by the exigencies of structural adjustment. Broader democracy introduces many new questions about governability, while structural adjustment policies require the state to embark upon a variety of reforms. Only two of these reforms have thus far been vigorously imposed throughout the region: the sale of state enterprises and the shrinking of public employment rolls. In some countries, however, the contemporary state is abandoning the social welfare gains of the organized poor or its populist predecessors. There, corporatist labor and social security structures are being undermined on the basis of yet to be demonstrated assumptions that market forces, fees for services, or NGO largesse will somehow fill the gaps. Clearly, reform can become a two-edged sword.

Beyond shrinking the public sector and off-loading certain state enterprise through privatization, I believe there is a need for legislative and judicial reform, administrative decentralization, geographical deconcentration, and democratization of the local state. Significant roles for municipal and regional governments can unfold to the extent that fiscal crisis is more realistically addressed. To move beyond rhetorical decentralization implies a serious attack on the fiscal incapacity of local governments, more enlightened approaches to revenue generation and revenue sharing, considerable investment in human capital and local capacity building, rediscovery of the principle of subsidiarity (superior units should not do what is readily do-able by inferior ones), and far more creative mechanisms for engaging citizens in the process. Legislative and judiciary reform are needed to counterbalance the long-term advantages of the executive branch and to introduce more effective checks and balances in the political system.

As part of the state reform package, social policy will require serious overhaul. New instruments have already appeared which are promising although insufficiently tested and assessed. Experimental programs like social emergency and investment funds mark new linkages among state, civil society, and market actors—diversifying and sometimes complicating the state by introducing parallel government structures between social sector ministries and investment funds. These programs have in some places restored a measure of legitimacy to states initiating unpopular reforms. Targeting techniques have improved the delivery of services to some of the needy and reduced leakage or "trickle-up," which too frequently distorts the purposes and performance of antipoverty programs. Joint ventures and partnerships in social service delivery, often with NGOs and for-profit, fee-for-service corporations, will test the imagination and skills of managers in effectively serving the needs of poor people.

Education and health policies must be devised that can ensure human and social capital adequate to the changing demands of productivity and competition in world markets. Technology challenges late-starters for whom comparative advantage has been an illusion. Legislatures and judiciaries require up-dating and rationalization if they are to begin to effectively balance the executive branch of government, which has hitherto received the lion's share of international assistance. The pathologies of fragile social structures added to the growing levels of anomic and systemic violence tax the state, both central and local, and raise questions of governability, civility, and containment of violence without indiscriminate coercion. The contemporary use of federal troops to police *favelas* in Rio de Janeiro is a painful case in point, while the appearance of neighborhood watch committees along Copacabana beach illustrates that citizens, rich, poor, and middle class, are ready to be more engaged.

Consolidating Civil Society—This Side of Utopia

In newspaper headlines around the region, civil society expresses ethical and moral claims regarding the state and its reform by denouncing corruption and demanding transparency. If civil society continues to expand its influence in the late nineties, it will be due in part to default by both state and markets; in part to growing levels of self-help and philanthropy and lessons learned; and in part to the tardy realization within the region that rights and responsibilities of citizenship belong to the majority. I often refer to NGOs as representative (though not sole) exemplars of civil society, which can be neither monopolized by nor reduced to NGOs. Abundant and heterogeneous, NGOs may be tested or opportunistic, competent or craven, autonomous or dependent. But civil society is far more textured, inclusive, and diffuse than NGOs alone. The warp and woof of civil society embraces a complex weaving whose strands represent NGOs, professional associations, producers' organizations, social movements, unions, churches, entrepreneurs, base communities, and mass media. What makes civil society unique in Latin America today is that impoverished citizens at last take part:

> Strengthening civil society is primarily a domestic process which cannot be imposed from outside. At the same time, it is a process in which all the agents in each society should be involved, governments, business, trade unions, political parties, churches, NGOs, foundations, intermediary and grassroots organizations and individual citizens. (IDB 1994)

Most would agree that each sphere—state, market, and civil society—is characterized by somewhat different dynamics and mechanics. The state, for example, is characterized by coercion, both actual and potential, and the market by never-perfect competition. Civil society, on the other hand, (at least for enthusiasts such as myself) operates through mechanics of dialogue and consensus. It is also self-limiting. As Diamond observes:

> Civil society is concerned with public rather than private ends . . . relates to the state in some way but does not aim to win formal power or office in the state . . . encompasses pluralism and diversity . . . and no group in civil society seeks to represent the whole of a person's or community's interests (partialness). (1994, 6–7)

The civil society-market-state nexus harbors both opportunity and challenge. Let me conclude this section by offering several propositions that take heed of the "self-limiting" dimension of civil society—that is, civil society makes only partial claims on citizens and, although capable of assuming certain functions in the name of self-help and citizen responsibility, is utterly unprepared for (indeed incapable of) becoming surrogate to either state or market.

- Civil society tends toward dispersion, diversity, and pluralism, unlike market and state, which tend toward concentration.
- Neither market nor state should disconnect from the moral, ethical, and normative content produced by civil society.
- Civil society cannot absorb all the burdens off-loaded from the state.
- State, market, and civil society potentially represent a healthy system of checks and balances hitherto lacking in Latin American societies.
- Many cultural taproots of democratic development may be found within Latin American societies themselves and need not be imported.
- Creativity and discovery take place at the margins, along the trio's borders, and should be encouraged and chronicled.

Civil Society Discernment

In the second half of this paper, I shall focus on civil society organizations (CSOs) and their relationships to state and markets. The borders between them are where the challenges lie and creativity beckons. Development and democratization are vulnerable and reversible. Managing the borders among state, market, and civil society seems to hold the key to their consolidation.

Conceptually, civil society is something of a catch-all. Some scholars in the United States prefer "third sector," others refer to "nonprofits." I will stick with Latin America's preferred "civil society" to emphasize the growing numbers of *private* citizens for whom *public* functions have grown routine. Civil society includes citizens propelled by concerns of race, gender, ethnicity, religion, and class. It embraces nongovernmental organizations that provide social services like primary education, day care, or health care; groups that promote micro- and small businesses; public policy advocates who aim to keep government and business on track; technical consulting firms that opt for the nonprofit side of the ledger; independent research and teaching institutions; cooperatives and credit unions with market as well as civil society interests; foundations and charities and churches that draw on long traditions of charitable giving; entrepreneurs crafting new approaches to development through philanthropy; business associations and labor unions that link civil society and markets; and social movements of organized and not so organized citizens.

Though civil society took shape in many countries of the region in frank opposition to governments, an uneasy but persistent trend toward partnership has begun to emerge. The precise contours of civil society and the intensity of civil society-state-market relationships vary greatly from country to country. I just returned from visiting six Central American countries. In Nicaragua and El Salvador international brokers like the United Nations, European Economic Community members, and US Aid for International Development (USAID), as well as the mechanics of the peace negotiations have conferred new status and legitimacy on the organizations of civil society. In Guatemala, site of one of Latin America's longest guerrilla wars, peace negotiations currently included ten sets of civil society actors, ranging from Indian organizations, women's groups, environmentalists, unions, business associations, NGO associations, researchers, and media to the churches. Whether in war or in peace, governments must take them into account as never before.

NGOs have multiplied indeed. The Inter-American Foundation (IAF) recently published a directory of NGO directories that listed more than 14,000. In recent years, nongovernmental development organizations have occupied portions of the space vacated by government and are increasingly labeled as part of civil society. To guide the reader through the alphabet soup, here is a list of some of the most frequently used terms:

CSO	=	civil society organization;
GSO	=	grassroots support organization;
MO	=	membership organization;
PDO	=	private development organization;
NGO	=	nongovernmental organization;
PVO	=	private voluntary organization;
QUANGO	=	quasi-nongovernmental organization.

Private voluntary organization (PVO) is the term most frequently used (in the United States) for U.S.-based international development organizations, with NGO more frequently used in other countries and by the United Nations overseas. Relatively well-organized, technically skilled grassroots support organizations (GSOs) provide goods and services to groups of the organized poor; membership organizations (MOs) like cooperatives, neighborhood associations, or ethnic organizations represent themselves directly; and the sometimes ephemeral, single-issue, and frequently vociferous social movements of the poor at local, regional, or national levels address particularly hot issues of the day.

The term "organizations of civil society" (CSOs) is increasingly used in North and South, thus avoiding the negative identification—non-governmental—and perhaps the negative connotation where NGOs are perceived as anti politics. If CSO represents the recently recognized and more inclusive genus, NGO is the older, more familiar but perhaps disappearing species. In these pages I will refer to the broad CSO category and restrict the NGO designation to internationally funded development organizations.

While organic metaphors for politics can be problematic, I like to think of CSOs and grassroots communities, popular associations, and social movements—the latter particularly significant in Mexico and Brazil—as the "capillaries" of civil society. Tiny, interactive, the beginning and end of a circuit—they are the points at which finance, information, demands, and supports (like wastes, oxygen, and nutrients for the body) are exchanged to keep democracy healthy. Clearly, there is abundant social energy available outside the state.

Discernment is called for, since NGOs are not necessarily virtuous nor always efficacious. In metaphor, if not in fact, NGOs are like mushrooms—*hongos* in Spanish—some attractive and healthy, others ugly and poisonous, and still others just plain hallucinogenic! The metaphor can be extended: "they grow in the dark, constantly multiply, and feed on crap."

Assessing CSOs and NGOs

Enthusiasm for NGOs in civil society must be tempered. Advocates of privatization and antagonists of government rhapsodize about the potential of NGOs, and indeed many of these organizations played pivotal roles in opposing authoritarian regimes and opening paths to democratic transitions. True, also, that nongovernmental development organizations can be effective laboratories for testing and delivering services to some of the poor. But microexperiments are not enough, given the scale of poverty and inequitable distribution. There are "universal" responsibilities to citizens that are rightly ascribed to governments. As Mario Padrón, a Peruvian spokesman for Latin American NGOs, remarked shortly before his death, "Don't ask us to carry more than our capacity, and then blame the failure of the next development decade on us—we can't carry the load."

Even if NGOs could shoulder such burdens, they resent implementing decisions made elsewhere. To become surrogate bearers of state services is not the goal of these men and women, especially when they have no say in policy formulation or program design. As international support decreases, NGOs must turn to local resource mobilization, sometimes contracting and subcontracting with the state and increasingly getting help from "good corporate citizens" and domestic foundations. They are ambivalent about accepting a role as surrogate service providers for a downsizing state, yet in need of new sources of support. Most would accept Keynes's dictum that "The important thing for government is not to do things which individuals are doing already, and to do them a little better or a little worse, but to do those things which at present are not done at all" (World Bank 1991, 128). NGOs do recognize their limitations and seek to build their capacity.

Civil society organizations have many strengths. Many of them are more closely identified with very poor populations than are government agencies. They often work with very low overhead thanks to exceptional levels of motivation and commitment. As sociologist José Pastore concluded in an evaluation of Brazilian NGOs, "They generally demonstrate high levels of commitment and of competence—but if forced to choose between them, I would choose commitment, since competence can be taught." While some CSOs have national and even international scope, most work on very specific issues at the very local level—hence their more frequent interaction with decentralized units of government.

Just as there are inefficient, opportunistic, and bankrupt states or markets, there are inefficient, opportunistic, and bankrupt CSOs. Social movements are frequently ephemeral. The levers of power within Latin American societies are not handled by CSOs or social movements, although these groups often deal with the unintended consequences of decisions made elsewhere. As political scientists worry about governability, the increase in anomic violence and threats to personal and collective security throughout Latin America suggest as well a breakdown in civility, a deterioration that CSOs alone cannot remedy.

Most NGOs have been supported by international donors in the past, some with their own political agendas. But international "largesse" is on the wane. What remains goes increasingly to the poorest countries. The organizations of civil society face a range of financial, political, and cultural challenges, with resource mobilization particularly acute. For example, the "Plano Real" program, structural adjustment, and fiscal austerity in Brazil have effectively reduced international support to NGOs by 40% in the past 12 months, forcing the downsizing of many NGOs and the closing of others and prompting discussions with the government about matching funds to fill the gap (interview with Silvio Caccia Bava, President of the Brazilian Association of NGOs, ABONG, 8 August 1995). Similar crises affect NGOs throughout the continent.

In many settings, the legacy of state–civil society antagonism lives on. Many political elites regard the NGOs with considerable disdain. They criticize NGOs for "antipolitics" posturing, for undermining fragile party systems, for keeping civil society a permanent political opposition force, for dependence on foreign funds, for their lack of transparency and accountability within the nation, for technical and professional shortfalls, or for their incapacity to translate protest into policy proposals. NGOs for their part question how far they should relate to governments. For example, Brazilian NGOs have struggled to define their role vis-à-vis government initiatives and, in a recent workshop, listed the following dilemmas:

- The first danger is the "cooptation effect," the risk that NGOs will lose their identity through close association with government organisms both national and international, thus converting themselves into "parastatals."

- The second stems from the proliferation of opportunistic NGOs spawned solely to get their hands on money from the SIFs (social investment funds); in other words, the funds may provide incentives for businesses to disguise themselves as NGOs.
- The third risk has to do with the real capacity of NGOs to intervene in the definition of social policies at the national level, given that historically it has been the municipality and sometimes state-level governments that have been the interlocutors with NGOs. (Rodriguez et al. 1993)

CSOs are often ill-prepared to scale up and tackle problems of large population groups let alone become "universalistic" service providers. Decades of distance from authoritarian regimes have left them ill-prepared for frequent interaction with government. Dependence on international donors has undercut their roots and fund-raising capacity within their own societies. Criteria for representation are elusive in the diversified and shifting coalitional world of civil society. Most NGOs recognize that they require greater professionalization and increased technical proficiency. The proliferation of civil society organizations in recent years spawned many spurious claimants. (A handful of "gender-specific" NGOs were created in Argentina two years ago with no weightier purpose than to hitch a ride to Beijing.) While their advocates—and I am one of them—celebrate CSOs, we must admit that CSOs do not corner the market on virtue.[3]

Sound research on civil society organizations has proliferated in the past few years. My own preferred approach has concentrated on CSO relationships with government actors like municipal governments or social investment funds and with market actors like corporations and foundations. Again, my theme: it is the borders with state and market that matter most. I shall begin with municipalities.

The Municipal-CSO Connection

As Latin America grows more urban and megalopolises explode, linkages between municipal governments and CSOs are multiplying throughout the region. I recently edited a volume on new paths to democratic development in Latin America (Reilly 1994, 1995) which analyzes the NGO-municipal government phenomenon in six large Latin American countries. The next few pages draw on some of those findings. We argued in the volume that municipal governments will increasingly become the setting where people who experienced secondary citizenship through membership in NGOs may graduate into a fuller realization of citizenship. Inherited from the colonial times, Latin America's centralized government models coexisted with formal though ineffective municipal government structures and very few citizens organizations. That scenario is changing dramatically.

Established NGOs are modifying their operations, their leadership, even their sources of financial support, while new NGOs spring up virtually overnight. Some, pushed by financial austerity or pulled by escalating human needs, have moved from confrontation to cooperation, engaging in joint ventures with local governments to provide goods and services to the urban poor. This alone is significant. But another unanticipated outcome of crisis, adjustment, and austerity will be the revival of city government. Could Latin America, like Italy, come to rely on a *sottogoverno* for stability, despite restive changes at the top?

As authoritarian regimes fade and economies founder, NGO-municipal collaborative ventures, contracts, and cost sharing will grow more significant—for both development and democracy. This paper aims to alert government policymakers and the development-assistance community to these emerging actors and relationships which can sustain more effective social policy.

The case studies in Reilly (1994, 1995) illustrate how grassroots collective action may stimulate at least a measure of change at the *meso* or intermediate level. From the perspective of policymakers and macrolevel donors engaged in policy dialogue and conditionality, the issue is not *whether* services should be provided but *who* should provide them and, to a lesser degree, how they can be financed. Whether NGOs and social movements are adversaries, collaborators, or surrogates for the local state; whether privatization is yet another instrument for excluding the poor majority; whether the survival strategies of the urban poor must be built on self-provisioning; whether joint NGO-municipal ventures are feasible and viable; and whether Latin American development in the postadjustment period will include growth in country economies as well as in the scope of citizenship benefits for the majority—these are the underlying questions. Although expanding and prolonging the productive potential of each society is fundamental, it is not the focus here. My emphasis is on expanding citizenship, human capital, and organizational capacity, all of which make increased and sustained production, as well as consumption, possible.

State, provincial, and local governments—all lacking resources—are now being asked by central government to shoulder more of the social and economic development burden. Even as most Latin American constitutions celebrate municipal autonomy, they contribute precious little to its vitalization. In most countries municipalities subsist on meager and dwindling transfers rather than on an independent tax base. Some countries are electing local officials for the first time, many of them riding to victory on reform platforms that stir high expectations. When they crash into harsh fiscal reality, stubborn bureaucracies, and empty coffers, disenchantment is often the first outcome.

Some municipalities opt to downsize, contracting services through nongovernmental organizations and unloading social services onto the nonprofit and for-profit private sector. (Social investment funds, to be discussed in the next section, have accelerated this trend.) Other municipal authorities, recognizing that informality in the economy contributes to endemic fiscal crisis, have begun to levy new taxes and to "formalize" even microentrepreneurs. The leaders of resource-poor major and mid-sized cities of Latin America are discovering too that demands and supports are often mediated, not by traditional parties but by nongovernmental development organizations rooted in churches, neighborhoods, and associations of people engaged in service delivery and productive activities. While the informal sector of the economy is being celebrated as the latest development fad, the informal sector of the polity based on informal associations deserves equal emphasis.

Shaping Social Policy for Diversity

Given such variation throughout Latin America, it may seem presumptuous to venture policy recommendations. There are limits to cross-national generalization and comparison, for in the final analysis the results of a policy or "authoritative allocation of resources" must be measured against specific people in specific contexts with specific problems. Paradigms, like policies and programs, are in flux. If austerity and program cutbacks constrict the fiscal landscape, new horizons open with pragmatism, experimentation, and the changing identities of the local state and NGOs. Intergovernmental relations must include more than revenue transfers, just as extragovernmental relations must encompass NGOs and social movements. Changing policy frameworks accompany democratization. Latin Americans are learning how to "muddle through the middle."

If market forces and the organized interests of civil society increasingly intrude upon policy-making at the regime level, how do they affect subnational politics? Decentralization and changing intergovernmental relations have dramatically altered the context of social policy in Latin America. The principle of subsidiarity has gained currency. The resources managed by local governments, traditionally based on transfers, will have to be increasingly generated locally. Local politics, usually associated with clientelism, may yet yield to more participatory arrangements, especially as NGOs and social movements grow more insistent about *making* as well as *taking* policy, proposing solutions as well as protesting problems.

A comparative reference may be useful to this discussion. For example, the democratic transitions of Europe and Latin America—usually compared only at the regime level—are equally if not more relevant for analyzing local policy and subnational politics. First comes the question of the level of analysis. Lowi's classic distinctions among distributive, regulatory, and redistributive policies look very different according to whether they are viewed from above or from below. Revenue transfers by the center (redistribution) are often viewed as regulatory in the periphery. However, regulation by the center may be the only way distribution can occur in the periphery. For example, tied and targeted ministry funding for primary health care clinics in outlying urban *favelas* or *villas* offers perhaps the only vehicle by which services get delivered. From a comparative perspective, localism in urban Latin America, as in parts of Europe, may in the long run become an asset rather than a liability for democratizing central government. As Ashford noted:

> both ideological and administrative values may be reversed in subnational politics, that is, the sub-units may be bastions of radical opinion and protection for good governments in the system rather than conservative and corrupt strongholds. Political stability owes more to the "sotto-governo" (undergovernment) — competent administration and routinized competition at the local level — than to constantly changing ministerial actors. (1976, 54)

In sum, the merging of frontiers between public and private sectors may contribute to strengthening participatory local government and lead to more inclusive, diversified social policy. Territory, like ethnicity and culture, has a way of resurfacing on political agendas from which it has long since been banished. Negotiations, pacts, and compromise happen more readily through the propinquity principle: face-to-face encounters, while they may not guarantee good results, do require policymakers and -takers to at least explore accommodation, for they will meet again tomorrow.

Collaborative Ventures

Faced by nearly overwhelming fiscal crisis, municipal governments are increasingly receptive to collaborative ventures in service delivery, often seeking to emulate NGO flexibility, innovation, client responsiveness, and programmatic effectiveness: they may contract for training and technical assistance or piggyback NGOs to obtain resources and fill service gaps. Reform and popular municipal governments are multiplying. New mechanisms have been created to institutionalize participation and add a deliberative character to city government through neighborhood councils and associations. Not surprisingly, increased frequency of meetings and daily exchanges on topics of mutual concern have reduced distrust and opened doors to shared efforts between these public and private actors. In many democratizing settings, for example, reform leaders emerged from popular movements and NGOs.[4] They are known quantities.

What else do the NGO and social movements bring to the policy-making table? What have they learned on their journey from protest to proposal and what more must they learn? Many have long experience in negotiating grants with international donors. But making pacts, contracts, and deals even with local and national officials is a relatively new experience for the organized poor and their advocates. Independent research centers and think tanks, another key set of NGO actors, supply social scientists and technical personnel who can chronicle negotiations, assess tradeoffs, and help accelerate the organizational learning curve. They encourage more systematic and programmatic learning, identify technical problems, and formulate alternative social policy. In the final analysis, the challenges confronting policy and science are identical—for both are reduced to humanity as their ultimate measures.

Some clear messages for policymakers have emerged from the case studies included in *New Paths* (Reilly 1995). Many of these recommendations are context-specific. For example, Mexican participants argued that membership organizations must make pacts with federal technocrats in order to counteract local clientelistic elites. Colombia recently celebrated local elections for the first time in its history and, despite a relatively decentralized tradition, observers there are less concerned than in Mexico about neutralizing excessive elite power at the local level. Chilean NGOs contract with the health ministry to provide primary health care, while Brazilians protest privatized (for-profit) health care, which excludes the poor—the protest more vehement where such health care was once more readily available from the state, as in São Paulo.

Administrative efficiency and social efficacy challenge NGOs and local governments alike. The researchers (Reilly 1995) cited many experiments and ideas for promoting greater management skills in NGOs, finding more creative domestic fund-raising strategies, opening more channels of communication through mass media to policymakers (and takers), and easing NGO pilot programs more directly into the social policy stream. Given the need, it is time to celebrate even small victories. The environment of social policy is expanding to incorporate interests and actors previously excluded. Both the rules of the game and the number of players have expanded.

Recommendations

During this research enterprise (Reilly 1994, 1995) a number of recommendations emerged that seem relevant to most countries for further expanding the social policy dialogue. These policy and programmatic recommendations fall into three groups: those directed at NGOs and other organizations of civil society, those treating the relationships between NGOs and local governments, and those relating to the policy environment—usually determined by central governments although sometimes by international or multilateral agencies. Among the propositions and recommendations for NGOs and organized social movements (as well as international donors who support them), the following stand out.

NGOs
- Support enhanced technical, management, and analytical skills among NGOs, MOs, and GSOs.
- Stimulate more cross-fertilization: the transfer of ideas, experiments, and social technology within and across national boundaries.
- Promote greater NGO sophistication in information management, communications media, and formation of public opinion.
- Encourage NGO effort and creativity in *local* fundraising to help invent domestic philanthropy or reorient it from charitable toward development purposes.
- Respect heterogeneity of NGO communities and their own determination of suitable timing and shape of second—or third-level association (federations, consortia, networks, etc.).
- Encourage greater programmatic focus within NGOs, since holistic approaches are frequently utopian.
- Promote multiple-issue movements to obtain multiclass support.

NGO–Local Government Relationships
- Support NGO projects that feed into or give direction to public social policy.
- Stimulate NGOs to act as laboratories of social experimentation, technical assistance, and training for local governments; document the experiences.
- Generate more information on functions of local government and examples of effective mechanisms for relating to civil society (neighborhood councils, associations, etc.).
- Recognize low skill levels and rapid turnover of local government personnel. Recognize, also, that although often short on managerial and technical skills, NGOs tend to be more permanent actors.
- Document successful tax reform, innovative transfer mechanisms, and those collaborative ventures that can reduce the endemic fiscal weakness of local governments.
- Encourage NGOs to be more flexible and less doctrinaire, open to negotiating ties to the state at every level.
- Explore how NGO international fundraising and technical assistance might be replicated by local governments, e.g., intergovernmental lobbies, Sister Cities International, Partners of the Americas, etc.
- Identify in each country the comparative advantage of public and private actors (for primary health care, housing, education, etc.). Who more effectively delivered what, to how many?

Policy Environment
- Pay more attention to state and local governments and to intergovernmental relations.

- Expand fiscal capacity of local governments, especially tax-gathering capacity.
- Permit NGOs autonomous space to function as mediating structures for the design and implementation of social policy.
- Simplify regulatory environments and procedures whereby NGOs are legally recognized and made accountable.
- Demonstrate where privatized social services effectively deliver services to the poor (rather than discriminating against or merely neglecting them).
- Experiment with mechanisms and incentives to make contracting, fees for service, and other types of private-public exchanges feasible and attractive.
- Design legislation and regulatory packages to distinguish those NGOs actually providing goods and services from for-profit ventures seeking tax shelters.
- In this global economy, recognize that NGOs can generate solidarity and revenues abroad without unduly threatening sovereignty.

Latin American urbanization is irreversible (although democratization and development are not). According to the United Nations Population Division figures for 1993, Venezuela (at 94%) and Argentina and Chile (at 87%) had much higher proportions of their populations living in cities and towns than did the United States (at 75%). Brazil reached 78% in 1990, and Mexico, now at 74%, is almost as urban as its North American neighbors. Colombia (73%) and Peru (71%) are not far behind. How are urban populations to gain the most fundamental goods and services? Where and how does their citizenship begin? These cases of NGO and local government conflict and collaboration illustrate how Latin American city dwellers are forging their own variations of Tocquevillian democracy through the "art of association" despite growing "inequality of conditions."

Social Emergency Funds (SEFs), Social Investment Funds (SIFs), and Citizens

One by-product of structural adjustment programs enjoined by multilateral banks and the IMF throughout the region has been the proliferation of social emergency and social investment funds. Set up by national governments, often with international support, the funds support projects of for-profit firms and civil society organizations as well as local and regional governments. The impact of such funds on poverty reduction, on civil society organizations, and on approaches to social policy is the subject of an ongoing collaborative research project cosponsored by CLACSO (Consejo Latinoamericano de Ciencias Sociales) and the Inter-American Foundation. Here are some thoughts and preliminary findings on this set of relationships.

The prospects for sustained growth, secure income, civil societies, and democratic institutions are uncertain. The division of labor among state, market, and civil society has accelerated. The welfare state yields ground to markets, social gaps multiply, and some assume civil society can fill the breach. Structural adjustment packages, the current recipes for righting economic "wrongs" and restoring (or initiating) economic growth, have exacted a heavy toll, especially on the poor, prompting yet one more round of attention to poverty alleviation and social policy. Economic reforms that promise yet do not always produce growth are coupled with social programs that "target" yet often miss the poor. Like shotgun marriages, not all will endure. But optimists (and only optimists work in development) argue that if social emergency and investment funds cannot ensure material well-being, they can at least cushion the painful effects of reforms and help deepen democratic institutions by bridging the fault lines between public and private spheres.

Some new answers have been forthcoming for the old question that drives public policy: who gets what, when, how? Social investment funds (SIFs) and social emergency funds (SEFs) have been constructed throughout the region, some orchestrated by multilateral donors to cushion adjustment policies, others wielded as development instruments of national governments or political tools of chief executives. Often labelled compensatory, these funds or safety nets aim to soften the social costs of reforms. The funds are changing the rules of the game, increasing the number of players, modifying government social welfare institutions, and redefining relations between state and citizen. They may even contribute to recovering notions of the public good through more responsive and responsible allocation of resources. But they are not panaceas:

> Safety nets should not be confused with what the market or the state is expected to deliver; namely, economic growth and production in the first case and basic social services in the second. Safety nets cannot substitute for coherent macroeconomic management or the effective provision of social services. (Graham 1994, 5)

The Funds in a Nutshell
In most Latin American cases the social investment funds parallel government social ministries, depend directly on the presidency, target specific poor populations, often implement through NGOs and local governments, are financial intermediaries rather than executing agencies and, not surprisingly, may sometimes be handled in clientelistic and partisan ways. In rhetoric, if not in fact, social investment funds claim to be "demand-driven," responsive to specific requests of local populations, and they "target" specific beneficiary populations (women, children, indigenous peoples, street-children, etc.). Although they are expected to contribute to more participatory development while softening the

hard edge of adjustment, the funds have thus far invested far more in physical than in human capital—they have built more roads than organizational infrastructure.

Though originally designed to create jobs and weave social safety nets for the "new" poor, unemployed by government downsizing and privatization, and for those left unprotected by social security or deprived of subsidies, many of the funds have since become routine tools for poverty reduction and government decentralization. During a period of rapidly changing social policy and state reform, the funds bring a new approach to local level development by targeting poor populations and offering a menu of financial options ranging from grants to loans to contracts. Projects supported by the funds include a mixed portfolio of job creation, social and economic infrastructure, social services, and credit for productive activities.

The specialized funds experiment with channeling resources through decentralized institutions, both public (municipal and regional governments) and private, civil society organizations, nonprofit and profit-oriented contractors. The lion's share has thus far gone to for-profits:

> Private contractors have carried out most of the projects financed by the social investment funds. Bolivia's FSE, for example, financed civil works and equipment contracts involving close to 1,300 contractors, and Honduras's FHIS financed projects carried out by more than 1,200 contractors and consultants. Similarly, Bolivia's FIS, El Salvador's FIS, and Nicaragua's FISE financed projects carried out by hundreds of contractors, many of them small enterprises that were performing work financed by a government agency for the first time. The significant role NGOs play in the operations of most social investment funds has been another way of involving the private sector. (Glaessner et al. 1994)

From a grassroots perspective, these funds have begun to alter the environment and financing of local level development. They bring new choices to citizens, micro- and small businesses, NGOs, and social actors of civil society about the terms of participation, funding opportunities, and perhaps empowerment. The funds seek to induce policy change along the perennially unstable fault line between the public and the private in Latin America. They demonstrate once again that public goods have many producers beyond the state.

The funds are both cause and effect of new relationships between governments and civil society. They have advocates and detractors. Carol Graham offers a positive assessment:

> The funds respond to proposals from local governments, nongovernmental organizations (NGOs), and community organizations and then subcontract them to the local private sector or NGOs for implementation. By avoiding partisan

politics and the state bureaucracy, and by accepting proposals from the bottom up, these funds not only respond to the demand for essential services but enable the poor to participate in the formulation of proposals and thereby increase their potential political influence. In other words, demand-based social funds establish links between the poor and the state by providing a new mechanism through which the poor can solicit services from the state. By requiring the poor to participate in and contribute to the schemes, funds avoid a host of unrealistic demands on the one hand and centrally imposed solutions on the other. One drawback to such schemes, however is that the poorest of the poor—who are at the margins of society because of poor health, low education or remote locations—are the least likely to present viable proposals. (1994, 5–6)

A less sanguine appraisal of the funds (and of the adjustment process that spawned them) is expressed by UNRISD's Jessica Vivian:

The "social investment funds" set up to channel funding for development projects to vulnerable groups have as yet had only very limited impacts—with even the largest of such programs reaching a very small proportion of the vulnerable population. In addition, while there are hopes that such an approach to funding may provide an efficient and holistic alternative form of social service provisioning based on participation and empowerment, some evidence suggests that they in fact work to undermine public institutions and create new forms of clientelism . . . Targeted interventions meant to protect the poor and vulnerable groups from the worst aspects of adjustment never reach all of the poor, and seldom reach most of the poor. (1995, 2, 9)

Typology of Funds
During the past decade variations on social safety nets have evolved in different settings. The modal pattern and sequence was to first design funds to attenuate the most damaging effects of adjustment on the poor, usually by emergency measures like job creation through public works. Programs of social investment and human capital formation appeared next, supporting projects contributing to longer-term community development and enhanced labor skills. A third variant appeared in Mexico during the Salinas administration called PRONASOL. It was a broad social action program under the presidency with multiple funds available for geographic and sectoral initiatives to reduce poverty while creating alternative channels of political mobilization. A recent entry, Brazil's Communidade Solidaria (CS) created in 1995, emphasizes *articulação* or coordination of social policy and problem solving through state–civil society partnerships. Inspired by a citizen-organized campaign against hunger and directed by First Lady Ruth Cardoso, the CS program exemplifies convergent public and private initiatives for grappling with poverty. Figure 8.3 shows the pattern and progression of such social funds.

Figure 8.3 Fund Types (In order of appearance)

> Social Emergency
> > Social Investment
> > > Social Action
> > > > Social Coordination (Articulation)

"Demand-based targeting" of poor populations with social emergency and social investment funds dates from the 1980s in much of Latin America. Joint ventures with civil society continue to multiply. In 1996, the Venezuelan government invited a number of CSOs and foundations to help design and administer a fund for the support of civil society which will be financed by an Inter-American Development Bank (IDB) loan guaranteed by the government—probably the first such fund in the hemisphere. The Guatemalan government seeks to support community initiatives through a similar fund in the "Peace Zone" as part of the reconstruction process following the accords signed in December of 1996.

Preliminary Assessment (From a Grassroots Perspective)
The World Bank and the IDB have been major contributors to the funds, and USAID has contributed as well. Many governments have created them as components of their antipoverty (or patronage) policy portfolio. As a general rule, they began as temporary or "emergency" funds, concentrating on job creation and infrastructural improvements in the initial stages of adjustment, to be subsequently modified with an emphasis on longer-term human or social capital formation. While designers from multilateral institutions conceived of them as temporary solutions to short-term adjustment problems, the growth promised by "adjusters" remains illusory in many places. The funds (like other organizations) tend to self-perpetuate. NGOs and community organizations and subnational governments need new sources of support, so funds are incorporated into the social policy of governments and become permanent features of the landscape. Whether permanent or temporary, the funds have definitely altered state–civil society relationships. "Politicization" and "partisan manipulation" are the most frequent criticisms of the funds by civil society actors. Patronage and clientelism are endemic throughout the Americas—we hope the funds might help break that pattern.

While Bolivia pioneered the social emergency and social investment fund concept with generous infusions of external financing, Chile's Social Investment and Solidarity Fund (FOSIS) financed NGOs, popular participation, and decentralization primarily from government resources. No fund has been as encompassing and political as the National Solidarity Program in Mexico during the Salinas administration. Most of the funds now operating in more than a dozen Latin American countries will impact on national policy, subnational governments, and civil society actors like NGOs, sometimes occasioning tension and always requiring negotiation.

Independent, empirical data about the impact of SIFs and SEFs on participatory organizations and the structures of government are still scarce. Some trends are already clear. The funds have accelerated involvement of municipal and regional governments—central government funds are more routinely transferred to support decentralized activities. The funds sometimes displace government monopolies in delivering social services, or they fill voids by supporting nongovernmental, for-profit and nonprofit service providers where government has failed to deliver. They sometimes introduce competitive bidding processes and diminish clientelistic controls. Not surprisingly, effective funds complement effective government programs—a vigorous state enhances the fund.

Many local level organizations and communities have learned that problem-solving now means writing proposals to justify support: the state–civil society relationship works through "grantsmanship" or "a culture of projects." We lack evidence on the degree to which the funds enhance efficiency by creating competition with the public bureaucracy, for example, or when they really duplicate functions and multiply inefficiencies. Whether these funds will become permanent features of the policy landscape rather than temporary measures will, of course, vary from country to country. Their persistence will be determined by factors including the polices of international donors, whether adjustment yields adequate levels of growth, and the political choices of the many new Latin American presidents elected in 1994–95. For the moment, demand-based approaches to poverty speckle the Latin American landscape.

Just as resource mobilization is the principal challenge for NGOs of civil society, so partisan political manipulation is the major criticism of the funds. The issue *does* boil down to policies, to politics, and to "who gets what." Loveman (1995) concludes his assessment of Chile's fund thus:

> Ultimately the fate of FOSIS will depend on Chilean politics. If the Social Investment and Solidarity Fund creates a diverse enough constituency, avoids political partisanship and patronage, and continues inventing social experiments that improve hundreds of thousands of Chilean lives, it will be difficult to eliminate—even if its mission is redefined within the fight against poverty or subsequent policy initiatives. If FOSIS is used by incumbent governments as a partisan political instrument or electoral device, fails to carve out a recognizable, distinctive and legitimate niche in the governmental social policy apparatus, it will become dispensable. In 1995, however, FOSIS' future seemed promising, a small but innovative element of the Concertación government's war on poverty.

Figure 8.4 Illusion of Progress?

---

from social emergency
    to social investment
        to social firemen and women
            to social insurance
                to social empowerment

A Digression?

At the risk of caricature, since images sometimes convey more than concepts, it might be useful to sketch a typology of those who advocate the funds. The architects of macroeconomic reforms and structural adjustment were among the first to encourage social emergency funds, especially job creation efforts. Sensitive to sinecures, if not Michel's "Iron Law of Oligarchy," multilateral reformers emphasized the transitional nature of the funds and opposed permanent institutions. Subsequently, in places like Bolivia where, despite compliance with all the prescriptions of adjustment, growth has not occurred, the designers reluctantly supported longer-term social investment efforts. Other advocates come from the "volunteer firemen" school. Alarmed by actual and potential social explosions, these *bomberos* would use the funds to pour water on social conflagrations. A subtler approach comes from those who use funds as insurance, targetting zones of potential unrest as a shield for the rest of society. (Some observers in 1992 speculated that Mexico's PRONASOL was a double indemnity insurance policy—against the unraveling of the PRI, on the one hand, and for building a well-endowed launching pad for a possible re-election bid by Carlos Salinas, on the other.) Armando Bartra (1992), referring to PRONASOL, captured the criticism of many SIF critics: "The solidarity hand of the regime consoles the victims of the neoliberal hand."

Finally, there are some who think of development and poverty reduction as a means to give the excluded poor access to the bases of social power (capital, information, organization, networks, time and space). Organizational experience gained through the funds might enable poor and excluded people to obtain a broader distribution of power and wealth within and across societies. Lasswell's query "who gets what, when, how?" refers to social power as well as financial assets. (The typology need not be sequential, though my Utopian tendencies and wishful political thinking would definitely prefer this sequence, skipping intermediate steps whenever possible.)

Finally, I would like to note new trends emerging where civil society meets markets and markets meet the state. In these boundary zones have appeared some of the most promising and long overdue coalitions which might make enormous differences in the long run. It is here that the need for "border managers" is most pressing.

Making Room for Philanthropy

In January 1995 a global citizen's alliance called CIVICUS held its first international meeting in Mexico City. Within the space of a couple of hours, the audience of several hundred representatives listened to talks by Mexican President Ernesto Zedillo, Nobel Laureate Rigoberta Menchu, three NGO leaders from Brazil, Saudi Arabia, and the Philippines (each had been a political prisoner under authoritarian regimes), and finally David Rockefeller. He congratulated and chided the organizers, noting that their conceptual walls dividing state and civil society and markets were too tall and seamless, leaving no doors for someone like his grandfather John D. Rockefeller to walk through, since he had been entrepreneur and philanthropist and citizen at the same time.

The borders and the overlaps among civil society and markets and states do indeed require more doors and windows and better charts. None of the triad makes sense independent of the others—and none of them works well alone. Markets are not magical; indeed they often do not work very well. The 1980s celebrations of microentrepreneurs and the informal economy (often masking vitriolic antistate positions) have been muted somewhat as the sheer enormity of the challenge to create decent employment opportunities has settled in. The informal economy is no miracle drug—among the first to recognize this have been local governments whose fiscal crisis is made more acute by "informals" who, by definition, pay no taxes.

Discourse on philanthropy has erupted in the region: research and public discussion on the prospects and limitations of charity, welfare, "assistentialism," and development appear everywhere. In the past year major conferences have been celebrated in Mexico City, Montevideo, Buenos Aires, and Cali to discuss philanthropy, more benign juridical frameworks for creating business foundations, modified rules of the games for tax incentives, and more discriminating legislation on the rules of engagement for nonprofits and for-profits. The duties and responsibilities of "good corporate citizens" have grown more widely accepted. Codes of corporate ethics have been ratified by many companies. The danger of "phony philanthropoids" is being slowly but creatively addressed through new legislation in a number of countries.

Besides legal and motivational challenges confronting Latin American societies as they reassess philanthropy, I sense a generational shift occurring among entrepreneurs. Competition, globalization, and flexibilization are buzzwords for phenomena that indeed significantly shape the business environment. But equally significant is a restored sense of localism, regionalism, and nationalism which in Brazil, for example, has prompted corporate, banking, and media elites to join forces under the leadership of civil society organizations and rally around a major "Campaign against Hunger" at the national level. Entrepreneurs, media moguls, and bankers support an energetic "Viva Rio" campaign to polish the image of and life chances of poor people in that splendid but beleaguered city. In Colombia a variety of imaginative and proven models for linking finance to development activities, such as the Social Foundation and the Foundation for Higher Education, have caught the attention of other Latin American economic and social entrepreneurs.

Space and my personal limitations will not permit me to further explore the market–civil society connection in areas like job creation, labor alliances, technology transfer, globalization, competitiveness, etc. Just like citizenship, philanthropy and domestic resource mobilization are blossoming, suggesting that market contributions too will be graced by a distinctively Latin rhythm and beat.

Conclusion

Democracy includes a reasonably well-known and agreed upon mix of qualities which continues to beckon each generation inspired by Tocqueville. Governments are expected to be responsive and accountable to their citizens and to ensure them at least a minimum set of rights. Citizens should enjoy space for meaningful participation, have ready access to government officials, enjoy certain basic conditions for living a decent human life, and be prepared to shoulder their own responsibilities in the form of self-help, taxes, and the like. Rights and responsibilities should be broadly shared. A considerable degree of transparency should pervade relations between state and citizen, with competition being one of the proven mechanisms for ensuring peaceful and regular transitions in the polity. More effective forms of representation must be devised to meaningfully include absent majorities in the same way that they have usually served influential minorities. Primers on citizenship and democracy are far easier to write than to practice.

Tocqueville, besides admiring New Englanders' ease of associability, was deeply impressed by the relative equality of the people he observed there. Herein lies the extraordinary challenge to Latin American civil society, municipalities, philanthropists, and technocrats. New policy instruments must be crafted for overcoming inertia and instigating movement toward greater equity in a region accustomed (and often indifferent) to extraordinary inequality.

Things cannot go on the same. The Latin American issue is *not* one of poverty, for poverty is more tolerable and tolerated than gross inequity. Albert Hirschman reminded us long ago of the "tunnel effect": when traffic is stalled people resign themselves for a time; but if one lane of traffic begins to move forward and another lane stands still, civility wanes, tempers fray, and violence is not far off.

If growth is the key (tempered by natural resource limits and future generations' claims), human and social capital formation must occur, accompanied by redistribution of wealth. Jobless growth is a specter with intolerable implications, nor is social apartheid a realistic long-term option. New formulae for generating and taxing wealth, increasing productivity, creating worthwhile jobs, and multiplying self-help initiatives must be devised. Better tools for customized and diversified social spending must be invented, tested, and improved to deal with the variety of needs in civil society.

Diverse needs exact plural responses, taxing the ingenuity and inventiveness of economic, social, and political entrepreneurs. Command and control models keep surfacing, despite their conspicuous failures (and despite persuasive hints of chaos theorists that the edges of chaos are patterned and hardly chaotic). Markets and civil society can teach states a great deal about diversity, flexible specialization, market niches, consumer responsiveness, and learning from failure. Social investment funds can become citizen-responsive tools for filling gaps and encouraging experimentation in public policy design, implementation, and reformation. Municipal government-NGO collaborative ventures are promising and productive arenas for democratic practice and poverty reduction. The reinvention of philanthropy in Latin America is an overdue but welcome new asset, challenging the affluent as well as those of us in the development business to rethink assumptions about hermetically sealed compartments separating welfare and sustainable development, relief and incentives.

Let us stop placing all our bets on one or the other, state, market, or civil society, one at a time. Destructive as well as constructive impulses are lodged in each of them. A lean, if not mean, state can move from privatization to better serving the public ("public-ization," if you will); global and national market leaders can take "good corporate citizenship" as seriously as they do consumers; societies can make themselves more civil through self-help and provisioning, distribution and redistribution of goods and of values, responsibilities and rights.

Bridges are linking state, market, and citizen, showing new routes to more effective, customized social policy. They are not nearly enough. Something more is needed. State and markets counterpoised with civil society are my prescription for a real and more sustainable "Inter-American (rather than Washington) Consensus." But let me refine the prescription with one more wise and elliptic verse from Tom McGrath entitled "Flint and Steel":

> Mountain
>   Mesquite
>   Sea
>   Star
>   Flower*
>
> All the imperial nouns
> In their presumed autonomy
> Waiting
> For the little verb that
>   will kindle the fire.

*Might I add state, market, civil society?

NOTES

The thoughts expressed in this paper do not necessarily represent any of the institutions with which I am affiliated. My thanks to Víctor Tokman for his helpful observations on the civil society universe as well as to James Joseph for his comments grounded in the Peruvian reality he knows so well. The two poems by Thomas McGrath, from his *Selected Poems 1938–1988* (Port Townsend, Wash.: Copper Canyon Press, 1988), are quoted here in their entirety by permission.

1. Civil society is indeed a complex concept. Widely diverging interpretations flow, for example, from whether you start the journey from Hegelian or Tocquevillian entry points. There is a rich literature and debate inquiring where to locate new and old actors like entrepreneurs or social movements in the scheme or how to determine when "political society" transforms into the state. In these pages, I have opted for a graphically simplified and operationally driven approach to civil society and its relationships with the state and markets. Resolving the conceptual tangle is a chore I shall leave to others.

2. The Washington Consensus endorsed structural adjustment, privatization, state-downsizing and other neo-liberal reforms; see Williamson (1994).

3. I would like to create an ethical Gini index for tracking the relative distribution of virtue and vice amongst CSOs, states, and markets, and if I ever get the damn thing perfected, will be happy to share it with you!

4. For the Chilean case, see Loveman (1991).

REFERENCES

Ashford, Douglas. 1976. *Democracy, Decentralization and Decisions in Subnational Politics*. Vol. 5. Beverly Hills: Sage.
Barta, Amando. 1992. *Desigualdad y democracia*. Col. Tabacalera, Mexico: El Nacional.
Bellah, Robert, Richard Madsen, William M. Sullivan, et al. 1991. *The Good Society*. New York: Alfred A. Knopf.
Carroll, Thomas. 1992. *Intermediary Organizations*. Connecticut: Kumarian Press.
CIVICUS (World Alliance for Citizen Participation). 1994. *Strengthening Global Civil Society*. Washington, D.C.: CIVICUS.
Cohen, Jean, and Andrew Arato. 1992. *Civil Society and Political Theory*. Cambridge, Mass.: MIT University Press.
de la Maza, Gonzalo, ed. 1993. El Sector No Gobernamental y los fondos de inversión social: La experiencia chilena. *Educación y Comunicaciones* (September).
Diamond, Larry. 1994. Toward Democratic Consolidation. *Journal of Democracy* 5, no.3 (July): 4–17.
Dresser, Denise. 1994. Neopopulist Solutions to Neoliberal Problems. In *Transforming State-Society Relations in Mexico: The National Solidarity Strategy*, edited by Wayne Cornelius, Ann L. Craig, and Jonathan Fox. San Diego: Center for U.S.-Mexico Studies.
Ford Foundation. 1994. The Ford Foundation Report (Summer). New York: The Ford Foundation.
Friedmann, John. 1992. *Empowerment: The Politics of Alternative Development*. Cambridge: Blackwell.
Fukuyama, Francis. 1995. *Trust: The Social Virtues and the Creation of Prosperity*. New York: The Free Press.
Glade, William. 1991. *Privatization of Public Enterprises in Latin America*. San Francisco: ICS.
Glaessner, Michael, Kye Woo Lee, Anna Maria Sant'Anna, et al. 1994. *Poverty Alleviation and Social Investment Funds: The Latin American Experience*. World Bank Discussion Paper no. 261. Washington, D.C.: The World Bank.
Graham, Carol. 1994. *Safety Nets, Politics and the Poor*. Washington, D.C.: Brookings Institution.
Hirschman, Albert. 1985. *Getting Ahead Collectively*. New York: Pergamon.
IDB (Inter-American Development Bank). 1994. *Summary Report of the Conference on Strengthening Civil Society*. Washington, D.C.: IDB.
Inter-American Foundation. 1990, 1995. *A Guide to NGO Directories*. Arlington: Inter-American Foundation.
Jarquín, Edmundo. 1993. *Modernization of the State*. Inter-American Development Bank Working Paper. Washington, D.C.: Inter-American Development Bank.
Jorgensen, Steen, Margaret Grosh, and Mark Schacter, eds. 1990. *Easing the Poor through Economic Crisis and Adjustment: The Story of Bolivia's Emergency Social Fund*. Washington, D.C.: The World Bank.

Loveman, Brian. 1991. NGOs and the Transition to Democracy in Chile. *Grassroots Development* 15 (2): 8–19.
———. 1995. The Social Investment and Solidarity Fund (FOSIS) and the Chilean Political Transition, 1990–1995. Paper prepared for the Inter-American Foundation, Arlington, Virginia.
Mesa-Lago, Carmelo. 1993. Safety Nets and Social Funds to Alleviate Poverty: Performance, Problems and Policy Options. Issues note prepared for UNCTAD (United Nations Conference on Trade and Development), Geneva.
Morley, Samuel A. 1992. *Structural Adjustment and the Determinants of Poverty in Latin America*. Inter-American Development Bank Working Paper. Washington, D.C.: IDB.
O'Donnell, Guillermo. 1994. Delegative Democracy. *Journal of Democracy* 5 (January): 55–69.
O'Donnell, Guillermo, and Philippe Schmitter. 1986. *Transitions from Authoritarian Rule: Tentative Conclusions about Uncertain Democracies*. Baltimore: Johns Hopkins Press.
Pastore, José. 1988. *Projetos de desenvolvimento de base—Um estudo*. Arlington: Inter-American Foundation.
Putman, Robert, with Robert Leonardi, and Raffaelay, Nanetti. 1993. *Making Democracy Work: Civic Traditions in Modern Italy*. Princeton: Princeton University Press.
———. 1995. Bowling Alone. *The Journal of Democracy* 6 (January): 56–79.
Reilly, Charles A., ed. 1994. *Nuevas políticas urbanas: Las ONG y los gobiernos municipales en la democratización latinoamericana*. Arlington: Inter-American Foundation.
———, ed. 1995. *New Paths to Democracy Democratic Development in Latin America: The Rise of NGO-Municipal Collaboration*. English version. Boulder: Lynne Rienner Publishers.
———. 1995. *SEFs, SIFs and NGOs: Who Gets What When, How?* Inter-American Foundation Working Paper. Arlington: Inter-American Foundation.
Rodriguez, Ana. 1993. *Las políticas de ajuste, los fondos de inversión social y las ONG: Conclusiones del seminario del Cono-Sur-Brasil*. Working Paper, June 28. Rio de Janeiro: FASE-ALOP.
Salamon, Lester. 1994. The Rise of the Nonprofit Sector. *Foreign Affairs* 73 (July/August), no. 4.
Salamon, Lester, and Helmut Anheirer. 1993. *The Emerging Sector*. Baltimore: Johns Hopkins University Press.
Vivian, Jessica. 1995. *Social Investment Funds*. UNRISD (United Nations Research Institute for Social Development) Working Paper. Geneva: UNRISD.
Williamson, John. 1994. *The Political Economy of Policy Reform*. Washington, D.C.: Institute for Policy Reform.
Wolfe, Alan. 1989. *Whose Keeper? Social Science and Moral Obligation*. Berkeley: University of California Press.
World Bank. 1991. *World Development Report*. Baltimore: Johns Hopkins University Press.

Part IV

A New Political Economy of Poverty and Equity?

9 | Jobs and Welfare

Searching for New Answers

VÍCTOR E. TOKMAN

This chapter is not a synthesis of the book nor does it pretend to draw the main conclusions. That is left to the readers. Our objective is to offer our own reading of the situation, to highlight some of the answers provided by the contributors, and to identify the main queries that, in our view, merit further attention.

This book is about ways to alleviate poverty in Latin America, which essentially involves job creation, investing in people, and implementing a welfare policy. These are traditional instruments for old problems. However, the challenge today is different. The economic scenario has changed and social demands are greater than in the past. New policies are desperately needed to create new jobs and ensure a decent level of welfare. Reinventing policy in the new economic and social setting includes considering new instruments and redefining some of the old ones. But in addition, and no less important, it requires a new, systemic look, since the old order is becoming outdated and the emerging trends are still unclear.

This chapter will first deal with job creation in the new context. Then, it will look into education and training, followed by a discussion of social policies. It will conclude with a discussion on poverty and equity. We will refer to chapter 4 for the first aspect and to chapter 5 for the following one. The discussion of social policies will be related to the contributions made in chapters 6, 7, and 8. Finally, we will return to the topics analyzed in chapters 1 to 3, which present a diagnosis of the evolution of poverty and equity in Latin America and their relations with the demographic factors and the political system and also focus on emerging trends and political coalitions that will shape the future economic and social order and its eventual outcomes in terms of poverty and equity.

What is the new scenario that establishes the need for reinventing policy responses? There is wide agreement that three main changes are key to understanding it. First, we are living in a more integrated world. This is usually referred to as globalization, meaning that people and countries are closer and more interdependent today than ever before. Second, the private sector is playing a more important role, with the corollary that governments are intervening less. Third, markets and civil society have an expanded role in the regulation of the economy. This triple process of globalization, privatization, and deregulation affects the way to create jobs and to protect people and, in fact, begins to configure a new economic and social system.

Jobs Creation in the New Context

Three main issues have been identified in relation to changes in job creation: the determinants of job creation, the functioning of labor markets, and the relations among government, the market, and civil society.

The Determinants of Job Creation: Growth and Employment Relationships Redefined

Economic policymakers generally agree that job creation is determined primarily by what is happening outside the labor market. Job creation depends on economic growth, which in turn depends on investment and savings. The process of economic growth in the new economic scenario has fundamentally changed. Growth possibilities in a globalized world are increasingly associated with trade and international finances, since the opening of economies means enlarged access to world markets and more mobile capital. In addition, privatization increasingly transfers the responsibility for investment from government to the private sector. Public employment is no longer a primary source of job creation, as it was in the past in Latin America; indeed, in most cases it is not creating any new jobs at all. These processes have at least three important effects on the relationship between economic and social policies.

First, as private entrepreneurs assume an increasing responsibility for the creation of new jobs, they will have to invest more, and this requires adequate incentives, in particular, a sound macroeconomic policy, attractive returns on investment, and stability. Stability refers not only to low inflation but, more comprehensively, to the rules of the game. These in turn are closely related to the degree of social commitment to ongoing policies. Such commitment requires a perception of fairness by all social groups, in the sense that everybody receives a fair share of economic progress. Fairness is difficult to achieve when there is widespread poverty, very low wages, inadequate working conditions, or unbalanced bargaining powers. In fact, the new situation implies the need for a strong interaction between economic and social policies to ensure its sustainability.

Second, labor policies can contribute to economic growth, particularly to savings creation and stability. For example, recent social security reforms have introduced new mechanisms for savings mobilization, and national tripartite consultations contribute to the achievement of macroeconomic balances by wage moderation and by explicitly indicating commitment to economic reforms. As Cortázar points out in chapter 4, this will diminish country risks and attract investments.

Finally, a more competitive international environment requires a closer monitoring of the labor dimensions of trade. As presently discussed in many instances, sustainable trade expansion cannot be based on exploited labor, since this will increasingly affect both the country where exploitation takes place and the trading partners. This is the justification for the argument that the introduction of new regulatory mechanisms to safeguard against obtaining trade gains based on labor abuses. The discussions on this issue in the International Labor Organization (ILO) and the World Trade Organization (WTO), as well as in regional integration agreements such as NAFTA and Mercosur, recognize this emerging link and are designing new machinery to ensure that the benefits of globalization are fairly shared by all at international and national levels.

Labor Costs and Productivity in International Competitiveness

The new scenario reinforces the interrelationships between economic and social policies, opening new possibilities for innovative labor policies that contribute to a better economic performance while being socially more efficient. Moreover, globalization imposes more rigid economic constraints on social policies and requires changes at the microeconomic level, in the firm and in the industrial relations system. Cortázar emphasized that, in the new economic environment, a stronger link should be established between wages and productivity. In more open economies wage adjustments cannot go beyond productivity gains without affecting the capacity for international competitiveness. In addition, he notes that moving collective bargaining to the firm level, with less governmental intervention, will achieve wage settlements in a more flexible framework. We will return to this issue below.

Globalization affects wage determination and increases the importance of labor costs as a key factor for international competitiveness. Countries can risk their access to international markets if they overprice or overprotect their labor. In Latin America today this argument has provided justification for policy reforms aimed at moderating wage adjustments and diminishing labor protection. Available data, however, do not support such a policy direction; wages in most Latin American countries are below 1980 levels and labor costs in the manufacturing industry are between one-sixth to one-eighth of those prevailing in the United States and even below those of the Southeast Asian countries (ILO 1995). Nevertheless, it is clear that international competitiveness is affected by the evolution of labor costs, their relation with productivity changes, and the impact of the new generation of macroeconomic policies. Labor costs matter, but it also matters whether or not they are accompanied by productivity increases. Furthermore, in most cases, exchange policies that resulted in overvalued national currencies or changes in relative prices during the opening of the economies were equally important determinants of competitiveness in the recent past (Martínez and Tokman 1996).

Productivity is low in most Latin American countries, and therein lies another important area for policy reform in the new environment. Enterprises in the region, following a world trend, have been rapidly adapting to the more competitive framework by following cost reduction strategies, mainly downsizing and reducing employment levels, favored by labor reforms geared toward introducing flexibility for firing workers. Apart from the social costs involved in this type of adjustment, it may allow for short-run increases in productivity but it does not ensure continued expansion in the future. On the contrary, international experience indicates that moving from a cost reducing to a productivity expansion strategy is a major challenge. While cost reduction may be needed, as the case of Fiat in Italy, among others, illustrates, it is not enough. Fiat reduced its personnel by 20,000 during the eighties with inevitable adverse effects on labor relations. In the early nineties it has had to reinvent an industrial relations strategy to ensure trade union support in the search for a new car design; its obsolete car had become out-marketed by competitors (Piore et al. 1995). There is then a strong case for giving priority to the promotion of productivity expansion, since cost reduction strategies and flexibility, while in some cases justified, will have to be accompanied by long-term productivity strategies. These, in turn, are related to training and the prevailing climate of industrial relations both at the country and enterprise level.

Restructuring Relations among Government, Markets, and Civil Society

A third aspect raised in this book is that a new consensus is emerging, based on new roles for government, markets, and civil society. Latin American history presents many illustrations of extreme strategies, from the predominance of government over civil society without due attention to markets, to neoliberal periods where the markets were supposed to substitute for governments. In fact, both extremes resulted in a weaker civil society, either because of too much interference or because it was envisaged as representing interest groups and, hence, as constituting distortions to economic efficiency. Today there is agreement that a strong civil society is needed. This should be accompanied by more markets and by a strong government.

In most countries we are witnessing a transfer of power from the government to society, particularly in the labor field. This has been happening in a general context where markets matter. In labor law this move is called the passage from heteronomy (where the state defines, sanctions, implements, and monitors the law) to autonomy (where society has more space for agreements, given a more general regulatory environment). This move toward social autonomy will enhance the capacity to respond to economic challenges, as both Cortázar and Reilly argue. This transfer of responsibilities, if accompanied by a process of decentralization, will ensure flexibility and more adequate responses.

A word of caution should be introduced at this stage, since the move cannot ignore that the prevailing structure of power is unbalanced. Indeed, labor legislation to protect workers emerged as a recognition of their weaker power in relation to employers. Unfortunately, the situation remains unbalanced, and the move from heteronomy to autonomy may end up reinforcing the power of the powerful instead of empowering those who could contribute to a more balanced bargaining process. The answer, however, is not to postpone the process of change but rather to complement this strategy with other measures.

An important starting point is to begin developing collective actors and empowering them with the capacity to represent and technically intervene in economic and social matters. This requires some form of protection, but the way in which the state intervenes to ensure such protection can either promote autonomy or result in subordination of social actors to government or ruling political parties, as unfortunately has happened in many past instances. Government should not replace social actors by decreeing fixed wages or forcing unionization. In so doing, it will contribute to weaker unions rather than to the reinforcement of unions' autonomy and, hence, their bargaining power. In the last ten years a new, redefined form of intervention has been happening in many Latin American countries; nine constitutional reforms and six labor legislation reforms have been introduced to reestablish the rights of freedom of association and collective bargaining. These rights, which are prerequisites for trade union development, were severely restricted during the long authoritarian period in the recent past (Bronstein 1995).

We cannot ignore the fact that the decentralization of collective bargaining to the enterprise level can affect the capacity of unions to influence national decisions, since their power base is partly derived from collective bargaining at sectoral and national levels. This, however, need not be the inevitable outcome, provided that union strategies adapt to the new industrial relations scenario. The new setting allows room for national actors and collective action, because only at the national level can they contribute to ensure solidarity and social incorporation in the economic system. Decentralization of collective bargaining should not be taken as synonymous with decentralization of collective action, nor should bargaining at the firm level be the unique level of negotiation. Federations and confederations of workers have a role to play in supporting negotiations at different levels, and new areas are opening possibilities for action at such levels (e.g., training and social security) where the execution of recent reforms has been displaced from government to the private sector.

The transformation of industrial relations encompasses more than collective bargaining. To be meaningful, the social dialogue requires the incorporation of the unrepresented, either through the existing organizations or other means. Unions and employer organizations are increasingly approaching workers in the informal sector while, as Reilly shows, nongovernmental organizations (NGOs) are becoming active participants and key actors on specific issues. The agenda for discussion will go beyond wages and include training, productivity, and organization of the labor process. Decentralization should not be restricted to the enterprise; the local community is becoming a more important space for dialogue and policy implementation, particularly in the social field, as shown in Raczynski's chapter.

Thus new rules and new possibilities exist for collective action. It is clear that decentralization will facilitate more rapid responses to economic challenges, but at the same time collective action at the national level can provide unique contributions to economic stability with social progress. The challenge is how to ensure consistency between the two.

Investing in the People

A second area of consensus identified in this book is the need to invest in people, particularly in education and training. This is an old area, but its priority and the way to approach it are affected by the changing world conditions.

The experience of recent decades is clearly showing that growth is increasingly knowledge intensive and that the more successful countries are those that have invested in educating and training their people. It is also becoming clear that the illiterate or those who do not have access to education are becoming the new marginalized. Investment in education and training is an essential requirement for the progress of individuals and nations in a globalized world.

The renewed priority in this area is accompanied by the need to adapt the traditional training model which, as Gallart described, has been organized in two layers. One, incorporated in the formal educational system as technical secondary education, is geared primarily toward the children of the working class. The other is based in large public institutions that train workers in the skills demanded by manufacturing expansion. This form of delivery is showing its limitations, particularly in relation to the relevance of training and its effective demand in the labor market but also in relation to the interactions with the educational system at the primary level.

Changes in the skill profile and job contents associated with the new wave of technological innovation are creating a demand for competences more than for specialized skills. These competences are related to abilities gained at the primary educational level; hence, the reform has to go beyond the technical training sphere. These basic abilities are developed in the early stages and constitute a prerequisite and a base for adaptation of skills, according to needs emerging from a more dynamic system. Adequate preparation of labor for the economy requires a new alliance among primary education, secondary technical education, and training.

The emerging model presents several additional characteristics that differentiate it from the prevailing one. To better respond to labor markets requirements, training must be demand—rather than supply—driven. This requires closer links between training and the enterprises. Secondary level education must be redesigned, since that level has proven to be important for countries experiencing productivity convergence (Tillet 1995). Vulnerable groups will require special public attention, in particular, youth from poor families, informal sector workers, and workers in need of labor reconversion, usually associated with privatization.

Two comments should be made in relation to the new configuration of the system. The first refers to the priority given to secondary education, particularly at the technical level, for this can be read as contradictory to prevailing wisdom about giving preferential attention to the primary level. For Latin American countries with almost universal educational coverage at the primary level, the challenge at that level is to increase quality and even out the differences between schools attended by children of the poor and the nonpoor. But, as argued before, the technical capacities demanded by modern enterprises are closely linked to an adequate secondary level education.

The second comment refers to the institutional redesigning that is taking place. Increasingly enterprises will play an important role in the training system to ensure a closer link with demand. Important externalities, however, will continue to justify public programs. Enterprises cannot be held responsible for all training, nor will they have the incentives to make the investment in an unstable labor market. Small and microenterprises are unable to deliver training by themselves and will require other arrangements. There is, finally, agreement in opening participation in training delivery to the private sector.

All these changes challenge the existing training institutions developed in the framework of the previous strategy. Should they be closed or is there room for institutional adaptation? Indeed, some are already adapting to the new form of operation and, particularly, trying to respond to the needs of the vulnerable groups. In addition, although training policies should probably be decentralized in their execution, mechanisms for orientation and monitoring will be necessary to ensure quality levels. This role constitutes a public domain and will have to be performed at a more centralized level by creating a space in the public administration or by reconverting the existing training institutes.

A New Generation of Social Policies

In the following discussion we refer to social policies from a comprehensive perspective because the issue, as correctly examined by Filgueira (chapter 6), Raczynski (chapter 7), and Reilly (chapter 8), is how to reconstruct—or create in countries where it doesn't exist—a welfare system that can respond to present demands and operate within the new constraints. This requires a systemic view, where poverty alleviation is a crucial strategic part but not the whole, and where efficient policies are important components for a workable system.

The welfare system in Latin America was never as comprehensive as in developed countries. Its coverage was limited, as a result of different structural characteristics and financial restrictions. It could only be applied to integrated segments of the population and coverage varied by country. To this historical feature is now added the questioning of the welfare systems within developed countries. The critique is based on the high costs and inability to cope with increasing demands for benefits in times of higher unemployment and aging of the population. This aggravates the redesigning task for developing countries which must cope with past and present challenges in a situation where resources have not been adequately managed during recurrent periods of rapid inflation and where contributions represent a significant part of labor costs.

The need for reform is beyond discussion; the issue explored in this book moves one step further, trying within a comprehensive approach to advance ideas about the general orientation of the reformed system: what and how to reform and the operational innovations that constitute best practices.

Given the financial restrictions, the general redesigning of the system has to make hard choices about focusing its impact on feasible options. Concentration on meeting at least a minimum of needs in a universal manner seems to be a first priority criteria. This includes covering specific risk-related situations, such as old age (pensions), health and nutrition, and coverage of other basic needs like establishing social safety nets to compensate for temporary lack of income owing to unemployment or insufficient incomes. At present these are largely covered by public systems and most Latin American countries offer wide-ranging coverage, except for safety nets. While coverage is wide, benefit levels are very low and the quality of services poor. Raczynski has raised the question of whether the sole purpose of the new system should be coverage for the poor and destitute or whether it should include other social objectives beyond poverty alleviation. In countries with unequal social structures and marked differences of income, a reformed system will need to cover people who, in some cases, are above poverty levels but are vulnerable. It must also include means to facilitate social integration.

Education
An obvious sector in which to ensure more equal opportunities is education, which should be an integral component of the social package. Again, the critical issues go beyond universal coverage of primary education and include strategies for narrowing the gap in educational quality differences based on income levels and introducing complementary programs to compensate for household constraints, which result in unequal opportunities. In addition, broader access to secondary education is needed to expand the opportunities to compete for better jobs. Just how far the focusing should go in terms of needs and groups of people to be covered is a crucial first decision to confront.

Reform
A second aspect very much present in today's debates and in several chapters of this book is *what* and *how* to reform. Here we must make an important distinction between persons already covered, particularly by mandatory social security and health systems, and those outside the systems, mostly people in rural areas and informal sector workers. The bulk of existing protection was designed in relation to jobs in modern sectors and was difficult to access for groups without formal employment. The reform process has so far concentrated on the former, largely overlooking the latter problem. This trend is not surprising, given the prevailing view of limiting public welfare to the poor. The key reform issue has been privatization, particularly how far the private sector should assume roles previously performed by public institutions. This is clearly illustrated in the case of social security and pensions. Cortázar and Raczynski have shown that the Chilean option has been for full privatization accompanied by a change to an individual capitalization system rather than the more traditional system of intergenerational transfers. More recent reforms, for instance in Argentina and Uruguay, have opted for mixed systems allowing for the coexistence of private and public, and for distributive and individual accounts. In most cases, the package is complemented with a welfare policy covering those outside the

system, although at very minimal levels of support. Reforms in the health sector have also faced the issue of privatization and private sector responsibility. The Chilean option was to privatize health care entirely for the middle and upper income groups, while Colombia chose a mixed system with a solidarity component.

Indeed, there are several options and the reforms are too recent to be able to evaluate results. It is already clear, however, that the reforms in the Chilean pension system are having an important positive effect on savings mobilization and on reducing the cost of the system. The level of pensions in the future will depend on return of the invested funds. The solidarity component composed of intergenerational transfers, albeit imperfect, built in the previous system, is absent from the new design. This is, perhaps, the main reason, apart from political conditions, that led other countries to go for a mixed system. The problem of solidarity transfers is, however, seen more clearly in the case of health, where higher income groups traditionally contributed to finance the health expenditure of the poor. By segmenting each group, the transfers are interrupted and the fiscal burden on general revenues increases. In addition, the coexistence of different systems in a market where interactions are strong affects both costs and expectations of the lower income groups. This is, then, the second issue on which policy options will have to be decided.

Extension of coverage to those outside the system raises an important pending social issue. The history of social security coverage in Latin America shows a progressive, although slow, inclusion of new groups that were able to successfully exercise pressure. The recent reforms will have indirect effects on the issue of coverage, but their outcome is yet unclear. On one hand, lowering the cost and transferring the entire contribution to the workers could facilitate access for those in informal activities. Yet the low level of income of informal workers and their precarious employment conditions, associated with instability of occupations and incomes, remain a problem. This situation provides neither the capacity nor the incentive to join a system that assumes a permanent income at an adequate level. Parallel to the reforms, several proposals are being analyzed to respond to the lack of coverage of informals. These include differentiating the benefits package according to contributions or by generating other mechanisms managed by civil society organizations. This issue cannot be left out of any reform with an inclusive social perspective; otherwise, social differences will be further institutionalized.

Operational Issues
A third element for consideration in the social protection reform process is to take advantage of innovations in operational aspects when executing social policies. There are at least four important aspects that the new generation of social policies is incorporating to different degrees. The first is privatization. As

previously discussed, it is clear that the private sector should participate more than in the past, but how much and in what way? In particular, can private and public execution of services coexist or should all social protection to the non-poor be completely privatized? Might the execution of publicly financed coverage for the poor be privately executed? Another issue under discussion is privatizing the decisions through transfers of income to the people who will freely select their coverage and the supplier, as opposed to a more restricted provision of specific services. These, as Raczynski correctly argues, are crucial choices which mark the differences between the prevailing approaches to privatization.

The second issue is decentralization. There is consensus on the efficiency of decentralization and yet there are many problems to be overcome in order to obtain the expected results. These include the complexity of relations among different government levels, the transfer of responsibilities without adequate transfer of resources, the lack of trained human resources at the local level, and the degree of community and NGO involvement at the local level.

The third operational issue on which there is agreement, in principle, is that of finance. Cost recovery should be the goal wherever possible, while public funds should be used to provide basic services for those who cannot afford to pay. Gray areas are those, like education, that can precisely make the difference between a social policy exclusively directed to the poor and another that promotes social integration. This is closely connected to the last operational aspect, targeting.

Although targeting offers the advantage of economic efficiency, there are important, socially grounded arguments to move with caution in this direction. In particular, coverage of vulnerabilities that correct gender discrimination (maternity benefits) or age (pensions), among others, while benefiting nonpoor groups are still important. The same can be argued in relation to some middle-income groups that in the last decade have been severely affected by targeting and cost-recovery policies on the social front and by loss of jobs due to the adjustment policies. As a result, societies have become more polarized.

We make two additional observations to end this section. One, introduced by Filgueira, refers to the different vulnerabilities; the other relates to differences among countries. Different groups are affected by diverse vulnerabilities, presenting different degrees of complexity. There are the traditionally excluded groups, mostly living in rural areas, whose vulnerability is well known but not addressed. These groups tend to contain concentrations of indigenous populations and other racial minorities; thus exclusion tends to be mixed with discrimination. A second, more recent vulnerable group is composed of those directly affected by the restructuring process: the unemployed from the public sector or from enterprises undergoing privatization or downsizing. This is generally a middle-income group, politically connected, highly organized, and traditionally well protected. Affected economically, and often psychologically, some try to react collectively by challenging the reform, while others opt out individually by resignation or by blaming themselves for societal effects.

The second observation is that, although there are some universal features of welfare systems among countries, unique characteristics within countries demand diverse responses. A country's size and degree of heterogeneity, its level and distribution of social expenditure, its stage in the reform process, and its political conditions will all shape different strategies. Hence, there can be no universal recipe for reform.

Poverty and Equity: Is There a Post-Adjustment Model?

We have saved the topic of poverty and equity for the final section of this chapter because the analysis of the main trends in poverty and equity leads to a key question that merits further discussion. In the remarks concluding his chapter Altimir asks whether a new, post-adjustment paradigm has emerged for distribution of income. This is a crucial issue, and although the available evidence is still too scant for a complete response, some preliminary comments can be offered.

Altimir clearly shows that poverty has increased during the adjustment period and that inequality is greater in most countries than it was previous to the debt crisis. Carvalho brings good and bad news about the effects of the fertility transition on poverty. Good for the near future, for the reduction in the child dependency rate will allow for better use of social expenditure oriented to the young; bad in the longer run, because there will be an increase in the elderly dependency ratio that will put additional pressure on already fragile social security systems. O'Donnell introduces the political factors hindering effective antipoverty strategies and suggests a potential alliance of the poor with middle classes as a basis for sustainable policies in democracy.

The trends shown in chapter 1 are well founded and not surprising. Anyone who has followed the adjustment period would expect this outcome since adjustment imposes a cost and, given the unequal society prevailing in Latin America, there are different capacities to compensate for such cost. The expected result is that the poor, who are the most vulnerable, will suffer more than the higher income groups, although every stratum will probably experience income reduction. In fact, what emerges from the data is that the main losers were the urban middle groups affected by unemployment, income deterioration, and reduced social expenditures. They constitute the new poor and accounted for most of the increase in poverty between 1980 and 1990. Eighty-eight percent of the 60 million new poor were in cities and, of these, 80% were nonindigent poor (Tokman 1995).

What comes next? To start answering this question, we will make two observations and a comment based on several points raised in the different chapters and on our own interpretations. This is, of course, geared to open rather than to conclude the debate on this issue.

The first observation is a methodological one. When analyzing poverty and equity trends, it is necessary to specify the reference of comparison. A country can have a good performance as compared to its past and still be one where poverty and inequity are very large. The usual methodological way out, by resorting to international comparisons, should also be handled with caution. If we compare Latin American performance with that of Asian countries (as has become fashionable), our region is indeed a poor performer. But such comparisons should not be extrapolated irrespective of cultural and institutional differences, which are determinant factors for policy, particularly when dealing with poverty and equity issues. Clearly, the NGO role and the organization of the community adopt different forms in different cultural environments. Income distribution is partly the result of the same factors. Institutions prevailing in Southeast Asia cannot easily be transplanted to Latin America nor to Switzerland or the United States. For instance, when comparing the distribution of income, one can find in Asia differences of 5 to 7 times between the income received by the highest 20% and lowest 20%. In the United States the same differential reaches 9; in Switzerland between 9 and 10; and in Latin America, where differences have been historically large, it is well into two digits.

The second observation regards whether we have countries in the region that are already in the post-adjustment era and what we can learn from their experience. Chile is often identified as a good example and considered to be a success story. It has been growing for a long period at fast and sustained rates without generating macroeconomic unbalances. It has lowered unemployment, increased real wages, and managed to substantially diminish poverty levels. Between 1987 and 1994 the percentage of households below the poverty line declined from 38% to 24%. These are remarkable achievements. Equity, however, is not improving along the same lines. Income differentials between the upper and the lower 20% remain constant around 12. Is that differential high for a country like Chile?

Despite our previous observation, taken with due care, it is interesting to compare Chile's performance with successes of the new Asian tigers. Malaysia and Indonesia, for example, have rapidly integrated into world markets and have registered sustained growth with low inflation in the last decades. Their record on poverty reduction is remarkable: between 1970 and 1990 poverty levels in Malaysia diminished from 49% to 17%; in Indonesia, between 1980 and 1990, the reduction was from 39% to 16%. In contrast with Chile both countries also managed to reduce income differentials, from 17 to 12 in Malaysia and from 7.5 to 5 in Indonesia. Why?

Another relevant comparison can be made between Chile and the United States because, while differences in the level of development are greater, institutions and policies are more similar. Surprisingly, the comparison shows that the income share for the bottom 20% is similar in both countries and has remained constant around 4% for decades. It also reveals that the upper 20% in Chile receives 55% of total income compared to 42% in the United States. The rich in the United States possess less relative income than in Chile. To find in the United States a share similar to the one prevailing in Chile, one has to go back to pre-1930. This comparison suggests that Chile seems to be heading toward a twenty-first-century capitalism with an early twentieth-century income distribution. It also suggests that the use of international comparisons for policy purposes when dealing with poverty should not be restricted to those regarding the poor but should consider those applied to the rich, particularly for purposes of tax policies.

The final reflection relates to policy implications in a broader sense. There is general agreement that, to deal with poverty, equity considerations must be introduced. But, although equity matters on ethical grounds, the risk is high of reverting to discussions from earlier Latin American periods when equity was postulated as a normative statement in a progressive environment without taking into account the economic feasability. The new structural context that is in the making and the substantial reform in policy management requires more than a restatement of the importance of equity.

The two pillars of the old system—the search for full employment and systemic solidarity—are under severe questioning and, in many cases, have been de facto abandoned as the result of the process of reform. The search for full employment was the most important instrument to incorporate people into good jobs and upward channels of mobility, resulting in greater homogeneity of society. Systemic solidarity was geared to correct social imbalances that could not be remedied through productive insertion, primarily through labor and welfare policies granted by protective laws and national institutions.

Full employment has been progressively abandoned owing to the overriding priority on stabilization, which has led to more restrictive policies, and because technological changes are enabling productivity increases without creating jobs. The present discussion of this trend of "jobless growth" or "the end of jobs" largely accepts that the search for full employment is no longer a feasible strategy.

Systemic solidarity has also been affected by several factors, particularly by the predominance of economic over social objectives. Globalization and privatization are leading to the adoption of more flexible labor policies and to the protection of entrepreneurs as the main actors responsible for job creation. This affects the government's capacity to implement redistributive fiscal policies, which are increasingly envisaged as antiproductive interventions. Social policy changes also affect systemic solidarity, both because public transferences become easy targets in time of priority concern about balancing the budget and because focusing, while justified on efficiency grounds, implies a redistribution from the middle to the bottom.

Individual action is gaining spaces over collective action. In the labor field, decentralization to the firm means weaker instruments for social mobilization and at the enterprise level, new technologies are replacing the collective worker by the individual one, since job diversity is making the identification of common interests more difficult. Similarly, social solutions to risk situations are increasingly transferred to individuals or the family, while collective action by the government is concentrated on the very poor. Indeed, economic efficiency considerations are important for maintaining a workable system in the new environment, but unless compensatory mechanisms are introduced, social disintegration cannot be ruled out in the future.

Does it matter? Large and even growing differences can coexist with successful policies of poverty reduction and with more efficient social targeting protecting the most vulnerable. How disfunctional is inequity and how far can it be tolerated? These are difficult questions to answer and we will limit our response to two final comments.

First, poverty and equity are not independent. The rhythm of progress in fighting poverty is linked to the capacity to change the distribution of income. If the rich cannot be taxed, there will be fewer resources to transfer to the poor. It is simple arithmetic: fewer resources mean longer periods of poverty. It is true that increased efficiency in the use of the resources can compensate to some degree, but it is also clear that it is becoming more difficult to introduce tax reforms, and the reforms that are adopted end up taxing everybody through indirect taxation rather than taxing incomes and capital gains. In addition, globalization is not only a phenomenon within the world of trade and finances but also in communications. The communications revolution has meant that people are closer than ever both internationally and within the same country. This leads to the homogenization of consumer expectations. Advertising and communications appeal to everyone to participate in the introduction of new products, a factor that, by itself, is the main avenue for technological innovation. Nevertheless, expectations are not equivalent to consumption, and the old dilemma of expectations unmatched by income possibilities is becoming more acute, even in cases where the incomes of the poor might be growing, because of the acceleration of expectations.

Second, we try to anticipate what kind of society is emerging. O'Donnell's analysis suggests that polarization is already happening. One group, with access to better jobs, is opting for exit as a means of protection: They live in separate urban areas, have special schools for their children and, increasingly, are creating their own police. Partly, this behavior is a reaction to increased urban violence and to the low quality of public services, but to a great extent it also reflects an economic and social option. The other side of the coin of course, is the majority of the people who can move only slowly, if at all. While some travel by TGV (high-speed train), others are still pulled by the old steam engines; a two-track society exists. Present differences may be transmitted generationally; children attending better schools will be better prepared for the future. Educational quality is increasingly the result of location, general environment, and quality differences between the public and private systems. The few available evaluations show higher levels of quality in private schools, and elites are no longer graduating from leading public schools, as they did in the past, where access was not dependent on socioeconomic background.

The contributors to this book suggest several answers to ensure a more integrated society. Job creation is a top priority for competing in the new international environment. Investing in people, particularly in education and training, is strongly supported as a means to expand opportunities, a prerequisite for more equitable social integration. Redistributive measures, especially tax reforms, were not ruled out of the agenda.

Two additional proposals are worth noting. The first envisions the creation, or preservation, of an institutional capacity in government and the recovery of public spaces for social coexistence. This does not mean a return to traditional public intervention; the new generation of policies incorporates the active participation of the private sector and civil society. It does, however, highlight the importance of institutional development, after a first stage of adjustment that largely ignored this factor, and it accents the need to recover the possibility of establishing free access spaces where people of different socioeconomic backgrounds can coexist and benefit from each other. Establishing these spaces would involve recuperating the quality of public education at both primary and secondary levels and maintaining public goods such as parks and media spaces, which provide opportunities for sharing.

The second proposal makes a strong case for empowering people, since policies cannot be successfully implemented without the involvement of and capacity to mobilize those who are to benefit. This is true for unions and for the community as a whole.

The proposals contained in this book constitute the basis for an emerging consensus that will require a different set of relations among the state, market, and civil society. This consensus will necessitate changes of policies and strategies of social actors and, to be politically feasible, it will have to build new coalitions.

REFERENCES

Bronstein, A. S. 1995. Societal Change and Industrial Relations in Latin America: Trends and Prospects. *International Labour Review* 134, no. 2.

ILO (International Labor Organization). 1995. Labour Overview '95. *ILO News*. Lima: ILO Regional Office.

Martínez, D., and V. E. Tokman. 1996. *Costo laboral en el sector manufacturero de América Latina: Incidencia sobre la competitividad en el sector y la protección de los trabajadores*. Lima: ILO Regional Office.

Piore, M. R. Locke, and T. Kotchan. 1995. Reconceptualizing Comparative Industrial Relations: Lessons from International Research. *International Labour Review* 134, no. 2.

Tillet, A. 1995. Commentary on the paper "Restructuring, Education and Training" by María Antonia Gallart, October, IDRC, Montevideo.

Tokman, V. E. 1995. *Pobreza y equidad. Dos objetivos relacionados*. Lima: ILO Regional Office.

Appendix

Poverty in Latin America: Issues and New Responses

WORKSHOP

I. General Trends in Poverty, Equity, and Employment in Latin America

   Chair: Vilmar Faria, UNICAMP; Special Advisor to the President, Brazil

   1. Inequality, Employment, and Poverty in Latin America: An Overview
      Oscar Altimir, CEPAL, Chile

   2. The Demographics of Poverty and Welfare in Latin America: Challenges and Opportunities
      José Alberto Magno de Carvalho, CEDEPLAR, Brazil

   3. Poverty and Inequality in Latin America: Some Political Reflections
      Guillermo O'Donnell, Kellogg Institute

   4. Issues and Policy Experiences in Various Countries

      Chair: Paulo Sérgio Pinheiro, USP, Brazil

      Discussants: José Márcio Camargo, PUC–Rio de Janeiro, Brazil
      Ulpiano Ayala, Former Deputy Minister of Finance, Colombia
      William W. Goldsmith, Cornell University

II. Globalization, Economic Restructuring, and Job Creation

1. Globalization and Job Creation

    Chair: Kwan Kim, University of Notre Dame

    Paper by: René Cortázar, CIEPLAN, Chile

    Discussants: Azizur Rahman Khan, University of California, Riverside
    Albert Berry, University of Toronto
    Rolando Cordera Campos, *Revista NEXOS*, Mexico

2. Restructuring, Education, and Training

    Chair: Jaime Ros, University of Notre Dame

    Paper by: María Antonia Gallart, CENEP, Argentina

    Discussants: Juan Antonio Aguirre Roca, Confederación Nacional de Instituciones Empresariales, Peru
    Norma González Esteva, Secretaría del Trabajo y Previsión Social, Mexico
    Anthony D. Tillett, International Research Development Center, Canada

III. Alternatives for Facing Poverty and Vulnerability

    Chair: Atilio Borón, EURAL, Argentina

    1. Welfare and Citizenship: Old and New Vulnerabilities
        Carlos Filgueira, CIESU, Uruguay

    2. The Crisis of Old Models of Social Protection and New Alternatives for Dealing with Poverty and Vulnerability
        Dagmar Raczynski, CIEPLAN, Chile

    3. Balancing State, Market, and Civil Society: NGOs for a New Development Consensus

        Chair: Ernest Bartell, C.S.C., Kellogg Institute

        Paper by: Charles Reilly, Inter-American Development Bank

        Discussants: Luis Fernando Cruz, Fundación Carvajal, Colombia
        Renato Poblete, S.J., Hogar de Cristo, Chile
        James Joseph, Centro Alternativa, Peru

IV. Wrap-up: Conclusions and On-Going Questions

    An Emerging System? New Roles for Social Actors; New Boundaries and Mixes for Governmental, Public, and Private Actions

Presenters: Víctor E. Tokman, International Labor Organization, Peru
Vilmar Faria, UNICAMP; Special Advisor to the President, Brazil

PUBLIC POLICY FORUM PANELISTS

Juan Antonio Aguirre Roca
Confederación Nacional de Instituciones Empresariales Privadas, Peru

Patricio Aylwin
Former President of Chile

Nancy Barry
President, Women's World Banking, U.S.A.

Rolando Cordera
NEXOS, Mexico

Vilmar Faria
Special Advisor to the President, Brazil

Jorge Garfunkel
Banco del Buen Ayre, Argentina

José Antonio Ocampo
Minister of Planning, Colombia

Rodolfo Paiz-Andrade
Former Minister of Finance, Guatemala

Renato Poblete, S.J.
Hogar de Cristo, Chile

Jorge A. de Regil
Partner, Baker & McKenzie, Mexico

Charles Reilly
Inter-American Development Bank

Benedita da Silva
National Senator, Brazil

Paulo Renato Souza
Minister of Education, Brazil

Contributors

OSCAR ALTIMIR
　Director of *CEPAL Review*, and former Deputy Executive Secretary of the United Nations Economic Commission for Latin America and the Caribbean (ECLAC), Santiago, Chile.

JOSE ALBERTO MAGNO DE CARVALHO
　Professor of the Department of Demography and the Center for Regional Development and Planning (CEDEPLAR), Federal University of Minas Gerais, Brazil.

RENÉ CORTÁZAR
　Former Minister of Labor and Social Security of Chile, Executive Director of Televisión Nacional de Chile and Associate Researcher at the Corporación de Investigaciones Económicas para Latinoamérica (CIEPLAN), Santiago, Chile.

CARLOS H. FILGUEIRA
　Director of the Centro de Informaciones y Estudios del Uruguay (CIESU), Montevideo, Uruguay.

MARÍA ANTONIA GALLART
Sociologist, Senior Researcher at the Center of Population Studies (CENEP), Argentina, and Coordinator of the Latin American Network of Education and Work, Buenos Aires, Argentina.

GUILLERMO O'DONNELL
Helen Kellogg Professor of Government and International Studies, and former Academic Director of the Kellogg Institute for International Studies at the University of Notre Dame, Notre Dame, Indiana, U.S.A.

DAGMAR RACZYNSKI
Sociologist and Senior Researcher at the Corporación de Investigaciones Económicas para Latinoamérica (CIEPLAN), Santiago, Chile.

CHARLES A. REILLY
Director of the Peace Corps in Guatemala and former Senior Advisor on Civil Society at the Inter-American Development Bank, and Vice President of the Inter-American Foundation, Washington, D.C., U.S.A.

VÍCTOR E. TOKMAN
Assistant Director General and Regional Director for the Americas of the International Labor Organization, Lima, Peru.

Index

adjustment process: changes in macroeconomic phases of, 8–10; cushioning, 194–96; effects during 1980s, 12
Administradores de Fondos de Pensiones (AFPs), 155
administrative decentralization, 181
age discrimination, 219
age distributions, 38, 39–40, 42 table 2.2, 43
Altimir, Oscar, xii, 54, 220
antipoverty strategies, and politics, 220
apprenticeship programs, 102–3
Argentina: adjustment process, 9; decentralized collective bargaining, 82; dualism, 54; education and training, 100, 103; income distribution, 11, 13; inequality, 11; job security, 82; labor force utilization, 10; old social protection model, 141; poverty during economic growth, 49; poverty identification, 124; reforms, 7, 83, 217; social expenditures, 19; social security coverage, 137 n. 14; stop-go growth, 16; total fertility rates (TFRs), 37; urbanization of population, 193; urban poverty, 7, 13; wages, 11, 14; welfare state, 49
Ashford, Douglas, 190
Asia, 221
authoritarian regimes, 57, 64 n. 30
automated technologies, 93
autonomy, passage from heteronomy, 213

Bamberger, M., 159
Bartell, Ernest, xi
Bartra, Armando, 199
Bellah, Robert, 178
birth control policies, 38, 39
births, 43. *See also* TFRs (total fertility rates)

233

Bolivia: old social protection model, 141; population growth rate, 38; social funds pioneering, 197; social investment, 199; social security coverage, 137 n. 14
Bradford, C.I., Jr., 148
Brazil: absolute poverty, 134, 137 n. 13; adjustment process, 9; Campaign against Hunger, 201; capital accumulation, 4; civil society organizations (CSOs), 185; Communidade Solidaria (CS), 175, 196; decentralized collective bargaining, 82; fertility decline, 39, 40, 47 n. 6; health care privatization, 191; income distribution, 11, 13; income inequality, 6; job security, 82; labor force utilization, 10; nongovernmental organizations (NGOs), 186–87; old social protection model, 141; Plano Real program, 186; population projections, 47 n. 6; Serviço Nacional de Aprendizado Indústria (SENAI), 105, 106–7; survey on poverty's effects, 65 n. 34; unemployment rates, 131; urban apartheid, 177; urbanization of population, 193; urban poverty, 7; Viva Rio campaign, 201; wages, 10–11; welfare state, 49
bureaucracies, 53, 56
businesses: adaptation to global economy, 77; social program interaction with, 56; state cooperation with, 51

capital accumulation, 4, 8
capital flights, 87
capitalist shock, 14
Cardoso, Ruth, 196
Carvalho, José Alberto Magno de, xii, 220

Catholic Church, influence on social policies, 141
CEMIT index, 124, 136–37 n. 4
Chiapas rebellion, 51
child dependency ratio, 43, 44 table 2.3, 46, 47 n. 7
child labor, 97
Chile: accumulation and growth model, 15; adjustment process, 9; aggregate social welfare, 10; comparison to Asian performance, 221; comparison to United States, 222; decentralized collective bargaining, 82; dualism, 54; economic growth, 146–47; emerging economic order, 15; employment, 13; equity and poverty reduction, 166 n. 5; health care privatization, 218; income concentration, 11; investment, 17; job security, 82; labor force utilization, 10; mother and child health and nutrition programs, 145; nongovernmental organizations (NGOs), 191; occupational training, 100, 105; old social protection model, 141; poverty during economic growth, 49; privatization, 156–57, 217, 218; real income, 11; reforms, 7, 83, 154–56; resource allocation instruments, 157–58; rural poverty, 7; social expenditures, 19; Social Investment and Solidarity Fund (FOSIS), 197, 198; social policies, 53, 143; solidarity transfers, 218; state and society relationship, 153–54; supply of education and training, 103; targeting, 158–60; total fertility rates (TFRs), 37; unemployment rates, 131; urbanization of population, 193; urban poverty, 7, 12, 13; wages, 10, 14; welfare state, 49
churches, 51, 56, 141

citizenship, 58, 120–21
citizens' movements, 173
CIVICUS, 200
civil service, 53
civil society: antagonism with state, 186–87; concept of, 203 n. 1; consolidating, 182–83; contours of, 183–85; origins of, 170; renewed attention to, 172–73; shifting boundaries of, 171, 173–75; working definitions of, 178–80
civil society organizations (CSOs): assessment of, 185–87; funding of, 193; municipal government linkage, 187–89; nature of, 183–85
CLACSO (Consejo Latinoamericano de Ciencias Sociales), 193–94
closed economies: employment in, 88 n. 7; labor demand in, 77
Coca-Cola Company, xi
coefficient of vulnerability, 127
collective bargaining: decentralization of, 82, 213–14; state intervention in, 85–86
Colombia: absolute poverty, 134, 137 n. 13; adjustment process, 9; aggregate social welfare, 10; emerging economic order, 15; employment, 13–14; fertility decline, 39, 40; Foundation for Higher Education, 201; income concentration, 11; inequality, 6, 11, 13; investment, 17; labor force utilization, 10; local elections, 191; mother and child health and nutrition programs, 145; occupational training, 100; old social protection model, 141; poverty during economic growth, 49; real income, 11; real wages, 10; social expenditures, 19; Social Foundation, 201; social security reform, 83; supply of education and training, 103; total fertility rates (TFRs), 38; urbanization of population, 193; urban poverty, 7, 13
colonial period, legacy of, 50
communications revolution, 93–94, 223
competences, of workers, 95–96
competitiveness: and equity, 100–102; in international arena, 211–12; and job creation, 224
compulsory basic education, 97
consumer expectations, homogenization of, 223
corporate ethics, 200
Cortázar, René, xii–xiii, 211, 217
Costa Rica: adjustment process, 9; education and training, 103; emerging economic order, 15; employment, 13–14; income concentration, 11; inequality, 6, 11, 13; investment, 17; labor force utilization, 10; mother and child health and nutrition programs, 145; old social protection model, 141; population growth rate, 38; poverty during economic growth, 49; real wages, 11; social expenditures, 19; social policy growth, 143; unemployment rates, 131; urban poverty, 7, 13
country risk, 87, 88 n. 2
Cuba, total fertility rates (TFRs), 37
culture of projects, 198

debt crisis of 1980s, 146
decentralization: about, 63 n. 12; administrative, 181; of collective bargaining, 82, 213–14; of education, 97; of social protection, 152–54, 219; of worker training, 84
demand-driven targeting, 194–95
democracy: commitment to, 58; linking with poverty, 57; transition to, 180

demographic factors, vulnerability influenced by, 129–30
dependency ratios, 43, 45 fig. 2.2, 46
destitution, incidence in 1980s and 1990s, 30 table 1.7
development: failures of, 172–73; postwar style of, 3–4; social organizations as threat to, 81; transformation of style, 7–8
Diamond, Larry, 179–80, 182
disinflation, and recovery, 25 table 1.2
distributive balance, of lost decade, 10–12
distributive trends, at full-capacity growth, 12–14
divorce rates, and vulnerability, 130
Dominican Republic, population growth rate, 38
drug trade, threats of, 59
dualism, 54–55

Economic Commission for Latin America and the Caribbean (ECLAC), 123–25, 134, 151–52
economic crisis, 124, 126
economic growth: employment relationship of, 210–11; inequality inimical to, 63 n. 14; and labor policies, 211; and poverty, 49, 62–63 n. 10, 146–47; social effects of, 126
economic policies: reforms of, 194; social policies gaining autonomy from, 56; and social protection, 151–52; strengthening, 53
economy: and globalization, 77–78; relationships with society and polity, 174; strategies of 1930s and 1940s, 141
Ecuador: old social protection model, 141; population growth rate, 38; social security coverage, 137 n. 14
education: age structure effects on, 43; critical issues of, 217; enrollment factors, 97; enrollment rates, 32 n. 10, 111 table 5.3; expansion in postwar period, 5; as fertility decline determinant, 39; financing of, 144–45, 158; inequality role of, 6; investing in, 214–16, 224; for new workers, 96; for productivity and equity, 102–7; public and private, 224; quality of, 50, 97–98, 224; reform of, 18, 87, 181; standards for workers, 94; state of, 96–100; subsidized university education, 145; supply of, 103; targeting, 160; in technical skills, 18, 215
elderly dependency ratio, 43, 44 table 2.3, 46, 47 n. 8
El Salvador: civil society organizations (CSOs), 184; population growth rate, 38; social security coverage, 137 n. 14
E-mail, and information flows, 175
emerging economic order, 14–16
employability, skills for, 101
employment: changes affecting vulnerability, 130–32; creation through growth, 16–17; during crisis and adjustment, 8–12; economic growth relationship of, 210–11; during full-capacity growth, 13–14; investment as determinant, 80; in open economies, 88 n. 7; in postwar period, 5; in public sector, 85, 131, 180–81, 210; search for full, 222; by small enterprises, 132; as social policy goal, 86
employment policies: agreement on, 79–80; disagreement on, 80–82; beyond labor market, 86–88; within labor market, 82–86
empowerment, 172, 224
England. *See* Great Britain
equity: and competitiveness, 100–102; education and training for, 102–7; and poverty, 220–24
Esping-Andersen, G., 127
estado de compromiso, 142

estado nacional-popular, 142
ethics, 179, 200
ethnic groups, vulnerability of, 125
European countries, fertility decline, 39
European Economic Community, 184
European Welfare State, fiscal crisis of, 146
experimental programs, 181
external adjustment, periods of recovery, 24 table 1.2
external shocks, 7, 9–10, 24 table 1.2
extragovernmental relations, 189

family, vulnerability influenced by, 129–30
family planning policies, 38, 39
Faria, Vilmar, xi
fax machines, and information flows, 175
fertility rates, 37–40, 40 table 2.1, 41 fig. 2.1, 47 n. 4
fertility transition, 36–40, 220
Filgueira, Carlos, xiii, 216, 219
fiscal balance, from 1987–1994, 79 table 4.3
fiscal discipline, 78
fiscal equilibrium, 177
fixed wage decrees, 213
"Flint and Steel" (McGrath), 203
Flora, Peter, 120
Fordist model of labor, 93, 130
foundations, 56, 184, 201
France, 64 n. 20, 104
Fujimori, Alberto, 64 n. 29
full-capacity growth, distributive trends in, 12–14, 33 n. 12

Gallart, María Antonia, xii–xiii, 215
Garretón, M.A., 141, 148
GATT (General Agreement on Tariffs and Trade), 173, 177
GDP, growth from 1980–1994, 76 table 4.2
gender, and vulnerability, 125

gender discrimination, 219
geographical barriers, transcendence of, 147
geographical deconcentration, 181
geographical targeting mechanisms, 161
Germany, training as social duty, 102
globalization: changes brought about by, 75, 77–79; and employment policies, 79–88; global economy, 55; and labor costs, 211–12; restricted definition of, 88 n. 1; and social policies, 211; and vulnerability, 123, 130, 132
government. *See* state
Graham, Carol, 195–96
Gramsci, Antonio, 175
grantsmanship, 198
grassroot support organizations (GSOs), 184
Great Britain: fertility decline, 39; poverty in, 64 n. 20; worker displacement by restructuring, 104
growth: and accumulation model, 14–15; distributive trends in, 12–14; pace of, 16, 33 n. 15; in postwar period, 4; and poverty, 16; beyond recovery, 25 table 1.2; sustainability of, 16, 33 n. 16
growth-with-equity view, of employment policies, 81
Guatemala: civil society organizations (CSOs), 184; total fertility rates (TFRs), 38; unemployment rates, 131

Haiti, 38, 39
health care systems, 19, 48 n. 11, 181
health insurance, privatization of, 156–57
health services, 145, 157–58
Hegel, Georg, 178
heteronomy, passage to autonomy, 213
high-productivity jobs, 17
Hirschman, Albert, 202

Honduras, 39, 137 n. 14
housing subsidies, 157
human capital, investment in, 151, 152
human resources, management of, 94–95

IAF (Inter-American Foundation), 184
IDB (Inter-American Development Bank), 100, 104, 124, 197
ILO (International Labor Organization), 80, 141, 211
IMF (International Monetary Fund), 62 n. 2, 124, 193
income distribution: comparisons among nations, 221–22; during crisis and adjustment, 8–12; in emerging economic order, 14–15, 33 n. 14; and labor situations in 1990s, 22–23 table 1.1; persistence of inequality, 134; post-adjustment paradigm of, 220; poverty linkage to, 223; social effects of, 126; in urban households, 112 table 5.5
income inequality: factors of, 6, 32 n. 3; in postwar period, 5–7
independent research centers, 191
Index of Unsatisfied Basic Needs, 124
India, democracy and poverty, 58
indigents, 49
indirect taxes, 65–66 n. 42
Indonesia, 221
industry, protection of, 3, 141
inequality: during full-capacity growth, 13; inimical to economic growth, 63 n. 14; relationship to real income, 11
infant mortality rates, 159
inflation: from 1980–1994, 79 table 4.4; during crisis and adjustment, 9; purchasing power of wages, 85
information flows, 175
information technologies, changes affecting vulnerability, 130
infrastructures, in global economy, 78, 85
Institutos de Salud Previsional (ISAPRE), 156
Inter-American Development Bank (IDB), 100, 104, 124, 197
Inter-American Foundation (IAF), 184
intergovernmental relations, 189
internal imbalances, 9, 24–25 table 1.2
international competitiveness, 211–12
International Labor Organization (ILO), 80, 141, 211
International Monetary Fund (IMF), 62 n. 2, 124, 193
international opinion, 57
interpersonal competences, 96
investment: as employment determinant, 80; in human capital, 151, 152; increasing levels of, 177; and national saving, 17–18; in social capital, 87–88
Italy, poverty in, 64 n. 20

Japanese factory model, 93
Jarquín, Edmundo, 176
job creation: as challenge, 75; determinants of, 210–11; factors of, 211–12; for international competitiveness, 224; and labor demand, 77; linkages of, 79–80; through modernization, 33 n. 19; through social capital investment, 87
job security, 81–82, 89 n. 11
joint factor productivity, 4, 32 n. 1, 32 n. 2
judicial reform, 181
judiciary systems, in global economy, 78, 85

Kellogg Institute, xi
Keynes, John Maynard, 185
kidnapping, fear of, 59
Kliksberg, B., 148

knowledge, rapid obsolescence of, 130
Kuznets, S., 14

labor: costs in international competitiveness, 211–12; demand for, 77; diminishing protection of, 212; legislation, 82, 83, 85, 89 n. 14, 144; policies, xiii–xiv, 211; and state intervention, 80–81; supply of, 78, 92; variables from 1980–1994, 24–25 table 1.2
labor force: changes in structure, 93–94; competitiveness in world economy, 52; displacement by restructuring, 104; female share of, 39, 43; growth of, 46, 48 n. 12; and restructuring, 93; training of, 63 n. 15, 83–84, 88 n. 3; trends in 1980s, 12; youth entering, 104
labor market: bottlenecks of, 100–101; changes in, 92–95; evolution from 1991–1995, 26 table 1.3; new rules for, 82–86
labor relations, 88 n. 3
language barriers, weakening of, 147
Lasswell, Harold Dwight, 175, 199
legislative reform, 181
life expectancy, and vulnerability, 130
local governments, 188, 189, 192. *See also* municipal governments
lost decade, 10–12, 92–93
Loveman, Brian, 198
Lowi, Theodore J., 189–90

McGrath, Thomas, 169, 171, 203
Machado, Antonio, 170
Machiavelli, Nicolo, 169
macroeconomic equilibria, 86
macroeconomic policy, 146
macroeconomic variables, 24–25 table 1.2
Malaysia, 221

market: emerging roles of, 86; relationship with state and society, 148, 151, 212–14; shifting boundaries of, 171, 173–75; working definitions of, 176–78
market-oriented policies, 57
market-oriented reforms, 7–8
marriage, postponement of, 130
Marshall, T.H., 120
mass media, globalization of, 78
mean relative incomes, 27 table 1.4
member organizations (MOs), 184
Menchu, Rigoberta, 200
Mercosur (South American Common Market), 177, 211
Mesa-Lago, C., 141–42
Mexican Labor Markets Modernization Project (PMMT), 105
Mexico: absolute poverty, 134, 137 n. 13; adjustment process, 9; capital accumulation, 4; civil society organizations (CSOs), 185; currency crisis, 15, 19–20; employment, 13; fertility decline, 39, 40; income distribution, 11, 13; income inequality, 6; inequality, 13; labor force utilization, 10; membership organizations (MOs), 191; National Solidarity Program, 198; occupational training, 100; old social protection model, 141; population growth rate, 38; PRONASOL, 196, 199; real income, 11; real wages, 11; social expenditures, 19; stop-go growth, 16; supply of education and training, 103; unemployment rates, 131; urbanization of population, 193; urban poverty, 7, 13
Michel, Louise, 199
microelectronic automated technologies, 93
microenterprises, 92, 107–8

middle sectors: linking poverty and democracy, 60–61; slide into poverty, 172; as social protection target, 159
Migdal, Joel, 123
military regimes, 57
minimum wages, adjustment of, 84–85
modernization: job creation through, 33 n. 19; of production process, 93, 107–8; and worker retraining, 105–7
Molina, S., 134
moral economy approach, 122–23
moral indignation, 50–51
morality, debate over, 179
mortality, rate decline, 37–38
mother and child health and nutrition programs, 145, 159, 160
municipal governments: civil society organizations (CSOs) linkage, 187–89; collaboration in service delivery, 190–91; and social funds, 198; and social protection, 152–53
Murray, John Courtney, 178

NAFTA (North American Free Trade Agreement), 83, 176–77, 211
Naim, Moisés, 53
national industry, protection of, 3, 141
National Training Agencies (NTAs), 98–100, 112 table 5.4
natural resources, export during postwar period, 3
needs, generated by poverty, 50–51
neoconservative view, of employment policies, 80–81
New Paths (Reilly), 191
new poor: emergence of, 55, 133–35; and poverty increases, 220; safety nets for, 195; slide into poverty, 172
Nicaragua, 38, 184
nonagricultural labor market, 131–32
nongovernmental organizations (NGOs): assessment of, 185–87; directory of, 184; as exemplar of civil society, 182; expectations of, 180; local government relationships, 192; in local politics, 189; municipal government linkage, 187–89; and policy formulation, 190–91; recommendations on, 192; roles of, 178; scope of, 179; and social funds, 194–96; social program interaction with, 56; state complemented by, 174–75; state cooperation with, 51
nonprofit sector, 178–79
nontariff restrictions, 75
North, Douglas, 88–89 n. 10
North American Free Trade Agreement (NAFTA), 83, 176–77, 211
Notre Dame Consensus, xiii–xiv
nuclear family, 135

occupational categories: changes in mean relative incomes, 27 table 1.4; participation in urban labor force, 28 table 1.5
occupational training, 99–100, 104–5. *See also* training
O'Donnell, Guillermo, xi, xii, 220, 223
Offe, C., 120–21
oil crisis of 1970s, 146
old consensus view, of employment policies, 80
on-the-job learning, 102–3
open economies, 77, 88 n. 7
open trade, 177
opportunity, structure of, 126–27
organizational learning curve, 191
organizational restructuring, 92, 93
Organization for Economic Cooperation and Development (OECD), 54
Oyarzo, C., 159–60
Ozlak, O., 148

Padrón, Mario, 184
Panama: income distribution, 11, 13; investment, 17; real wages, 10; unemployment rates, 131

Paraguay, unemployment rates, 131
passive poor, 162–63
past, lessons from, 169–71
Pastore, José, 186
pensions, 19, 155–56
people, investing in, 214–16, 224
Peru: adjustment process, 9; fertility decline, 39; Fujimori government, 64 n. 29; income concentration, 11; old social protection model, 141; real wages, 11; social security reform, 83; urbanization of population, 193; urban poverty, 7
philanthropy, 200–201
Piñera, S., 134
Polanyi, K., 119
policy environment, 192–93
political repression, 123
politics: and antipoverty strategies, 220; coalition of political and social forces, 59–61; disenfranchisement of poor, 51
population: aging of, 40, 46; estimates for 1994, 110 table 5.2; growth of, 33 n. 17, 38, 39; or working age, 17; projections for Brazil, 47 n. 6; urbanization of, 143, 193
populismo, 142
postwar development, long-term trends in, 3–7
poverty: changing profiles of, 143; chronic, 133; conceptualization of, 161–63; during crisis and adjustment, 8–12; in economic growth periods, 49, 62–63 n. 10; and equity, 220–24; incidence in 1980s and 1990s, 30 table 1.7; income distribution linkage to, 223; indices of, 124–25, 133; linking with democracy, 57; measurement of, 162; and pace of growth, 16; in postwar period, 7; reduction with economic growth, 146–47; survey on effects, 65 n. 34; trends in 1980s, 12; and vulnerability, 123–27, 132–33

PREALC, 131
preferences, in global society, 78
private consumption, expansion in postwar period, 3
private education, 224
private investment, 17–18. *See also* investment
private sector wages, 85
private voluntary organizations (PVOs), 184
privatization: advocacy of, 176; of health care, 191, 218; as key reform issue, 217; of public enterprises, 92; of social protection, 78–79, 154–57, 218–19; of state enterprises, 180–81; of training institutions, 78–79, 84
privileged class: appealing to fears of, 51–52; democracy's effects on, 57; isolation of, 55, 59
production, 93, 107–8
productive transformation, 126, 147
productivity: education and training for, 102–7; and human capital investment, 152; in international competitiveness, 211–12; promoting expansion of, 212; restructuring of, 17, 33 n. 18; wages linked with, 77, 78, 80, 84, 89 n. 13, 211
provincial governments, 188
public education, 224
public opinion, 52, 61
public sector adjustment, 92
public sector employment, 131, 180–81, 210
public sector wages, 85
public services, reforms in, 92
Putnam, Robert, 179

quasi-rents, appropriation of, 4, 6
quotient of vulnerability, 127

Raczynski, Dagmar, xiii, 159–60, 214, 216, 217
real income, 11

real wages, 10–11
rebellion, 51
recession: during crisis and adjustment, 9; due to internal imbalances, 24–25 table 1.2; effects during 1980s, 12; social effects of, 126
recessive adjustment, to external shocks, 24 table 1.2
recovery: periods after external adjustment, 24 table 1.2; and periods of disinflation, 25 table 1.2; periods of growth beyond, 25 table 1.2
reforms: adoption during 1980s, 7–8; cushioning effects of, 194; of education, 18, 87, 181; issues of, 217–18; Notre Dame Consensus suggestions, xiii–xiv; political economy of, 13; of public services, 92; of social policies, 181, 216–17, 222; of social security, 83, 154–56, 211; of social welfare systems, 19; of state, 180–82; of taxation, 152
refractory poor, 163
regional governments, 198
regional trade blocs, 176–77
Reilly, Charles, xiii, 188, 190, 214, 216
relative income, in urban labor force, 29 table 1.6
relative wages, 14
remedial actions, 50–51
research centers, 191
restructuring, effects during 1980s, 12
revenue transfers, 189–90
"Revisionist Poem: Machado" (McGrath), 169, 171
robotization, 130
Rockefeller, David, 200
Rockefeller, John D., 200
Roman Catholic Church, influence on social policies, 141
rule of law, 59, 65 n. 33
rural poverty: in Chile, 7; trends in 1980s, 12; urban poverty compared with, 134, 137 n. 12

safety nets, 19, 151, 180, 194–95
Salamon, Lester, 178–79
salaries, 95. *See also* wages
Salinas, Carlos, 196, 198, 199
savings, 17–18, 177, 211
Schlabach, Joetta, xi
Schumpeter, Joseph, 58
"Scientific Management" (Winslow), 113 n. 1
SEFs (social emergency funds): about, 193–96; advocacy of, 199–200; typology of, 196–98
self employment, 92
service economies, spread of, 177
Serviço Nacional de Aprendizado Indústria (SENAI), 105, 106–7
severance payments, 82, 89 n. 11, 89 n. 12
SIFs (social investment funds): about, 193–96; advocacy of, 199–200; typology of, 196–98
Singapore, 64 n. 30
single-parent households, 130
skills, supply and demand, 18, 100–101
Smith, Adam, 169, 170, 178
social autonomy, 213
social capital, investment in, 87–88
social citizenship, 120–21
social coexistence, 224
social competences, training in, 104
social conflicts, state intervention in, 85–86
social funds. *See* SEFs (social emergency funds); SIFs (social investment funds)
social mobility, in postwar period, 5
social movements, and policy formulation, 190–91
social norms, 83
social organizations: emerging roles of, 86; and globalization, 78–79; viewed as threat to development, 81

social policies: autonomy from economic policies, 56; Catholic Church's influence on, 141; content of, 161–63; ECLAC report on, 151–52; growth of, 141–43; implications of new demographic pattern, 43, 46–47; improvement of, 53–54, 189–90; to increase learning, 55, 56; investing resources in, 51; new generation of, 216–20; Notre Dame Consensus suggestions, xiv; operational issues of, 218–19; origins of, 141; reform of, 181, 222; scope of, 18–19

social protection: conceptualization of poverty, 161–63; decentralization of, 152–54, 219; economic and social policies, 151–52; emerging trends of, 146–48; expenditures on, 19, 31 table 1.8; funding of, 219; market mechanism incorporation, 157–58; models of, 149–50 fig. 7.1; old model of, 141–46; privatization of, 154–57, 218–19; state, market, and society relationship, 148, 151; targeting, 158–61, 163

social security systems: challenges to, 46; financing of, 145; history of coverage, 218; impairments to function, 130–31; privatization of, 78–79; reform of, 83, 154–56, 211; types of, 48 n. 10; weak points of, 89 n. 15

social services, 19, 143–44, 144–45
social stratification, 135–36
social vulnerability, 121–22, 125. *See also* vulnerability
society: polarization of, 223–24; relationship with state and market, 148, 151, 212–14
soft technologies, 18
sottogoverno, 188, 190
South American Common Market (Mercosur), 177, 211
Souza, Herbert de, 175

Spain, poverty in, 64 n. 20
state: and businesses, 51; corruption in, 179; disappointment with, 176; emerging roles of, 86; funding of training, 108; and globalization, 78; increasing burdens on, 188; interventions by, 80–81, 85–86; privatization of enterprises, 180–81; reforms of, 180–82; relationships of, 148, 151, 174, 186–87, 212–14; responsibilities of, 176; shifting boundaries of, 171, 173–75; social programs of, 119–21, 143–44; strength of, 52–54; working definitions of, 175–76

stock of capital, 77, 88 n. 2
stop-go pattern growth, 16
subsidies, 145, 157
sustainable human development approach, 88 n. 8
Sweden, fertility decline in, 39
systemic solidarity, 222–23

targeting: cautions about, 219; demand driven, 194–95; in social protection, 158–61, 163; techniques of, 181; of training, 101, 103–4
tax incentives, 200
tax systems: in global economy, 78, 85; improvements to, 51; reforms and social protection, 152
Taylor, Frederick Winslow, 113 n. 1
Taylorism, 94
technical vocational schools, 97, 98–100
technologies: automated, 93; changes resulting from, 92, 130, 215; and labor-intensive growth, 177; progress in postwar period, 4; social effects of, 126, 128, 147; soft, 18
teenage pregnancy, 130
television: as fertility decline determinant, 39; social integration potential of, 166 n. 3

territorial targeting mechanisms, 161
TFRs (total fertility rates), 37–40, 40 table 2.1, 41 fig. 2.1, 47 n. 4
think tanks, 191
third sector, 178–79
Tocqueville, Alexis de, 169–70, 178, 180, 201
Tokman, Víctor E., xi, 32, 55
Tomassini, L., 148
total dependency ratio, 44 table 2.3, 46, 47 n. 9
trade blocs, 176–77
trade schools, 98. *See also* vocational schools
trade unions, 61, 88 n. 9, 177, 213
training: demand driven, 215; funding of, 100, 104, 106, 108; gap with available jobs, 177; investing in, 214–16, 224; for new workers, 96; of poverty-level populations, 104; problems of, 107–8; for productivity and equity, 102–7; target populations of, 101, 103–4
training institutions: challenges to, 84; privatization of, 78–79, 84; quality of, 89 n. 16
trends, in long term development, 3–7
trickle-down effects, 134, 146

underemployment, 5, 88 n. 6
undergovernment, 188, 190
unemployment: causes of, 137 n. 7; implications of, 177; rates of, 76 table 4.1, 110 table 5.1, 131; social effects of, 126
unemployment insurance, 82, 88 n. 6
unions, 61, 88 n. 9, 177, 213
United Nations, 184, 193
United States, 53, 222
university education, subsidies of, 145
urban apartheid, 177
urban households, mean relative incomes, 27 table 1.4

urban labor force: in expanding market, 92; occupational categories in, 28 table 1.5; relative income by educational levels, 29 table 1.6; underutilization during 1980s, 10; unemployment rate in 1992, 110 table 5.1
urban poverty: during full-capacity growth, 13; rural poverty compared with, 134, 137 n. 12; trends in 1980s, 12
Uruguay: adjustment process, 9; education and training, 103; emerging economic order, 15; employment, 13–14; income distribution, 8, 11; inequality, 11, 13; market-oriented reforms, 7; poverty during economic growth, 49; real wages, 11; reforms, 217; social expenditures, 19; social policy growth, 143; social security coverage, 137 n. 14; stop-go growth, 16; unemployment rates, 131; urban poverty, 7, 12, 13; welfare state, 50
US Aid for International Development (USAID), 184, 197

value-added taxes, 65–66 n. 42
Venezuela: adjustment process, 9; income distribution, 11, 13; inequality, 6, 11; labor force utilization, 10; population growth rate, 38; real wages, 11; social expenditures, 19; unemployment rates, 131; urbanization of population, 193; urban poverty, 7
Vivian, Jessica, 196
vocational schools, 97, 98–100
vulnerability: areas of, 121–22; changes in structure, 129–36; groups affected by, 219–20; and industrial sector, 125; new and old, 128–29; and poverty, 123–27

wages: fixed wage decrees, 213; policies for, 84–85; productivity linked with, 77, 78, 80, 84, 89 n. 13, 211; protection of, 212; real wages, 10–11; relative wages, 14; salary negotiations, 95
Washington Consensus, 170, 203 n. 2
wealth, distorted distribution of, 177
wealthy. *See* privileged class
Weber, Max, 175
welfare: during 1980s, 10; reform of, 19; responsiveness of systems, 216
welfare state: challenges to, 135–36; expansion of, 119–21; origins of, 122–23; and poverty increases, 49–50
Wolf, Eric R., 123
women: gender discrimination, 219; in labor force, 39, 43; occupational training of, 104–5; and vulnerability, 125
women's rights, as fertility decline determinant, 39
workers: hierarchy of qualifications, 94; protection of, 81–82; qualifications and competences, 95–96
working-age population, expansion of, 17
World Bank, 62 n. 3, 100, 124, 197
world economy, 75. *See also* globalization
World Trade Organization (WTO), 211

youth, entry into labor force, 104

Zedillo, Ernesto, 200